THE PEOPLE ARE THE NEWS

Grant Pick, 2004

THE PEOPLE ARE
THE NEWS

Grant Pick's Chicago Stories

Grant Pick

**Edited and with an introduction
by John Pick
Foreword by Alex Kotlowitz**

Northwestern University Press
Evanston, Illinois

Northwestern University Press
www.nupress.northwestern.edu

Printed in the United States of America
10 9 8 7 6 5 4 3 2 1

 ISBN-13: 978-0-8101-2445-5
 ISBN-10: 0-8101-2445-9

Library of Congress Cataloging-in-Publication data are available from the
Library of Congress.

Jacket design: Marianne Jankowski
Book design: Beth Herman Adler
All art by Kathy Richland except images on pages 5, 14, 30, 118, 132, 201,
and 221.

Contents

Crime

Death

Foreword

Alex Kotlowitz

Grant Pick had this wonderful laugh. It would percolate just under his breath, as if he was trying to keep it to himself, like a teenage boy trying to muffle his giggles during class. But Grant couldn't help himself. The laughter would escape his attempts at concealment. And then everyone around him would burst out along with him. His writing has the same effect. I dare you to read these stories without laughing, without trembling in indignation, and in a couple of cases—including a tribute to a local newsman—without wiping away a tear or two. Grant knew how to spin a yarn, and he knew how to do it in a way that made it seem like he was letting you in on a secret, as if he was taking you— and only you—by the hand for a long stroll through the nooks and crannies of his city, Chicago.

Chicago has had its share of chroniclers: Mike Royko, Ben Hecht, Nelson Algren, to name just a few. Add Grant Pick to that list. I read most of Grant's articles when they ran in the *Chicago Reader,* the weekly for which he did most of his writing, but reading them here, one after the other, has the effect of making you giddy with excitement as you revel in the discoveries, along with Grant, of the city's gritty and eccentric inhabitants. I don't know that Grant intended it this way, but his stories, one on top of the other, create this magnificent structure that serves as a portal into the ultimate decency of people—even people who at first glance might seem a bit kooky or off-kilter. That's the other thing about Grant:

his head was often cocked to the side, as if he were trying to compensate for a listing world, as if he were trying to make sense of our all-too-human digressions and frailties.

Unlike his predecessors, Grant was not an oversized personality. To the contrary, he ambled around in the background, listening to and watching all that unfolded before him. He had the keen eyes and ears of a novelist; nothing escaped him. In one profile he described a homeless person lying on a bench. It's not enough that we know the man is perusing a newspaper; he's reading Michael Sneed, a gossip columnist. Such detail connects us to him, and him to us. Or consider Grant's profile of two transgender friends. We learn that one of them preferred silicone forms for breasts since they tend to absorb body heat. Grant didn't miss a thing. And he did it all with such understatement, such modesty. It was rare that he appeared in his pieces. But those who knew him weren't fooled by his insistence that he wasn't part of the story. He poked and prodded, pushed and pulled. He challenged people to consider who they were and who they wanted to be. He didn't let people off the hook. Grant's presence is felt in every moment, in every line of his stories.

One of my favorite portraits in this collection is that of Bill Tomes, a lay Catholic who strolled through the housing projects dressed in a cassock, convinced that he held the key to reducing gang violence. When the gangs started shooting, Tomes would amble into the middle of the gunfire, seemingly immune to the bullets flying about him, certain that just his presence would subdue the hostilities. It did. Mostly because no one knew what to make of this robed white guy who introduced himself as Brother Bill. "I'm just a regular guy, a simple shit," Tomes told Grant.

Grant had an uncanny ability to get people to open up to him, often in this brutally honest manner. Part of it, I'm sure, was that laugh of his that drew you in. You wanted to tell him things. At one point, Tomes confided in Grant that the love of his life, a nurse, had left him for another man. Tomes, who could be a bit melodramatic, informed Grant that no one compared to that nurse "except Jesus." To which Grant deadpanned, "Tomes realizes that his present lifestyle is not what every woman dreams of." I read this particular story in envy. Years ago, when I was hanging out in the projects, I met Tomes. I thought the guy was nuts and steered clear of him. My mistake. Grant knew that there was something there, that there was more to Tomes than met the eye. Grant didn't judge people. Or at least he didn't judge them harshly. And so he met Tomes and saw a guy who, eccentric or not, had found respect among many of the gang members and had done a great deal of good. Grant hung out with him and, beneath those flowing robes, found a remarkable human being. I can picture Grant, stoop-shouldered, trailing behind Tomes in one of the most dangerous, run-down neighborhoods in the country—all the while laughing in amusement at the incongruity of this man dressed in medieval garb trying to connect to young men slinging dope in the breezeways of the high-rises. And I have no doubt that before long Grant had Tomes laughing right along with him.

Grant Pick is a Chicago treasure. He's our Joseph Mitchell, someone who found poetry in the quotidian, who saw the extraordinary in the ordinary. His writing inspires—and should serve as a model for any aspiring journalist. Grant saw the best in people, and yet he let us see them as he did, squarely and honestly, without sentimentality, without condemnation. When an American Nazi learned that Grant was Jewish, he told Grant that he'd continue talking to him as long as Grant was fair in his reporting. Grant told him he'd try. And from his portrait there's no doubt that he did. In the classic novel *To Kill a Mockingbird*, Atticus Finch tells Scout that you can never understand a man until you crawl into his skin. Well, that was Grant's strength, his ability to stand in someone else's shoes, to try to understand what motivates, propels, and inspires that person. And he did it with such generosity and such humor. Grant rejoiced in the resiliency of the human spirit, and he got us to celebrate along with him.

Grant died far too early. He was only fifty-seven. A vigorous fifty-seven. To those who were fortunate enough to be considered a friend, he was deeply loyal. And a straight shooter. He was someone I leaned

on constantly. I knew he'd ask tough questions—the same tough questions he would ask of his subjects. There was not a hint of falseness about him. And he kept us all laughing. He was amused by himself (he was one of the most self-aware people I've known) and amused by the world around him. He saw the best in all of us. After he passed, one of the people he wrote about, Katie Thomas, a transsexual, said that Grant told all of us what "transgendered people are really like. And it was done with such grace and dignity that our community will be forever grateful."

We're richer for the people whom Grant has introduced us to: richer for their company, richer for having Grant as our guide. We're *all* forever grateful.

Introduction

John Pick

After my father died suddenly in February of 2005, one thing felt unresolved: he'd always wanted to write a book; he just never had the right idea. He pitched and he pitched, but he could never get anyone to fully bite. He pitched *The Cop and the Killer,* a book about two men whose lives diverged from eerily similar upbringings. He tried to work a book out of the 1950s television puppet show *Kukla, Fran, and Ollie.* He thought early twentieth-century Jewish gangster Julius "Dolly" Weisberg would make a good subject. But nothing flew.

Sometimes it was hard to understand the nexus of one of my father's stories. Often he would present his ideas to the Pick family dinner table, where, after a lengthy explanation, a teenage version of my sister or me would roll our eyes and say, "Why is that interesting?" or "So what, Dad?" But as I set to task on this project, I came to realize my youth and ignorance. I hadn't read a lot of his stories, ostensibly because I was too young, they were too long, or I was off in another state or country. Certainly I would hear about them in his letters or over meals, but, as was often true, my father was much better writing about something than explaining it verbally.

So I pored through three decades of his stories, reading almost everything he ever wrote: from where to take a toddler in Chicago on a Saturday in the early 1980s to an ode to a tree dying in front of our house. He produced hundreds of stories about a wide assortment of people: from the woman who cut newspaper clippings for the city to the first African American to circumnavigate the globe. He wrote about a feud tearing apart an upscale beauty salon and about a man who ambled around the South Side looking for keys to add to his collection. Often it would seem as if my dad would turn a corner, happen upon someone he couldn't believe he'd found, and simply want to tell you about this person. I like to think of my dad as an urban fisherman, venturing out with a net for a tale and returning to prepare the fish on his typewriter or marginally defunct laptop.

The process of exploring my dad's work has offered great solace. As is often the case after the loss of loved ones, one looks for signs of them, places where they still live. Combing through his work, I realized I could simply look into his file cabinet and hear his voice: his curious nature, his sense of humor, his passion for justice. And going back years, I could find my father when he was closer to my age, ripe to adult life and eager to earn his stripes, if a bit confused.

My father was faced with challenges early in life—he lost both his parents by the time he was fifteen. He was sent off to boarding school and, over the next decade, struggled to find his way. For college, he decided on Roosevelt University, and there fell for Chicago's spirit and eclectic characters. After college, after mopping up blood as a male orderly and dropping out of law school, he decided to be a reporter and enrolled at Northwestern's Medill School of Journalism. After Medill, he took a job writing for the Chicago Lung Association's newsletter and later edited the *Beverly Review*. Then, in the late 1970s, he found a home at the newly formed *Chicago Reader*.

The editorial staff at the *Reader* offered my father the freedom to do the profile work he wanted to. He started to churn out stories: the host of the lowest-rated television show in Chicago; the homosexual bar owner who partied his way to his death at thirty-eight; the former CTA [Chicago Transit Authority] worker who lived in Lincoln Park. He wrote more: the restaurant owner who fought to keep her doors open; the social worker forced to reconcile his son's murder while working with gangsters; the importance of a Laundromat to a struggling community.

Into his stories are stitched recurring themes: death, loss of home, community, and, overall, the struggle to maintain and persevere amid adversity—all themes that echoed his own life. My dad wanted to connect, and to do so he offered his subjects an attentive ear and a sharp, nonjudgmental eye. He sought to give voice to the voiceless, to chronicle the struggles of the ordinary. I like to think that my father didn't choose his stories; instead, they found him.

My dad was a very emotional man. He cried a lot, he laughed a lot, and he listened hard. He believed in people and their potential, and he used storytelling to convey that belief. Often he would return to speak at Medill to the class of his close friend and colleague Bob McClory, a professor of journalism at Northwestern.

The well-trained students would be inclined to ask, "But Mr. Pick, what's the news peg?" My dad, as I understand it, would softly reason back. "There is no news peg," he'd say. "The people are the news."

The stories included in this collection will hopefully add to Chicago lore. They are tales of a timeless Chicago. They are about people who worked in buildings that are now torn down and replaced by condos. They are about people who made their way, who made news with their little victories. I'm happy to be able to give my dad a little victory: a place on the shelf in the public library. We just had to get the right idea. ■

THE PEOPLE ARE THE NEWS

Drifters

THE RAG MAN OF LINCOLN PARK

His name was Jim Northcutt. He graduated from the University of Cincinnati with majors in philosophy and economics. He served during the Korean War and worked in the planning department of the CTA. This is his story.

The man was probably in his fifties, but his lined face and matted hair made him look older. He was standing in a small plaza across from Columbus Hospital in Lincoln Park one recent weekday afternoon. The hat he wore read, "I'm not completely worthless. I can always serve as a bad example."

"Who runs those things?" he asked, motioning toward some paddleboats bobbing in the lagoon behind him. He seemed to be just making conversation.

"That restaurant over there rents them out on weekends," I said.

"Oh," he said, then walked away, leaving the plaza to other men. At the rim of the plaza, inside a red-roofed gazebo, an unshaven guy in a black leather jacket and jeans walked in circles. Another man lay on a bench just outside the plaza, smoking a cigarette and reading Michael Sneed. His belongings were wrapped in plastic in a shopping cart parked by his side.

The weather was cold enough that the small cement drinking fountain in the middle of the plaza had been turned off for the season. Locust and hickory leaves filled the basin.

If I hadn't been looking for the plaque on the side of the fountain, I would have missed it. The bronze rectangle was a little larger than an index card, and the inscription began with a line from the book of Isaiah: "All you who are thirsty come to the water." It ended with, "In memory of Jim Northcutt, 1929–1988."

———————

Jim Northcutt

Jim Northcutt began appearing at Saint Clement's Church in Lincoln Park sometime in 1984. He was a bearded, heavy man in his fifties, garbed in a rubber poncho even in warm weather. He'd come for the 7 A.M. weekday service and take a seat in the rear pew. When he sat down, so did his companions—two wire baskets filled with junk. Northcutt never took communion, although whenever the congregation knelt in prayer he too got on his knees.

In many ways Northcutt's presence proved an affront to his fellow worshippers. He often gave off such a foul odor that people moved to the front of the church to get away from it. On Saturdays he came for the morning service and stayed for the weddings, which provoked a few incidents.

One afternoon in late 1984 a father of the bride saw Northcutt in the back of the church and approached Father Robert Oldershaw, then associate pastor at Saint Clement's. "Get rid of that bum," the man demanded.

"That's not a bum," said Oldershaw. "That's one of our parishioners." Oldershaw refused to evict Northcutt, whom he knew only as Jim, although he did convince Northcutt to slide his baskets underneath the pew.

Oldershaw became Northcutt's defender. One time some Saint Clement's youngsters on break from choir practice were making noise in the main sanctuary. "Don't misbehave in God's house," yelled Northcutt from his pew. The kids fled to Oldershaw to complain about the "bum." Oldershaw paused. "Well, wasn't that man right about what he said?" he asked. "Let's talk about 'bummery,' shall we?"

"Jim just made you think," says Oldershaw. "He was troubling. Sometimes I'd look at him and think, gee, if I could just put you in a washing machine then you'd conform to our norms. But maybe Jim wasn't meant for that."

At first Northcutt's place of residence was the red-roofed gazebo in Lincoln Park, but in the spring of 1986 the police forced him out of the park. So he set up on the corner of Clark Street and Deming Place, near the Itto Sushi restaurant. Ironically, the block to the west counts as one of Chicago's wealthiest; it is dominated by several mansions, a Ronald McDonald House for the families of hospitalized children, and Saint Clement's.

Northcutt's home consisted of the bench he sat on and his baskets, which held old newspapers, magazines, two German prayer books, a notebook, and two plastic bottles—one to hold water and a second into which he urinated. In the winter Oldershaw would leave the west door to Saint Clement's open, but otherwise Northcutt lived exclusively on his corner bench.

Northcutt asked for neither food nor money. If someone offered him money he spurned it, although Kathy Burke, a Saint Clement's parishioner who took an interest in Jim, says that if you left him something to eat he would consume it. Mostly, she says, Northcutt combed Dumpsters for food.

Beginning in early 1985 Saint Clement's offered its basement as a community shelter for the homeless during the cold-weather months, and Northcutt sometimes came inside to eat. However, since he stank so, he was barred from staying the night; instead, he'd huddle by the church entrance.

Northcutt usually avoided making eye contact, even with people he knew. He spoke sparingly, seldom acknowledging his audience. When he did connect with a person he'd say, "God's peace be with you." An exception was Kathy Burke's son, whom Northcutt addressed by name when he saw the boy. "Be good, Abe," he used to say.

Because Northcutt often spiced his remarks with German phrases, people assumed he came from Germany. But he told Oldershaw he came from Kentucky. He also told the priest he had been in Chicago for seventeen years—an understatement, as it turned out. Oldershaw discovered Northcutt's last name, but kept it to himself because he felt to share it would violate Jim's privacy. Other priests at Saint Clement's learned that Northcutt harbored certain political opinions. Once he informed Father John Fahey, then head priest at the church, that "they should blow up abortion clinics." When the cleric argued for a kinder approach, Northcutt revised his opinion. "You changed my mind, Father," he said. "They should shoot the doctors."

In general, Jim's relative silence was seen as menacing, and his appearance as unsettling, especially to the well-heeled residents of Lincoln Park. "There was a real uneasiness about him," says Jeff Zaslow, at the time a feature writer for the *Wall Street Journal* who lived on Deming Place. "Here was a guy who urinated in bottles and had those ugly carts. People got on their buses to go down to LaSalle Street, and there he was." Jim was unwanted. "There was a feeling among businessmen especially that he was bad for business," says Kathy Burke.

On the night of July 15, 1986, someone set fire to Northcutt's bench. When the neighbors found him in the morning, Northcutt was sitting on the remains of the bench and his carts were gone. Northcutt's arm and shoulder were seared, although not severely. The police took him to the hospital, but not before he, weeping, told Burke, "They don't want me around anymore. I'm going to have to go away."

Afterward Northcutt moved his base of operations about a mile northwest to Saint Alphonsus Church. For a year and a half, when it was cold, he slept in the side vestibule of the church; the rest of the time he roosted on the church steps. He took supper with a senior-citizens group at the church, and he patronized the German service held each Sunday. Father Bernard Guenther, a retired priest affiliated with the church, took pity on Northcutt and gave him a rubber mattress. Guenther marveled at Northcutt's belongings, stowed again in baskets. "It was junk, but these things were Jim's treasures," says Guenther. "He was a nice man, but peculiar in his ways."

Jeff Zaslow, who now pens a personal-advice column for the *Sun-Times*, happened by Northcutt's bench on the day it was burned. He was intrigued by Northcutt, who waved away any inquiry, and wrote a story for the *Wall Street Journal* that dealt not only with Northcutt but with the reaction of the upper middle class to the homeless. It ran in the *Journal* on December 1, 1986.

When *Sun-Times* columnist Tom Fitzpatrick wrote a spin-off story and revealed Northcutt's last name, it jogged the memory of Harry Hirsch, director of operations planning for the CTA. He told Glenn Andersen, then a CTA equipment engineering supervisor, that the person Fitzpatrick had described sounded an awful lot like their old colleague Jim Northcutt. Andersen knew Northcutt's sister Gail and called her at her home in Detroit. A high school math teacher, she had been searching for her brother for years.

Jim Northcutt was born in Cincinnati, Ohio, on August 8, 1929, and grew up in nearby Covington as the oldest child and only boy in a blue-collar home. His father, Galen, was a sheet-metal worker; his mother, Catherine, became a switchboard operator once her five children were off at school. The household had some tenuous ties to Germany, since Northcutt's maternal grandfather, born in Alsace-Lorraine, spoke German and passed along a few phrases to the children.

Brainy and motivated, Jim skipped straight from sixth grade to high school at Covington Latin School, a Catholic facility for bright youngsters. Following high school Jim went to the University of Cincinnati, where he earned a bachelor's degree, with majors in philosophy and economics. He also developed a proficiency in French and Greek.

There were troubles, however. Sometime after Northcutt left high school, says Gail Northcutt, "there was some estrangement with the family. He had a troubled relationship with his father, and he pretty much denied he had a family." Catherine Northcutt, now an eighty-nine-year-old widow, disagrees with her daughter's assessment: "I don't think Jim and my husband had a strained relationship. They had a good relationship—Jim just preferred living somewhere else." That somewhere else was first Cincinnati, where Gail remembers passing her brother on the street and him not recognizing her, or pretending not to.

Northcutt served in the army during the Korean War, perfecting his German while on duty in Europe. Afterward he worked for the Cincinnati transit system for a few years, and then was hired by the Chicago Transit Authority in February 1958. Assigned to the planning department of the CTA, Northcutt oversaw, among other things, the installation of the authority's first computer system. He left the CTA in 1962 and spent three years with the engineering firm DeLeuw Cather and Company, advising them on bridge and mass-transit projects in Australia, New Zealand, and Europe. But he tired of being in other people's employ and in 1965 turned to independent consulting.

Andersen recalls Northcutt as a talkative, jovial man, five feet eight inches tall, with a handlebar mustache, longish hair, and a sloppy appearance. He was always overweight, tipping the scales at two hundred pounds or more, and he seemed to own just one suit. "He was a very open, very friendly person," says Harry Hirsch, who started in management training at the CTA at the same time Northcutt did. "He took a lot of kidding over his appearance, but it rolled off his back." Hirsch says Northcutt's superiors took a dim view of his appearance, but he was too stubborn to change. "He always declared himself as a hillbilly," says Andersen.

In his off-hours Northcutt cultivated an interest in Chicago's ethnic churches, attending a different one every Sunday. He also went to church picnics. Another passion was railroad history. He lived in Lincoln Park and turned half of his Bissell Street apartment, which backed up to the El, into a mini-museum, piling it high with railroad books, pictures, movie reels, maps, and even roadbed ties. He was an avid member of the Central Electric Railfans Association.

Northcutt never married. "He was interested in girls, but I didn't know of him having had any long-term relationships," says Andersen.

In 1967 Northcutt seemed to withdraw more and more from society. Andersen is still mystified at the cause of his decline; all he knows is that Northcutt turned inward and became more eccentric. "One night I went down to see him, and he thought his phone was bugged," Andersen says. Gail Northcutt would call and find a monosyllabic sibling on the other end of the line. "He'd say 'yes,' 'no'—practically nothing," she says. "I don't think he was able to keep up with his bills." Finally, in either 1968 or '69—Gail's and Andersen's recollections differ—Northcutt's phone was disconnected. Andersen then found Northcutt's apartment vacant, and the woman across the hall told him Northcutt had been evicted.

"In my subconscious I feared Jim was having severe mental problems," says Gail, who's now fifty-one. "He had always been strange, but when you are a little sister looking up to an older brother, strange sometimes passes for brilliant. When he disappeared, I first thought, oh well, he's just sick of his family again."

From what she was later able to determine, Northcutt went to living on the street and in state mental hospitals, including Manteno and Chicago Read; doctors diagnosed him as paranoid schizophrenic. He eluded contact with his friends and family. Andersen figures Northcutt's former coworkers must have passed him countless times without recognizing him. "Middle-class people just don't look at the homeless unnecessarily—they don't make eye contact. His friends might have seen Jim a lot. I might have."

Northcutt's family did what they could, from a distance, to locate Jim. In 1979, after one Northcutt sister read a newspaper story about a Chicago railroad organization, Gail made some calls about Jim and finally connected with Andersen, who is also a train buff. Gail had weathered cancer surgery and wanted to find her brother, but she and Andersen had little luck.

They did discover, with the help of Michigan senator Carl Levin's office, an uncashed Social Security check made out to Northcutt in October 1979. But Gail grew more and more pessimistic, and in 1984 she finally donated Northcutt's railroad memorabilia to the Illinois Railway Museum. Then came the *Wall Street Journal* article and Andersen's call.

On January 13, 1987, Gail slid into the pew behind her brother at Saint Alphonsus Church. It had been twenty-eight years since she had seen him. "I was overwhelmed," she said. "I knew it was him." Northcutt eyeballed her and then rose to do the stations of the cross. "He walked right by me. I just wanted to embrace him." But sensing his displeasure, she held off.

The next day she approached him in front of the Golden Nugget Pancake House. "*Guten Morgen,*" she said, which means "good morning" in German. He spat in her face. "It broke my heart," she says. Minutes later she walked up to him in church. "Jimmy," she said, "I'm your sister, Gail, and I've been looking for you for years." He yelled at her and made a gesture as if he was going to throw something at her.

She returned to Chicago that April on her spring break from teaching. After examining his records at Chicago Read, she began proceedings to become his guardian. In a hearing that August, at which Northcutt failed to appear, a circuit-court judge granted her that status. Two days later Jim and Gail had their first friendly interchange, after she presented him with some sandwiches at the church. "Thank you," he responded.

For a month that fall he was hospitalized at Chicago Read and then released to Arlington House, a retirement facility and halfway house in Lincoln Park. He had developed what was first thought to be anemia, but in December 1987 doctors at Grant Hospital diagnosed him as having acute myeloblastic leukemia, an insidious form of blood cancer. Chemotherapy was begun.

"We talked, or rather I did," says Gail. "I told him about school, about my work. I never asked him where he had been all those years. I didn't want him to be under strain. I told him about his sister, about his nieces and nephews. He just closed his eyes. But I know he looked forward to my visits. We had good visits."

According to Father Oldershaw, Northcutt started to take communion in the hospital during this period. Released to a nearby nursing home, Northcutt did not fare well. He developed a cyst on the left side of his head, and his gallbladder began to fail. On February 17, 1988, he reentered Grant Hospital for gallbladder surgery. Three days after his operation he lifted his oxygen mask and looked directly at Gail. "Celebrate," he told her.

"When?" she asked.

"Tomorrow," he said. He died the next day, February 29, at 6 P.M.

"Two days before Jim died he knew I cared for him," says Gail. "He looked touched as I was crying, and I told him I cared for him."

The funeral took place on March 5 at Saint Clement's, with Northcutt's mother, Gail, and another sister in attendance. Father Fahey delivered the homily. Northcutt was buried at Mount Olivet Cemetery on the South Side. "*Gruss Gott,*" reads his headstone, which means "Praise God."

The next month Gail Northcutt returned to Chicago to attend a benefit for Thresholds, a social-service agency that had helped her with Jim, when the idea of some memorial to him "just popped into my head. I didn't want his life to have been in vain. I didn't want him to be forgotten." She cornered Forty-third Ward alderman Edwin Eisendrath, who happened to be at the affair, and convinced him to assist her. Liz Rothman, an aide to Eisendrath, subsequently suggested dedicating an existing water fountain to Northcutt. It was arranged with the Chicago Park District to name the fountain in front of the Lincoln Park gazebo after him. Gail agreed to pay for the plaque, but Eisendrath's office has yet to forward her the forty-dollar bill.

The dedication ceremonies occurred on June 24 at 11 A.M. in the plaza adjoining the gazebo. It was a hot day. A representative of the Chicago Park District spoke, and so did Rob Buono, another assistant to Eisendrath. Then came Oldershaw's turn.

"Jim was the rag man of Lincoln Park," said Oldershaw, now pastor at Saint Nicholas Church in Evanston. "Jim, clad in rags and loaded with his stuff, was a parable. He disturbed us, troubled us. We who don't live on the streets or in the parks or on bus-stop benches, we who live in comfortable homes, have much to learn from the homeless.

"See, people were at first scared of Jim—bearded, berobed, Moses-like patriarchal figure that he was. But we came to respect and love this man who troubled our consciences and threw us off balance.

"Oh God, we ask your blessing on this fountain, that has provided refreshment for countless people. We bless and thank you for Jim Northcutt—friend, prophet, parable, Christ figure. Keep Jimmy always in your heart and help us all who are refreshed by these waters to open our eyes to the plight of the homeless and our ears to their cry of pain."

Oldershaw then invited the thirty people in attendance to drink from the fountain. As they drank, he sang an impromptu song about Northcutt to the tune of "Michael, Row the Boat Ashore."

"The next day, on Sunday morning at five o'clock, I walked over to the fountain," says Gail. "Some guy stopped by who looked like he had been up all night. He grabbed the fountain with both his hands and took a drink. Boy, I said to myself, I'm glad that fountain is here."

There are those who don't see the reason for the dedication of the fountain. "Jim Northcutt was homeless, but he wasn't helpless," says Father Guenther of Saint Alphonsus. "He could have worked or gotten Social Security. He was just mentally unbalanced. We are making too much of a fuss over the man."

"No," says Gail. "The fountain gives dignity to the memory of my brother and to the homeless. We must remember that each of them is unique."

BROTHER BILL

"The history of the Catholic Church is a history of exotics and eccentrics. These are figures impassioned to meet God in other people, and in every culture people emerge to do this in lavish proportions. Bill is one of them."

What strikes you first about Bill Tomes is the look of the man. He is fifty-five and overweight. He wears glasses with clear plastic frames. His sandy hair is graying, and it's thinning at the temples and the crown. This spring he was sporting a Band-Aid on his brow, covering the spot where a skin cancer had been removed. "Too much sunshine, too little moonshine," Tomes told anyone who asked.

His clothing consists of dark pants, a blue oxford-cloth shirt, and black tie shoes that he shines almost every day. But these are merely undergarments to a hooded cassock made entirely of blue-jeans patches. The original cassock was fashioned of ten worn pairs of jeans, "but there's almost nothing left of the original," he says. "I've patched up my habit a whole number of times." The cassock is cinched at the waist with a rope belt from which a rosary and a crucifix hang.

Tomes's manner makes him seem to regret that he's taking up your time. He speaks haltingly. "Sor-ree," he is apt to say before saying anything else. He burdens his conversation with "oh-oh"s and "oo-ees"s—little notes of self-effacement. Occasionally, from out of nowhere, a spate of oaths will issue. "Hah-hah," Tomes usually laughs after swearing. "Sor-ree."

People who first encounter Tomes don't quite know what to make of him. Is he a fugitive from a halfway house? A madman attempting to resurrect the Middle Ages?

No, Tomes—or "Brother Bill," as he is invariably called—is a youth worker

13

Bill Tomes

employed by Catholic Charities. He is assigned to work among street-gang members in housing projects and poor neighborhoods, and where you'd expect the young toughs of the city to treat him with derision, what he receives, instead, is reverence.

He's earned it. Since 1983, when Tomes first ventured out among project kids, he has become their accepted friend. Every afternoon and evening he travels the city in his '82 LeSabre, engaging in brief chats with kid after kid. He exchanges gang handshakes, finds out if killings are going down, takes youngsters for rides, and—sometimes against his better judgment—loans them money from his paltry salary. He never tells the kids that they're bad, only that they're good. When violence breaks out, Tomes stands between warring factions. When someone is wounded, Tomes speeds to the scene; later he'll take up a vigil at the hospital. When someone dies, Tomes goes to the funeral and to the burial.

He never proselytizes. "I treat the kids with respect, that's all, and that gives them self-respect."

"The history of the Catholic Church is a history of exotics and eccentrics," reflects Father Tom O'Gorman, pastor of Saint Malachy's, the West Side church that is Tomes's base. "These are figures impassioned to meet God in other people, and in every culture people emerge to do this in lavish proportions. Bill is one of them."

"Oh no, oh no," says Tomes. "I'm just a regular guy, a simple shit."

The black LeSabre lumbered through the streets of Cabrini-Green one afternoon in April. The windows were down, despite the cool weather. The radio was punched to WFMT. The Buick's radio has five buttons: two are tuned to classical stations; the center button is keyed to an easy-listening channel that Tomes's mother likes; the last two buttons punch up black rock stations.

"Brother Bill, hey Brother Bill," came a cry, and Tomes curbed his sedan. Five boys in their early teens rushed the car, and Bill offered to give them a ride. A really skinny kid got in the front seat. The other four climbed in back, wedging in alongside Tom Garner, a Jesuit seminarian who frequently works with Bill. A boy in a windbreaker took his time getting in; he was on crutches—he'd been shot recently in the leg.

These were Vice Lords riding with him now, and Tomes carefully navigated the Buick through territory occupied by rival gangs, Disciples and Cobra Stones. He headed east on Division Street.

"I don't know if you'd like to stop for a second and say hello to the seals at the Lincoln Park Zoo?" Tomes wondered.

One boy grunted.

"Are things peaceful for you?" Tomes asked.

"Nope," said a kid in the backseat.

"But is anybody shooting?" inquired Tomes.

"No, it's cool," said the same boy.

The Buick wound through Lincoln Park, nearing the zoo. When Tomes asked if anyone had summer plans, there was silence. "I was in the zoo for a while," Tomes said, "but I was eating too many bananas, so they threw me out." The boy in front chortled, and Tomes pulled into a parking space. "Is this all right, to go in and see the seals?" he wondered. "Maybe you can feed me to the seals."

Everyone got out of the car and walked over to the seal tank. Rocking up and down on their Nikes, the boys took a long look at the animals. Tomes asked if he could take a group shot. "Fine by me," said a youngster in a white cap, and Tomes pulled an Instamatic from the pocket of his cassock and made Garner and the boys move in tight. "Smile," he said, and pressed the shutter.

The kid in the white cap wanted to visit the reptile house, but it was closed. Soon the Buick was rumbling toward Cabrini. Tomes punched up WGCI-FM, and the boys hooted to the music. "If the other gangs are bothering you, I'll be around," said Tomes before the boys got out. "Bye, Brother Bill," they said in unison.

Tomes admitted that he didn't know the boys' names—he seldom does. "But I know their faces," he said. "They are my friends."

Tomes did know the name of the kid sporting a Bulls cap who now approached him. "Floyd [the name's been changed] and I are old friends," Tomes said. "We've known each other since he's been thirteen." Once Floyd, who's now eighteen, gave Tomes a school picture of himself inscribed "To my good friend." Floyd wanted a ride to the Logan Square nursing home where his mother works. "My grandmother died," Floyd said. "Oe-oe, sor-ree, bud-dee," said Brother Bill, reaching a hand into the backseat and gripping Floyd's.

Tomes detoured to a car wash on the edge of Humboldt Park. The car wash was recently opened by two brothers, Ralph and Juan "Papito" Rios, who named the place in memory of their slain brother, Edgar. Edgar died last December 28. Police said he was sitting in a car at midnight with three other men and one of them began firing. Nicola Incandela, a cook, was charged with triple homicide. Police told reporters a drug deal apparently had gone sour.

At the time, Tomes didn't know any of the Rioses. "Brother Bill just showed up at our house the day after Edgar died," said Ralph Rios, who lives with his relatives, including Edgar's pregnant girlfriend, in a Logan Square two-flat. "Bill rang the doorbell, and, believe me, when we looked out we didn't know who the hell this was. We just gaped—we were shocked. But he came to the funeral, and he spoke there. Afterwards we all went to the auto show together. Our family likes to rent videos—we're real couch potatoes—and Bill comes by all the time and just hangs out. He has been our strength. He's been especially good for Papito, 'cause he took Edgar's death real hard. Bill keeps telling him Edgar is in a better place."

At the car wash Tomes shook hands with Ralph and Papito and asked how business was going. "Well, it's OK," reported Ralph, "but it's not great. It should pick up with summer coming." Tomes nodded and said he had to go—Floyd needed to get to his mother.

Conversation in the car drifted here and there. Tom Garner explained that it will take him eight more years to become a priest. Tomes talked about a twenty-year-old woman with two children who'd been shot to death a couple weeks earlier outside a public-housing building on South Prairie. "They were trying to shoot her boyfriend," Tomes said, "except they shot her three times in the head." The next night Tomes returned to the building and stood guard there until after midnight. Some time after nine o'clock a van drove slowly past, Tomes said, putting him on edge but doing no harm.

The story reminded Floyd of something. "One day my auntie was going to visit us from St. Louis," he said. "She was telling a friend about coming, and she was shot in the head. She was my favorite auntie."

Floyd said, "You remember 'Poodle,' Brother Bill?"

"Yeah, sure," Tomes said.

"He's dead," Floyd said.

"How'd he die?" Tomes asked.

"They say somebody strangled him."

Before Floyd got out, Tomes loaned him twelve dollars to buy shoes for his grandmother's funeral. Later, Floyd would confess that his grandmother never died at all. Floyd used the twelve dollars to help settle a drug debt.

In 1983, when Bill Tomes showed up at Saint Malachy's, a onetime Irish parish now serving the Henry Horner Homes, the church was converting its gymnasium and garage into a shelter and soup kitchen. A year earlier, Mother Teresa had sent Saint Malachy's six nuns from the Missionaries of Charity. "Bill told me he wanted to work among the poor, too," remembers Father Stephen Mangan, pastor of Saint Malachy's at the time. Tomes volunteered at Saint Malachy's a couple of days a week, staying in the gym at night to keep it safe.

Soon he became a pastoral associate at the church; he received room and board and, eventually, pay. He took over a room on the third floor of the rectory. The small room contained a chair, a bed, and a television, but Tomes removed them. "I wanted to participate with the poor," he explains. "I wanted to give up material things as a sacrifice." Over the four years Tomes called the room home, it was bare except for a telephone and a rug, on which he slept.

Tomes did odd jobs for the church, like helping to restore the stained glass and pink marble in the sanctuary, but in time "he started working the neighborhood," says Father Mangan.

One day Tomes came downstairs to find Mangan completing the church bulletin. "I'm going to call you 'Brother Bill' because you need some form of religious identification," Mangan said. When Tomes pointed out that he wasn't a member of any religious order, Mangan replied that he was a brother in the sense that "everybody in the world are brothers and sisters," Tomes remembers.

He assumed the blue-jeans cassock as a tribute to Francis of Assisi, who was wellborn but took a vow of poverty, cared for the destitute, and in Egypt during the Crusades moved between warring armies. Mangan encouraged Tomes to wear his cassock constantly. "That might save you," Mangan told him. "People will perceive you as the salt of the earth. They are victims, too."

Tomes wears the habit whenever he's on the streets—in rain and snow, during the hottest days of summer and the coldest of winter. When it's soaked, so be it. Claiming the cassock's sleeves are long enough to protect his hands from the cold, he never wears gloves. He also never wears a hat. "Can you think of a proper hat to go with this outfit?" Tomes says.

His first day at Henry Horner, Tomes strode the length of the project. The teenage boys there had never seen anybody like him, and the next day, according to Tomes, the council of the Disciples gang took a vote on whether he should be killed. "But they thought I was a good guy and agreed to protect me," Tomes says. Whatever verdict the council rendered, the run-of-the-mill gang members had their own opinion. "We thought he was crazy," says Demetrius Ford, a Disciple who has since gone to work at Saint Malachy's. "What the fuck would *you* think?"

Gradually, Tomes established an identity as a welcome piece of landscape. He recalls an early game of basketball behind Saint Malachy's in which he confounded his own highest expectations. "It was like a miracle," he says. "I made five free throws in a row. One shot I watched as it went up to the left and then curved into the basket." Odd as Tomes seemed, it became clear to the kids that here was a nonjudgmental, friendly, even helpful presence. "Brother Bill hung around," says Demetrius Ford, "talking to people, taking 'em to McDonald's or out to the sand dunes. He became just Brother Bill. He's cool, a nice man of God who is out for peace."

Tomes is ignorant of the gang hierarchies that newsmen like to display in charts on television, but he knows all the insignia and handshakes; he says hello with them. "For me they [the handshakes] are a matter of reality," Tomes says.

"Other people might want to change these kids," Tomes says, "but I recognize them for who they are, and for how great they are as children of God. They need to respect themselves; it's when they don't that they shoot at each other." Tomes never issues advice except when asked. "I give information, is all," he explains. "I don't make a recommendation except if I think the person is ready to follow my bullshit anyway." If he overhears some lethal plan he will intervene in his way. "Once I overheard some guys plotting to kill somebody," says Tomes, "and so when the hit was supposed to go down I went back and just stood with them. It was twelve thirty in the morning. The boys involved went off in separate directions."

Passive intervention has become, more than anything, Tomes's signature. When gangs are fighting, he stands between them to still the violence. One summer afternoon a half-dozen years ago, Demetrius Ford recalls, some Disciples and Vice Lords were shooting it out on the blacktop behind two buildings at Henry Horner. "Bill just came right up through the middle," says Ford, who was standing on the periphery. "Nobody wanted to hit a white-man priest and go to jail for any murder, so there was a cease-fire."

In 1984, Cardinal Bernardin asked to meet Bill Tomes. Tomes made such an impression that Bernardin put him on Catholic Charities' payroll as a consultant. The agency allowed him to expand his turf to include Cabrini-Green as well as Henry Horner.

"I went to a Cobra Stones building, then a Disciples building, and I got . . . um . . . a cold reaction," says Tomes, recalling the first day at Cabrini. "Some drug dealers gave me the silent treatment." The one bright spot was an encounter with a young man named Elbert O'Neal, a Cobra Stone who lived with his mother and siblings on the fifteenth floor of 1150 North Sedgwick. "You are a sign from God," O'Neal told Tomes. No, Tomes said. "Yes, you are," said O'Neal. "God sent you as a sign so I'd change my life."

O'Neal became Tomes's protector. "Elbert was the only kid who welcomed Brother Bill to Cabrini," says the boy's mother, Bessie O'Neal. "Elbert would take him into our building and keep the other young men from doing anything to him." At the outset the gang members took Tomes "for a crank out to get their money," says Darryl Webster, a Disciple. But in time, Tomes was again accepted.

Consider his relationship with Webster. Webster dropped out of school in the twelfth grade, not for academic reasons but "'cause I got shot in the stomach and legs." At twenty-four, he's been a cook and a salesman in a video store. "Currently I'm looking for a job," he says. His nickname is "Doorknob," which, he says, stems from the fact that "all the ladies get a turn." Webster, a Disciple, has been shot twice in the last two years; each time, Tomes visited him in the hospital. "He holds my hand and prays with me," says Webster. "He is my homey." "Homey" is gang lingo for friend.

"Other times Brother Bill'll ride us around, and we'll say a prayer together," says Webster. "He'll say it with the Cobra Stones or the Vice Lords, it don't make no difference. He treats everybody the same." (Tomes even used to drop by the El Rukn's South Side headquarters to wish the ruffians a happy new year.)

Sometimes, gang members don't want Tomes around, particularly when he positions himself in the middle of their gun battles. Having kept count, he says bullets have whizzed by in his vicinity a total of twenty-eight times. Mostly they shoot at him to force him out of harm's way, Tomes figures, but the tactic doesn't work—he keeps coming. "That's my vocation," he says, "to love people and to be in conflict situations to prevent violence. Only if I'm willing to die for these kids can I change attitudes. If I do die in this way, it's God's pleasure." He says he isn't afraid when violence erupts; on the contrary, he feels immense joy, since he's convinced he's doing the Lord's bidding.

The most dangerous turf at Cabrini-Green was long said to be Hobbie Field, an expanse of blacktop near adjoining buildings ruled by three separate gangs—the Disciples, the Vice Lords, and the Cobra Stones. On warm-weather afternoons and evenings, battles would break out there with bottles, pipes, and sometimes guns. In 1986, Jerry Drolshagen, a Jesuit seminarian, was skinned on the arm by a bullet while with Tomes at Hobbie Field. "We were with Vice Lords," says Tomes, "and some Disciples ambushed us. We went back that same night to show we weren't afraid."

Tomes's mission is not just to stop violence but also to minister to its victims. Since 1983, he says he has lost seventy-five "bud-dees" to murder, kids under twenty-five years whose violent deaths rarely made the papers. Tomes keeps a thick stack of funeral programs. Sometimes he is listed; when asked, he takes a part, usually reciting from the beatitudes. "Blessed are the poor in spirit, for theirs is the kingdom of heaven. Blessed are they that mourn, for they . . ."

Tomes remembers all the dead, the troublemakers as well as the blameless. Laketa Rodgers, for example, perished on August 5, 1985, at Cabrini-Green. She was nine years old. "She used to run out to us; she was so sweet," says Tomes. "She was killed out on the blacktop. Some gang members were shooting at each other, and she got hit. Afterwards, I went to see the boy that killed her. He didn't mean to do it. He got eighty years."

In August of 1986, Johnny Bates, who was twenty-one, was shot on a seventh-floor balcony at Henry Horner. He tumbled into the stairwell, crumbling on the landing a half floor down. "He gave out the most horrible scream you ever heard in your life," says Tomes. "I got to him five minutes before he died. I tried to prepare him for death. 'God loves you,' I told him."

In December of 1988 a twenty-five-year-old named Sammy Hatcher was gunned down in an entranceway at Cabrini. Tomes baptized him with a handful of snow before Hatcher was hauled away to Northwestern Memorial Hospital, brain-dead on arrival.

Aron Buckles, a Disciple, used to call to Tomes across Hobbie Field. "Brother Bill, give me some love," he'd say, and Tomes would respond by putting one fist on top of another, which is the gang symbol for love. "Aron was a tough guy, but we were close friends," Tomes remembers. "He wanted to go straight. They killed him for trying to leave." He was shot to death on a Thursday; the next day he would have started a job with the city. Buckles was twenty.

Two deaths hold special meaning for Tomes.

Dwayne "Chico" Harris was a resident of Henry Horner. "Everybody knew him," says Demetrius Ford. "He would get high and freak around a lot, but he wouldn't hurt nobody." At four o'clock one August morning in 1987 someone shot Harris, twenty-five, as he slept on a park bench yards away from Tomes's room at the rectory.

"Bill felt terrible about Chico," recalls Father O'Gorman. "Chico wasn't Catholic and, to be honest, he wasn't my favorite. When Bill asked me about burying him at Saint Malachy's I found it a bit unorthodox, but I said, 'By all means.' It was important, I felt, to placate the neighborhood grief. So Chico was waked here, and I said the funeral Mass. The church was jam-packed. Chico got the same send-off that Mayor Daley or Cardinal Cody would get."

The other was Elbert O'Neal. In the spring of 1985 Tomes's protector told him he expected to die soon. "Oh no, Elbert," Tomes sighed, but O'Neal was convinced. O'Neal was trying to keep his distance from the Cobra Stones, and various Stones were leaning on him. It was a bad situation, one that concerned Tomes all the more when he found out that O'Neal had received a college grant. One afternoon, O'Neal interfered with some toughs beating up another young man in the lobby of O'Neal's building. One tough, Washington "Snake" Green, pulled a gun and shot O'Neal in the mouth, chest, and stomach.

Tomes rushed to Henrotin Hospital and found his friend in a coma. For two weeks Tomes stayed with O'Neal, passing the nights on the floor by his side. Tomes insists that O'Neal knew he was there, for whenever Brother Bill walked away from Elbert's bed the boy would squeeze his hand. Because he thought O'Neal would want it, Tomes baptized him using a rag and water from the sink. O'Gorman delivered the last rites, and after O'Neal died the funeral was held at Saint Malachy's.

Washington Green remained at large. After he was finally apprehended in

Wisconsin and charged with O'Neal's murder, Tomes went to visit him at the Cook County Jail. Green, twenty-one, entered the visitors' room, saw Tomes across the bullet-proof glass, and turned on his heel. Eventually Green was sentenced to thirty-eight years in prison.

Tomes and Bessie O'Neal bought Elbert a tombstone. "Beloved son and brother," it says, "never be afraid to die." O'Neal is buried at Queen of Heaven Cemetery in Hillside. Every year on his birthday—June 6—Tomes takes some of O'Neal's friends to the grave and throws a party. They say a prayer, reminisce, have pop and Burger King hamburgers, share a cake, and sing "Happy Birthday" to the gravestone. "It's a mixed-bag event," Tomes explains. "There are tears on some people's part."

For all this Tomes earns fourteen thousand dollars a year, plus mileage. He figures he spends more than four thousand dollars a year on his kids. He takes them to his alma maters—the University of Notre Dame and Loyola Academy in Wilmette—to speak on gang life, buys them meals at McDonald's, and—as hard as he resists it—lends them money that is seldom repaid.

A couple of years ago, Tomes and a fellow youth worker, Jim Fogarty, founded a two-man religious community they called the Brothers and Sisters of Love. Fogarty, thirty-two, a thin man who doubles as chaplain at Saint Bernard Hospital, wears the same kind of habit as Tomes and patrols mostly in the Rockwell Gardens project. To fund the Brothers and Sisters of Love, Tomes set up a not-for-profit foundation that raises money by sending out a newsletter twice a year. But contributions are small—about two thousand dollars raised per newsletter—and Father Larry Reuter, the president of Loyola Academy and the head of Tomes's foundation, is after Brother Bill to come up with a more productive approach. Or at least to print more newsletters.

Tomes feels he has better things to do. From 2 P.M. until after midnight every day but Sunday, he can be found wheeling his Buick through the city's poorest neighborhoods, sniffing out friendships and trouble. Since his father died in 1988, he has lived in Evanston with his eighty-four-year-old mother. He hasn't taken a real vacation since 1977. "He has no downtime, no personal life," says Walter Ousley, Tomes's supervisor at Catholic Charities. Tomes's universe now encompasses the Henry Horner, Cabrini-Green, Stateway Gardens, and Robert Taylor projects, plus Logan Square, Humboldt Park, and anywhere else he's of a mind to go. These fields of his grow even more fertile with the night.

A squad car's Mars lights ripped through the dwindling light of day on Pershing Road. Cruising Stateway Gardens at dusk, Tomes saw the flashing lights and gave chase—as much chase as a Buick with 139,000 miles on it can muster.

The cop car stopped in front of some four-story buildings at the Ida B. Wells project. The cops got out and went inside. Tomes, who keeps his distance from police officers, waited on the sidewalk out front in case he was needed.

"Who you? Jesus?" asked a ten-year-old boy looking up at Tomes.

Tomes told the lad he was with Saint Elizabeth's Church on Forty-first Street, and this was partly true. For the last couple of years Tomes has joined Father Donald Ehr, the pastor of Saint Elizabeth's, in a walk through Stateway Gardens and Robert Taylor each Tuesday afternoon.

"You got no gym shoes on," the boy pointed out.

Tomes stuck out a black shoe. The boy smirked.

It turned out that nothing much was going on at Ida Wells. Tomes fired up the Buick, and a teenager on the sidewalk gave him the finger. Tomes jammed on the brakes. "I never accept an insult," he explains. "I always try to make friends." The teen and his friends, whose hats were pitched to the right, Disciple style, greeted Tomes suspiciously, but within minutes everyone was gabbing. Tomes promised to return another night.

Minutes later, Tomes pulled up in front of a high-rise in Stateway Gardens. The night before, a twenty-five-year-old woman had fallen to her death from a twelfth-story apartment, and now Tomes wanted to be of service to the survivors. But the people gathered in the darkened building's entryway told him none of the family was home. Tomes managed to find out the time and place of the funeral.

A few minutes later, Tomes ran into Debra Jones, the youth minister of Saint Elizabeth's, and found her musing on the death. "In two years she's the fourth person who jumped out the window at Stateway," said Jones, an outgoing woman with large hoop earrings. "People were shocked that such a young woman—with children, too—would fly right out. She had six kids, and now who's going to raise them?

"Kids are going crazy. They get in gangs because there's no one to guide them. They don't have father figures, so you can't expect them to have pride. Drugs are flowing. It hasn't even begun to get really hot yet, and already the kids are going crazy. Girls are out prostituting. I don't know, Brother Bill, I don't know. . . ."

"I'll be around," promised Bill. And now he was headed north, to Cabrini-Green.

The news there was grim. A reputed Cobra Stone nicknamed "June" had been gunned down by Disciples two days earlier in a project parking lot. "This is going to increase my business," Tomes remarked darkly, and he set off in search of more information. The man on duty at Johnson's Funeral Home on North Avenue was not much help—the name "June" was nowhere on the register—but later a Cabrini kid told Tomes that the full name was Lugene Tanner and that the funeral was scheduled for the coming Saturday.

Rounding a corner, Tomes spotted one youth giving a karate kick to another.

He bounded from the car, the flaps of his habit flying in the lamplight. He needn't have bothered—the kids were only goofing off—and Tomes went on. He spent another twenty minutes giving four Cabrini kids a lift to a house in Lincoln Park, the home of one boy's grandmother.

It was after ten o'clock when Tomes tapped on the door of the flat belonging to Lugene Tanner's mother. It was dark inside. The little boy who opened the door agreed to summon Mrs. Tanner. "I'm sure June is fine," said Brother Bill, who could not recall ever meeting Lugene Tanner, but nevertheless believed him now safe in heaven. The woman nodded wearily.

His next stop was the Logan Square two-flat occupied by Edgar Rios's family. Brothers Ralph and Juan were standing in the backyard when Tomes arrived, working on cars under floodlights set on the porch. Ralph pointed out the motorcycle that had belonged to his late brother. "Jeez, I feel like I knew Edgar, even though I didn't," offered Tomes. "I love him, especially when we all go out to the grave to visit him."

Brother Bill directed the conversation toward which gangs were operating in the area. "Don't know," said Ralph, "except they killed a kid over on Drake Street over a damn dog." Tomes nodded evenly, like he'd just been told tomorrow's weather.

"Bye-bye," Tomes said finally, and he moved off to his car, chatting for a moment with Edgar's girlfriend, who was sitting on the front stoop.

Then Tomes drove over to the building where Johnny Bates had died in 1986. He climbed to the seventh-floor landing. "Here's where I talked to him about God for the last four minutes of his life," he said. On the cement wall, surrounded by graffiti, were the initials "BT JB," which Tomes had written there. "Sometimes I just come here to pray," said Tomes. "It's a holy place—maybe not for you, but it has meaning for me." He bowed his head.

Bill Tomes was born in Akron, Ohio. Growing up, he moved to Cleveland, to Philadelphia, and finally to Chicago as his father, an industrial engineer named W. Wylie Tomes, changed jobs. Bill's given name is William Wylie Tomes Jr. "My father was a man of great integrity," he says. "I'll never be able to be as good as my father. All businessmen held him in high esteem. When he went golfing, no one would use a bad word in front of him."

Tomes graduated from Saint Athanasius Catholic School in Evanston and entered Loyola Academy. As a boy Bill was "quiet, always neatly dressed, and rather studious," recalls Dan Cotter, a childhood friend who's now a businessman. "He was a nerd," says a woman who knew him as a boy, "and the last person you'd ever think would be doing what he's doing today."

Tomes studied English and philosophy at Notre Dame, later returned there to earn a master's in counseling, and then began a sixteen-year tour as a counselor for Catholic Charities. Once a year he'd travel to Europe for a month at a time, preparing a doctoral thesis on psychotherapeutic services in eighteen countries. Ultimately, he abandoned the project. "I thought, is this going to make a difference in helping people?" says Tomes. "I figured no."

Tomes never married. He was briefly engaged in college, but his true heartbreak came in 1966, when Bill was thirty-one and fell in love with a nurse from Minnesota. They dated for a year and a half and were to the point of looking at rings and furniture when Tomes left on one of his European excursions. When he returned, the nurse had married somebody else. "Oo-ee, I went into a real depression," Tomes says. "It made me distrust people for quite a while." There has been no one since to compare with the nurse—"except Jesus." Tomes realizes that his present lifestyle is not what every woman dreams of.

Painting had been Tomes's longtime avocation—three of his oils of Paris hang in the Snite Museum of Art at Notre Dame—and in 1978 he gave up his job at Catholic Charities to try his hand at doing portraits. It didn't work out financially, and by February of 1980 he was looking for work. His options came down to an airline job out at O'Hare Field and a counselor's slot at Saint Mary of Nazareth Hospital. On the way back from an interview at O'Hare he stopped at Saint Joseph's Ukrainian Catholic Church to think matters over.

"When I knelt down," Tomes said in a 1988 interview with the religious periodical *Witness*, "everything in the church that was in color went black, and everything that was white stayed white. Everything was sort of fuzzy except a picture of Christ which hung by the altar. Christ began speaking from the picture and said, 'Love. You are forbidden to do anything other than that.'

"It was such a surprise. I had never experienced anything like that. I started to write down what He was saying. I asked Him if I should take the job at the hospital. He said, 'I'll lead, you follow.' I asked Him again and He said, 'I'll lead, you follow.' Even though I thought I might anger Him I asked, 'Should I take another job?' Deliberately but not angrily He said, 'I'll lead, you follow.' Several times He told me not to be afraid. At that time I didn't understand what there was to fear. I do now.

"The conversation lasted forty minutes. Somewhere during that time I told Christ that I had to go because I was expected at my sister's house for dinner. He responded by saying, 'Stay with Me. Rest with Me.'"

Tomes was not a devout person (he had even considered himself an atheist briefly in the sixties), but now he started to experience what he felt were messages. One day he picked up a Bible and opened it to a passage that read, "Take nothing with you for the journey." Twice more he opened the Bible and found the same command in other places. What does this mean? he eventually asked the pastor at Saint Athanasius, Father Tom Ventura, and Ventura said it meant Tomes was being told to rid himself of his belongings. Later, Tomes opened a picture book on Francis of Assisi. The caption before him read, "Take nothing with you for the journey." Tomes concluded that Ventura was correct.

First went Tomes's possessions, then his Evanston apartment. He accepted food as payment for odd jobs and lived in the basement of a sympathetic neighbor, sleeping on cardboard. "The spiders were really getting to me," he told *Witness,* "and one night as I was about to kill one it jumped across the room. So I got down on my hands and knees and decided to love him. I looked at him real hard, and he didn't jump away. From then on, spiders and I lived at peace with one another."

Tomes was still finding messages in the Bible and conversing with pictures in churches the day he read a *Tribune* article about Saint Malachy's. The story described it as the poorest parish in Chicago, and this appealed to Tomes—he felt that's where he should be. He was employed part-time at a White Hen in Schiller Park when he started volunteering at the parish.

Over time, Tomes has enjoyed a higher and higher profile. Go to a project now—especially Henry Horner or Cabrini-Green—and everyone knows him. Each Good Friday, Tomes and other clerics lead a march through Cabrini-Green; carrying a cross, they stop at each of fourteen stations for responsive readings. This year's Good Friday dawned cold and drizzly, and only two dozen or so people joined the march. At least that number of spectators hung from their windows watching the parade. "Hey, Brother Bill," some yelled. "Come down and walk!" he shouted back, although none did.

Tomes's moment of greatest public recognition came in November of 1985, when he was honored with the Daniel A. Lord Award by Loyola Academy. A one-hundred-dollar-a-plate, black-tie dinner drew seven hundred people to the Conrad Hilton. "I was so nervous about this talk tonight that I went to Cabrini-Green to settle down," said Tomes, beginning his remarks. Then he held up his funeral programs and talked about the kids he had buried, including Elbert O'Neal, dead just that May. Tomes spoke of God's command that we love our fellow men, and he invited the audience to devote themselves to others. When he finished, some people had tears in their eyes. Afterwards, a man approached Tomes and pledged a gift of five thousand dollars to Loyola, for Tomes's use.

Tomes feels that he puts whatever money he receives to good purpose. He thinks he has saved "hundreds of lives." But whether Tomes has curbed violence in the main—rather than just in specific circumstances—is open to question.

At Henry Horner, says Demetrius Ford, the violence is off "100 percent from what it used to be," despite the 405 violent crimes, including five homicides, that police reported there last year. "All the guys who used to shoot are either dead or in jail," Ford says. (Thirteenth District police commander Don Torres says the same thing.) There are simply fewer people at Henry Horner now: of 1,774 units, 815 stand vacant, according to the CHA [Chicago Housing Authority].

On the other hand, a peace treaty between the Disciples and the Vice Lords forged two and a half years ago at Horner was assisted by Tomes. When the agreement was pending, "Brother Bill walked around and asked everybody what they thought," remembers Ford.

At Cabrini-Green, "the carrying-on is less now," says Darryl Webster. "Now something happens once every blue moon. But the shooting ain't going to stop unless the gangbangers want it to." In other words, Webster credits the decline in fighting more to the gangs' own machinations than to Tomes's influence. (Ray Risley, the Eighteenth District commander, says reduced occupancy is the big reason.) Steve Pedigo, pastor of the Fellowship of Friends church in the development and an admirer of Tomes, thinks violence has diminished in large part because city police and CHA officers swept and secured five troublesome buildings.

Tomes sometimes faces the accusation that in mingling so closely and lovingly with gang members he is sanctioning antisocial behavior. He understands he's been criticized for knowing gang symbols.

Tomes responds by saying that he just does Christ's bidding. "I'm not allowed to think about changing them. All I'm permitted to do is love. God has perfect love for these boys, and we are simply vessels for His love." And when pressed, Tomes argues, however modestly, that he does make things better. "We accept the kids and love them as they are, and that brings some change," he says. "They feel better about themselves. They develop higher self-esteem." Finally, he exhibits a touch of rancor: "There is the view that I ought to change these guys, but they are tough fellas—they kill and do drugs. Are *you* out here getting jobs for them?"

"If nothing else, he is helping kids discover that they have value," contends Father Tom O'Gorman. "At least someone—Bill—sees goodness in them. If he preached against their lifestyle, it wouldn't make any difference. You don't alter your behavior on account of words from other people. Does Nancy Reagan affect a soul with her Say No to Drugs campaign?

"The most positive thing about Bill is that he disintegrates the anonymity of gangs," O'Gorman goes on. "Through him I've met hundreds of individuals who, before, I just thought of as 'members of gangs.' Now I know them as people. I can look out my window at Saint Malachy's on a summer day and see a gang member stealing a woman's purse—and be enraged by it—but that's only part of the story. The other part belongs to Bill."

"When I first met him, I thought to myself, 'Who is this nut?'" reflects Father Donald Ehr of Saint Elizabeth's. "But I had an intuition that he wasn't a nut, and that turned out right. He shows people that they don't have to kill and do drugs. He hasn't been here long enough for me to say he's made a tangible difference, but in time I'm sure he will have an effect. He is a gift from God, I think. I might have doubts about him if he wasn't willing to put his life on the line, but he is—when cops and firemen crouch behind cars, he's out there. And so far, thank God, he has had God's protection."

This spring Tomes worried that God might be about to remove His shield. "Most people think I'm going to get myself killed," he mused one day. "I always seemed to be the only person who wasn't feeling that way, but a couple months ago I started to wonder." So he made advance arrangements for his funeral, which will take place at Holy Name Cathedral, with Catholic, Lutheran, Quaker, Presbyterian, and Missionary Baptist clergy participating. Holy Name makes sense to Tomes because it doesn't sit in gang territory, which will allow all his kids to come and mourn him comfortably.

"Probably nothing's going to happen," he said, "but I've been with other guys who thought nothing was going to happen—and it did."

The funeral of Lugene Tanner took place at the Johnson Funeral Home on a Saturday morning in April. A hundred mourners entered the chapel and approached the open, blue-sided casket. They found Lugene lying peacefully in a white jogging outfit, a white cap lying on his stomach. Lugene's mother and a brother took their places on folding chairs at the front. Bill Tomes, whom Mrs. Tanner didn't know but "had seen around a lot," sat in front, too, but across the aisle.

Normally Tomes might have spoken; but the Tanners were Jehovah's Witnesses, and Tomes explained that their funerals are conducted by a member of the church. "The purpose of life is to accumulate a limited amount of knowledge," said the preacher, "to grow old, and eventually to die—some prematurely, as in the case of Lugene Tanner." That was the only mention of Tanner.

Thereafter, the preacher recited passage after passage from the Bible. In the middle of the service, a girl in a pink dress shrieked and fled. Tomes ran out after her. Lugene's soul is still alive, he told her.

Afterward, the mourners poured out onto North Avenue. The family climbed into a pair of limousines. Tomes gathered together a half-dozen Cobra Stones, friends of the deceased, and offered them rides to the cemetery. The sun shone brilliantly as the funeral procession headed east toward Lake Shore Drive. The black Buick was the sixth car in line.

LIKE A ROLLING STONE

Arrest after arrest, Kent Fly always winds up back on the streets he's called home for more than a decade. What are we to do with a guy like that?

Kent Fly was bobbing on his feet in front of the Pearl art supply store on Chicago, announcing that a sale was going on inside even though it had ended. It was early March, and a cold wind whipped down the street. Fly, who had a crack running through his lower lip, was dressed in a black vinyl shell with a sleeve that had been ripped during a fight. A hood belonging to some long-gone jacket covered his head, and he had his hands stuffed in the pockets of thin tan pants. "I ain't got no gloves," he said.

Fly is thirty-eight, yet he looks older. He's balding, with gray hair and a gray beard. He's bowlegged, and his toes have been amputated, which makes him hobble.

"Help the homeless, my brother," he said to a long-haired man scurrying into Pearl. The man took the wrong door, and Fly, a veteran panhandler skilled at being agreeable, directed him to the other one. "This side, sir," he said.

Fly broke into a soulful version of the song "I'm Crying" until he saw a woman approach. "Help the homeless," he said.

The woman responded with a tight smile.

"Maybe you can help me when you come out," he said, but she'd already gone inside.

He cupped his hands around his eyes and peered through the window, scouting

29

Kent Fly

his prey in the store aisles. Soon the long-haired man reappeared. "Sir, a little help," Fly said. But the man beat a hasty retreat.

"I need ten dollars," Fly said, sighing. He explained that it would go toward the cost of a room at the New Ritz Hotel, at Eleventh and State, where he often spends the night. The sun had begun to fade, and Fly hadn't yet secured enough money.

"For the bulk of people, homelessness is a relatively brief experience," says Brooke Spellman, director of the city's Family Support Division of the Human Services Department, which encompasses services for the homeless. "It's a transitional stage they grow out of." But Fly, who's at once dim and crafty, has been a resident of the public way for nearly a dozen years, longer than most of the other homeless people in Chicago. He does get off the street, although it's usually because he's in jail. He's been arrested scores of times, mostly for misdemeanors, and he swings in and out of the justice system with a startling blitheness.

"Kent talks like he's never done anything wrong," says Jerry Fluder, a police lieutenant who heads the community policing program in the Eighteenth District and has known Fly for years. "He is real good at making it on the streets. He has an upbeat personality, and he doesn't seem unhappy at all with the lot he's pulled."

Fly likes to panhandle along a route that runs west on Chicago from the Pearl store, at Franklin, to the Shell station at the corner of Orleans, then swings north a half block to a building that houses a Bally's Total Fitness. Sometimes he materializes on Rush Street, at the Jewel [grocery store] at Clark and Division, or outside the rock-and-roll McDonald's. His usual hours of operation are from noon until dusk, but you can look for him for days at the regular times and find no trace of him.

For three months in 1993 Fly was licensed to sell *StreetWise,* but he lost his badge for violating the rules, which require vendors to use "professional language and attitudes" on the job, cooperate with other solicitors, and not be on drugs while working. *StreetWise* executive director Anthony Oliver says the paper has no record of why Fly lost his badge, but Fly has a version: "I was at Sixty-ninth and the Ryan in a McDonald's, and this dude gave me a dollar for a paper. I had one in my hand, and he said, 'Keep the paper.' But then he called to complain because he said I wouldn't give the paper up, and somebody came to McDonald's and took my badge. I've been selling without a badge since then. My friends give me extra copies."

Oliver says Fly can get away with selling the extras "because we don't have the resources to police adequately illegal vendors." And the police usually have better things to do than make arrests for failure to have a *StreetWise* badge. When Fly can't get extra papers, he just asks for donations.

Fly speaks in a halting manner, and he can be testy when confronted. Yet he can also be engaging, with an aw-shucks smile and a courtly, subservient way of addressing potential customers or donors. "A lot of people help me out because I'm a nice person," he says. "That's the thing." He has regular patrons, particularly when he's trolling the Rush Street area. "I don't know their names, but I know them when I see them," he says. "I remember faces, not names. They're white, and they call me Fly, not Kent."

Fly says many people who buy the paper give him more than a dollar, and some are very generous. "A dude gave me twenty dollars on North Avenue last night. I bought a steak at Ronny's Steakhouse, and I went and got a room at the Ritz. Once I was up north on Dearborn, and a Mexican dude with a three-piece suit came by. He and his wife, in a black-and-white dress, were celebrating their seventh wedding anniversary. I said, 'StreetWise. Help the homeless.' The man said, 'How much do you need?' I said, 'One hundred dollars.' And he handed it to me. If I'd have asked for more, he'd have given it to me."

On a good day, Fly grosses one hundred dollars, although his usual take is around fifty to sixty dollars. He also gets a $494 monthly disability check from the Social Security Administration, although it's stopped when he's in jail. The check is sent to him through one of his half sisters.

Fly uses his panhandling money to buy meals—he favors quarter-pounders with cheese, fries, and a drink—and drugs. "I go into the projects and buy drugs. I know what cribs to go to," he said in late January, listing addresses in Cabrini-Green where he'd bought and smoked crack and marijuana. But a few weeks later he said he'd been off drugs for a year. "I don't buy that shit now," he said. "I just don't."

In early 1999 Fly was riding the Howard El when another passenger noticed that he seemed to be in pain. "The man asked me what was wrong, and I said, 'My feet is cold,'" he says. "The man asked to see my toes, and they turned out to be black. He was a white guy, a nice fellow, and he gave me twenty dollars and took me to the hospital for frostbite."

Fly was hospitalized for two days, and his toes were amputated. He spent a month at a rehabilitation center learning to walk again. "A woman at rehab took me to a Chinese restaurant," he says. "She told me I could order anything I wanted." He doesn't know who paid for his treatment but believes it was the passenger who took him to the hospital.

When he's panhandling, Fly keeps an eye out for the police. "They always bother me," he said one afternoon while huddled in the doorway of the Orleans Street Bally's. "They tell me I have to move on." But he readily admits they often do more than that, saying, "I've been arrested thousands of times." Police records show that since 1981 he's been arrested 185 times, frequently on multiple charges—almost certainly the record for a homeless person in the city.

Most of the charges are for misdemeanors or quasi-criminal violations related to vagrancy. He's been hauled in for hassling someone when he was panhandling, giving a store owner a hard time, and selling *StreetWise* without a license. In February 1997 he was nabbed for offering to perform oral sex on an undercover officer for forty dollars, and three years later he was cited again when he approached the same officer with the same offer. He was arrested in October 1999 at Bally's after being "warned numerous times by security, police and Spectrum [the building's owner] to not be on the premises."

Last year he was arrested twenty-five times—for disorderly conduct, criminal trespass, prostitution (the oral-sex charge), battery, assault, and possession of crack. The year before, he racked up twenty-four arrests. In 1998 he was arrested just eleven times, but only because he wasn't let out of the penitentiary until August. He'd been arrested in October 1997 in an abandoned building in Cabrini-Green carrying a Ziploc bag containing crack and found guilty after a bench trial in January 1998; he was sentenced to two years in prison but got out early because of good behavior and credit he'd earned for days already logged behind bars.

Lisa Lefler, manager of the Shell station at Chicago and Orleans, knows Fly as "Foots," the name her employees gave him because of his uneven gait. Fly begs from Lefler's customers, frequently sweetening his requests by offering to pump their gas. "He's been a pain in the butt to me," says Lefler. "When I ask the guy to get off my property, he just looks at me and smiles. Then he limps away." He often returns as soon as he notices Lefler pulling away in her Cadillac. "We've called the cops on Foots probably fifty times and had him arrested ten times," she says. "He's my worst experience in eleven years with Shell."

Misdemeanor cases involving Fly routinely turn up in the misdemeanor court at Belmont and Western. Fly tends not to show up for hearings, and then a warrant is issued for his arrest. When he comes to court his case is made by an assistant public defender, for whom he's merely another name on a long list. The only lawyer Fly mentions by name is a private attorney who represented him twenty years ago and with whom he's had no contact since.

Judge Mark Ballard, who has heard many of Fly's cases, considers him "a pest" but is amused by his manner. "Ah, judge," Fly has told Ballard, smiling, bowing his head, and rocking on his feet. In Illinois a misdemeanor carries a maximum penalty of 364 days in jail and a $2,400 fine, but Fly escapes heavy punishment by pleading guilty in exchange for a reduced or suspended sentence.

"I always plead guilty because I did it and I don't want to lie," he says. "So the judge will give me a sentence of time served or it's an SOL," meaning "stricken off with leave to reinstate," legalese for a dismissal, usually granted because the complaining witness or the police officer hasn't come to court.

"In the end, being arrested doesn't mean anything to him," says the Eighteenth District's Jerry Fluder. "The worst thing that happens to him is he'll have a place off the street to stay for a few days, and he'll get meals. He's using the system."

When he's not enjoying the county's hospitality, Fly stays overnight at the New Ritz or, he claims, with Laura Ball, "my ex-lady." He also claims that he and Ball have a daughter and a grandson. "I don't know my grandson's name," he says. "I ain't been told it yet." Ball, who lives in Cabrini-Green, says she knew Fly when they were both young and living on the South Side. "But I had no relationship with him," she says. "I don't have no daughter by him, and he doesn't stay by me." Fly also claims he has two daughters with a woman who now lives in California, although he can't remember her name.

Fly sometimes says he has lots of friends and girlfriends, but at other times he says, "I'm by myself a lot. I don't like to be with anybody." And he often lashes out at his associates. "That black nigger, I don't like him," he said one afternoon outside Pearl. "And the other one over there is crazy."

On the weekend Fly usually stops in to see a woman I'll call Pat Redmond, his youngest half sister, a bank clerk who lives with her two boys in a South Side high-rise. Redmond lets her brother sleep on her couch, and she feeds and cares for him. "People say, 'Why do you put up with Kent?'" she says. "He's my brother, we grew up together. I hate to see him out there on the streets."

Yet Fly taxes his sister's devotion. "You can see that he's filthy," she said one morning in her small kitchen. "I try to get him to take a bath, because he leaves an odor here. All those germs he picks up are jeopardizing my kids. I got him to take a bath yesterday, but he needs to do that every day." Fly insists that he showers daily.

It irks Redmond that Fly asks for money for washing the dishes and that he sells off the shoes, jeans, pants, and sweatshirts she buys him. And she says that when she slips him a little money he misuses it. "I gave him money yesterday to clean out the trunk of my car," she says, "but once he got it he went over to the projects along State Street to spend it on drugs." She also gets tired of Fly's fits of anger. "Kent has a temper," she said in late February. "If he can't get what he wants, he just goes off on you." As soon as she stopped speaking, Fly got up from the couch and asked for a couple bucks for the El. Redmond said no. "I need carfare!" he shouted at her and slammed out of the apartment.

Fly has six siblings, but Redmond is the only one who routinely takes him in. She's also the person he calls when he lands in jail. "He calls me collect," she says, "I tell him, 'What do you want me to do?'" She says she can't afford to bail him out.

Kent Lewis Fly was born in 1963 in Shaw, Mississippi, a poor community of bean and cotton growers twenty-five miles north of Greenville. His father was Truly Anderson, a truck driver, and his mother was Henrietta Fly, who would later marry a construction worker named Willie Silas.

In a court report prepared before a sentencing in 1998, Fly described his childhood as "good" and said he saw his father every week. "I was glad to stay with him," he says. Anderson died a couple of years ago, when Fly was in jail. "I wanted to go to his funeral," he says, "but they wouldn't let me."

Fly's relationship with his mother wasn't particularly warm. "They were 50 percent close," says Bobbie Jean Hardy, another of Fly's half sisters. "She and my stepfather had problems. She didn't talk to Kent in the usual way. It was 'Kent, don't be doing this and that' instead of real talking between mother and son." She says Fly was much closer to his maternal grandmother, who also lived in Shaw.

Fly didn't get along with his stepfather. "I didn't like him a lot," he says. Hardy says Silas treated the children who weren't his own differently, especially Fly, who had learning problems. She says Silas would tell him, "Get away from me, you crazy boy. You ain't got no sense." Silas also verbally and physically abused his wife and the children. Fly says that one night when he was a teenager he and one of his brothers got into a fight, and Fly drew a knife to defend himself. Silas hit him in the head with a two-by-four.

Hardy describes the young Fly as "a good neighborhood kid—mowing people's lawns, taking out their trash. Anything that needed doing, he'd do, even if he wouldn't be paid. He was more settled back then." Pat Redmond describes him as "playful, fun to be with." Cynthia Hawkins, the current Shaw city clerk, remembers him from high school, where he was in classes for kids with learning disabilities. "He was nice," she says. "His attitude was pleasant. He was real bowlegged—his legs were so wide you could crawl through them. Kids would pick on him, 'cause kids can be nasty, but that didn't seem to faze him. He laughed it off and kept going. He also would get into little things at school—this or that, being disruptive—and he'd have to go down to the principal's office. And he did a little stealing—picking up gum in the store—but it wasn't like he broke into a building or anything. Just little misdemeanors."

Fly says he dropped out of high school when he was a junior so that he could have an operation to correct his bowed legs. "They broke my legs and then fixed them," he says. "I had to stay home because I had casts." When he could walk again he took a job pumping gas.

In August 1980 Henrietta and Willie Silas brought their children to Chicago to join other members of the family, settling into a second-floor apartment on South Aberdeen. Fly, then seventeen, soon got into trouble. "He had no direction," says Hardy. "Somehow he got drawn to things of the street. Next thing we knew he was into drugs." Fly says he started with marijuana, liquor, and cigarettes, then moved to crack. His mother told him to stay away from his new friends, "but he was hardheaded and wouldn't listen."

In October 1981 Fly was charged with taking "indecent liberties" with a child, attempted rape, and aggravated kidnapping. "A lady two doors down said I had assaulted a little girl," he says. "I didn't do it. Somebody else did, a guy down another street. He was in a gang—I wasn't in no gang. I pleaded guilty because I was facing six to thirty" years in prison. He got off with four years' probation.

At the time of his arrest Fly had been working as a janitor and stock clerk at a grocery store. After he was sentenced he worked as a delivery driver until his company's distribution routes were sold, and the next summer he worked for a South Side car wash. Other than his brief stint selling *StreetWise* legally, he hasn't had a job since.

Fly went to prison for the first time in 1989, on a three-year sentence for delivering cocaine to an undercover officer in the gangway outside his family's apartment. Released early in 1990, he moved in with his mother and Silas, who was then on disability. Fly too started getting disability, having been found to have "a form of mental retardation" while he was in prison. He had another operation on his legs at Cook County Hospital. "They took a bone out," he says. "I still have the scars." He says he also earned his GED.

Family members say that during this time Fly stole a TV, telephones, money, a radio, curtains, and curtain rods from the house. "The neighbors had seen Kent do it," says Hardy. "He wouldn't fess up, but it got to where you didn't feel you could put your purse down in your own home—you always had to look out." His mother says she tried to get him into drug counseling. "But he was crazy, and he wouldn't do it."

Fly first appeared in the South Loop in the early nineties, panhandling and selling *StreetWise* in the morning along Dearborn from Dearborn Station to the Dunkin' Donuts at Jackson. Sometimes he went farther afield, trolling in front of the McDonald's or the Walgreens on State. He says if he was lucky he could make twenty dollars an hour. "He was super aggressive," says Jerry Fluder, then a tactical-team sergeant in the First District, "and he'd get in people's faces."

At night Fly often stayed at the Pacific Garden Mission on South State, which housed up to six hundred "overnight guests," about half of them homeless. The mission required guests to listen to dawn and late-night sermons, and Fly says he didn't mind. "I didn't like that shelter because I couldn't sleep there. I'd wake up dizzy." Yet when he was arrested for selling *StreetWise* illegally or for harassing passersby, he would list the shelter as his place of residence.

Fly often encountered the police on his rounds. "A lot of those who live on the street don't want contact with us," says Bill Ross, a veteran sergeant in the First District who now heads its CAPS program [Chicago's community policing initiative]. "Kent Fly didn't care." Ross says that for a time Fly lived in a rag-filled box on Lower Wacker—Fly denies it—and Ross offered to get him help. "He said, 'Get away from me.' He wasn't interested. Yet he'd ask for money from us. 'A couple of bucks, officer. A couple of bucks,' he'd say. And he didn't care if you locked him up."

The charges varied. Police records show, for example, that in December 1994 he sprayed tear gas into the eyes of a "pedestrian" and a "banker" at the First National Bank branch on Dearborn. In March 1995 he was hauled in for trying to sell the *Chicago Jewish Star,* a free bimonthly newspaper. That May he got picked up for stealing a *StreetWise* badge belonging to a vendor, and in June he was arrested for having crack paraphernalia stowed in his shoe. In April 1996 he was taken in for urinating in public, exposing himself, and blocking the street "in such an unreasonable manner as to alarm and disturb the peace." Early on, court clerks knew who he was—"the famous 'Super Fly' Kent" is scrawled on the file jacket of a case from 1994.

Meanwhile he'd become unwelcome at the Dunkin' Donuts—"The supervisor never liked me," he says—and at the White Hen Pantry at Dearborn and Harrison. The convenience store's manager, Robert Boone, says every day there's an incident with a homeless person, many leading to arrests. "At first I tried to hire these people," he says. "Well, one stole from me, the next was a drunk, and the third announced flat out, 'I'm going to start dealing drugs, I'm going to steal from your store, and this isn't going to work out.' I have a three-strikes-and-you're-out rule. After the third guy, I stopped hiring the homeless."

Boone never considered hiring Fly. "It's a nonstop hassle with this guy," he says. "He's a particular pain to women. I don't know if you've ever seen him, but he's just disgusting. Plus he can get very aggressive. He'll talk back to you, cuss at you. When he gets how he gets I just walk him out of the store. He just doesn't get the fact that he isn't wanted." Luis Montano, one of Boone's shift managers, says that he sometimes confronted Fly and that Fly responded with racial slurs or shouted, "Go back to your own country."

At SRO Chicago, a sports-themed grill just down the street from the White Hen, Fly got a marginally better reception. The owners, Dino and Tommy Bezanes, would have Fly arrested if he badgered their customers, but they also made deals with him. When the garbage collectors threw the garbage cans around, the brothers paid Fly five dollars to line them up along the curb. "I remember one time this guy outside was pulling his pants down," says Tommy. "We had Kent go over and tell him that that wasn't acceptable behavior and that he'd better get moving."

When the brothers saw Fly getting into it with Boone or Montano, one of them would walk out and signal Fly to stop before he ended up in more trouble. "We were able to communicate with him nonverbally," says Tommy Bezanes. "We had a détente, an understanding. We had a strange affection toward him, because we'd been through so much together. Sure, he was loud, obnoxious, and dirty, but to us and the beat cops he was just Kent." He remembers Fly fleeing a beat officer after allegedly stealing something from the White Hen. "The cop was a young guy, but he couldn't catch Kent," he says. "Kent just jumped the rail of a parking lot and was gone."

When Tommy Bezanes's name comes up, Fly says warmly, "Yeah, Tommy. He looked out for me a lot. He'd give me five dollars, ten dollars, fifteen dollars to get a room."

In February 1995, Judge Janice McGaughey sentenced Fly to a year of conditional release on a battery charge; he was supposed to stay away from the complaining party, First National Bank, and to undergo alcohol treatment and psychological counseling. But Fly, accompanied by his mother, kept only one appointment with a social worker, who referred him to a hospital to "address health issues." Jesse Reyes, director of the court's social services department, says, "We had minimal contact with him. He simply wouldn't come."

Between February 1 and August 15, 1996, there were fourteen court hearings involving the case, none of which Fly attended. McGaughey issued three separate warrants for his arrest, and he finally was picked up. She entered a guilty finding, and he spent sixty days in jail. ("I don't remember him," says Judge McGaughey, who saw up to two hundred defendants daily.) "Trying to handle a case like this—the toughest kind we have—is like handling Jell-O without a bowl," says Reyes. "There's nothing to grab on to."

In 1997 Fly suddenly vanished from the First District, and the shopkeepers and police wondered where he'd gone. He'd moved to the Near North Side, where, he says, "You can get more quick money." His move soon showed up on his rap sheet, as he began being arrested in the Eighteenth District. A couple of years ago Jerry Fluder transferred to the Eighteenth. "I happened to be the watch commander one night, and they brought me a report of the arrests," he says. "I saw Kent Fly's name. 'I thought you disappeared,' I said when I saw him. He said, 'Nope, I just got out of the First District.'"

Last October, Lisa Lefler had Fly arrested again for panhandling, bothering a customer, and refusing to leave her Shell station lot. This time she'd had enough, and the Eighteenth District police decided to treat Fly as a chronic offender, requiring him to post bond and telling prosecutors to take his offenses more seriously. Lefler, accompanied by Jim Gelbort, a CAPS volunteer advocate, showed up twice in misdemeanor court. Then Fly demanded a jury trial, and the case was transferred to the courtroom of Marvin Luckman, at Thirteenth and Michigan.

On the morning of January 18, Lefler was sitting on a spectator's bench with Gelbort when she thought she heard Luckman's clerk call Fly's name. "Excuse me, should I go up there?" she whispered to the sheriff's deputy, who told her harshly to be quiet or she'd be thrown out of court. "This is her case—she's a witness," Gelbort told the deputy, who ignored him. Lefler says, "He just continued to go off on me."

When Fly was brought before the judge, Lefler rose and came forward. "Don't stand there and make faces to this court," the judge told her. Lefler had no idea what he was talking about. "What kind of face would a thirty-seven-year-old woman make in a courtroom?" she asks.

Through his public defender, Fly waived his right to a jury trial and pleaded guilty to criminal trespass, and Luckman handed him a 150-day sentence—thirty days less than he could have received. "I'm telling you now," the judge said, "when you get out of jail you stay away from that gas station. If you don't, I'll give you the maximum."

The public defender then said that Fly wanted the judge to know he'd finished a drug program during his time in jail.

Luckman contemplated Fly, then said, "I want to compliment you, sir. In Illinois we believe in rehabilitation as well as punishment. I hope you keep this up, so that I won't ever have to see you again in this courtroom." Luckman told Fly he had thirty days to withdraw his guilty plea, then, as Fly was being led off, added, "And stay away from that Shell station."

Lefler walked out of the courtroom angry. "I didn't mind having to go to court, because I want people like Kent Fly off the streets," she said. "But when you're treated like this it turns you off. I was totally disgusted. Kent Fly gets a nice thank-you for taking a drug class, though he'll be right back on drugs. The judge treated me like a kindergartner. I was humiliated, treated like shit, with no thank-you." Luckman says he doesn't remember Lefler. The sheriff's deputy says he was just doing his job.

Fly seemed about to prove Lefler wrong about him. He'd felt encouraged by his addiction counselor, Nancy Abram, and a few days before he pleaded guilty he said, "Miss Nancy and I have been talking about drugs, about changing my ways and my attitude—about doing life right." Abram had advised him to seek treatment at the Roseland office of the Human Resources Development Institute, which addresses drug addiction and mental-health problems on an outpatient basis, and Fly said he intended to go there as soon as he was released.

Jeremy Unruh, an assistant state's attorney who has handled cases against Fly, calls the way vagrants like Fly continually move between the courts, jail, and the street "aggravated mopery." He thinks the problem exists because of a change in public policy in the 1970s that forced mental hospitals to release their less-impaired patients into the community. "The institutions had to release all borderline people," he says. "Kent would have been one of them. He doesn't really belong in jail, but he doesn't belong in the general public either." Unruh thinks Fly should be examined thoroughly by a mental-health professional. "A public defender could have him undergo a mental-health exam," he says. "But because he's always brought in for an offense like disorderly conduct, his case never gets that far. It's dismissed or he pleads guilty."

Fly remembers having only one psychological exam in all his years passing through the courts. "I went to see a psychiatrist in the county jail," he says. "They wanted to put me in the psych ward, but they found I didn't need it. That was a long time ago."

"Look, Kent Fly isn't crazy or slow," says Lisa Lefler. "He understands. He knows how to play the game. So he finishes four weeks in jail. Big deal. Put him in a boot camp, make him clean bathrooms, give him some kind of community service. What they're doing with him now isn't helping him—it's only turning into a handicap." Robert Boone, the White Hen manager, says, "He's the pink elephant in the room. Society doesn't want to look at him, nor do the courts. But someone has to—it's part of being a humane society. I think they need to get him into some type of program where he can put his time to good use and improve himself. Maybe jail is the answer, a place where he's controlled. Or they should test him to see if he belongs on the street. If I was crazy, I'd want to be put in a mental institution."

"Homelessness is only a symptom of a larger problem," says Ervin McNeill, pastor of the Pacific Garden Mission, who was once briefly homeless himself. "The problem could be mental illness or the deception that being a vagabond frees you from the responsibility to love, work, and contribute to society. Many creatures of the street—and I know some have been out there seven, fifteen, or twenty years—have been seduced by their desire to withdraw from society. It's a tough cycle to break, but God gives you freedom of choice to do that." He thinks that the Pacific Garden sermons Fly once heard are a bomb inside of him: "It will go off sometime and somewhere. Maybe it will go off too late—maybe when he's standing in line waiting to enter hell—but it will go off."

Police officers don't believe they can do much to change the lives of disruptive vagrants such as Fly. "We arrest them for disorderly conduct or begging, and we lock them up," says Gary Szparkowski, the lieutenant who now directs the tactical unit in the First District. "Then they're gone. We don't see them because they're in the courts, and in time they're back. It's a revolving door, and there's nothing much we can do about it."

Judges don't think they can do much either. "There are a couple of things that don't happen when you put on a robe—your IQ doesn't go up, and you don't have ultimate power," says Judge Luckman. "You have to do things strictly within the law. My concern—my obligation—is to protect the citizens of the state. What can we do with him [Fly]? A judge is limited to whatever the penal statutes of the state say."

No legal organization seems to have studied the issue recently. "This isn't something that we've dealt with during my tenure," says Pamela Wolf, chairman of the Chicago Bar Association's criminal-law committee. The Cook County Court Watchers, a group founded in 1975 by the League of Women Voters that's now under the umbrella of the Better Government Association, doesn't even have enough volunteers to post observers in city courtrooms. "This is not something we've been able to look at," says Wendy Sadler, chairman of the BGA's court-activities committee.

According to the Chicago Department of Human Services, some twenty-eight thousand people signed in at the city's overnight shelters last year. Many of those names are duplicates, yet it's still safe to assume that thousands of homeless now live in the city. Of those, says Brooke Spellman, head of the city's family support services, some 15 percent are categorized as "episodic," or repeatedly without shelter; 5 percent are "chronic," hard-core cases such as Fly. The city spends fifteen million dollars annually to provide overnight shelters and services for the homeless, including outreach teams that walk the streets, and it can make referrals to four thousand subsidized apartments and rooms. Spellman says that the episodic and chronic homeless get 80 percent of service resources. "If we don't solve those cases," she says, "we will never end homelessness." At a January retreat, a consortium of city agencies and provider organizations set a goal to rid the city of homelessness by 2010.

The consortium's most promising venture is a pilot program set up by Thresholds, a psychiatric rehabilitation center, in conjunction with Cook County Jail. The project is offering extra assistance and counseling to forty-five released offenders who have problems such as schizophrenia and bipolar disorder, most of whom are homeless. The program is expensive—$450,000 a year—but it has cut jail recidivism and rehospitalization rates of participants who've been involved for a year by more than 80 percent. "These are people who believe that nothing good is going to happen to them," says Jerry Dincin, executive director of Thresholds. "The trick is to meet them on their own terms. Maybe they don't want counseling. Maybe it's a shelter or maybe a delousing. But they have to want some help."

Some police, faced with mounting complaints from residents and merchants, are trying a different tactic. Last June and December the First District police invited local homeless people to a site in Grant Park, where they were offered jobs, housing, physical exams, flu shots, and drug rehabilitation—all with no strings attached. More than two hundred people responded. The Eighteenth District police had their own "special services day" in August in Washington Square Park.

Fly didn't make any of the gatherings. Occasionally he says he wants to better himself—his life's ambition is "a job in shipping and receiving"—or to accept an outstretched hand, but the sentiment rarely lasts. Sometimes he acknowledges his dependence on drugs, sometimes he doesn't. Sometimes he accepts that he's responsible for the behavior that leads to his arrests, sometimes he won't. "It's not right to lock me up for nothing," he said one day. "I think that's a disgrace." Then he paused. "It's their fault," he said, referring to the police and the merchants who lodge complaints against him. "I'm not in front of businesses, and they call the cops on me. They say I harass their customers, but I don't. Sometimes I just stand there, and the cops tell me to leave. I just stand there, and I go to jail—for no reason."

His relatives say they've tried many times to get him to straighten up, all to no avail. "He just doesn't think he has a problem," says Pat Redmond. "He's in denial. You can't help somebody who doesn't want to be helped—if you do, you put a jinx on yourself."

Willie Silas died in 1995, and Henrietta—who suffers from failing kidneys, high blood pressure, and asthma—now lives in a spare studio apartment in a church-run building in the New City neighborhood. "Kent won't listen to anybody," she says. "He wants to do things his way. He makes himself homeless." When Kent called her one day this winter, she pleaded, "Come see your mama." But he rarely goes. Redmond tells Henrietta when Fly ends up in jail, and Henrietta says she responds, "Lord Jesus, what did Kent do now?"

"It's a decision he's made to be on the streets," says his half brother Clifton Silas, a sheet-metal worker who lives in the suburbs. "He has an attitude with us. I love my brother, but I can't talk to him straight." Bobbie Jean Hardy says,

"This has been going on for years with Kent. There's only one way out of here, and that's death. That's my greatest fear."

Fly was released from jail on February 5, but he hasn't yet gone to the drug-rehabilitation facility as he promised. "Miss Nancy set me up for that," he says. "She told me to see this one person. But I haven't gone there yet because I've been running the streets."

Fly started training to get a new *StreetWise* license, then lost his training badge twice; he says he can't afford the twenty-dollar replacement fee. On February 7 he was arrested for illegally selling a free publication and for impeding pedestrians. A week later he was nabbed for harassing customers exiting the 7-Eleven on North State. "We have people arrested every day for begging and harassing," says Brian Kongnaewdee, the clerk who filed the complaint against Fly. "The only thing that changes are the faces." In court on March 8, both charges against Fly were dismissed because neither witness showed up.

Fly was soon back panhandling and selling *StreetWise* in front of Pearl, and he kept turning up at the Chicago Avenue Shell station. "He gives you a smart-ass grin, as if to say, 'Here I am again,'" says Lisa Lefler. Jerry Fluder ran into him crossing the street at Ninth and Wabash. He was wearing a three-quarter-length leather coat and carrying copies of *StreetWise*. Fluder, startled to see Fly outside his normal North Side territory, asked, "What you been up to?" Fly told him, "Doin' my usual." Fluder asked if he needed any help. Fly replied, "I do OK."

In April, Fly pleaded guilty to trespassing at the Dominick's on Division. He spent ten days in jail, where he celebrated his thirty-eighth birthday. "I told everybody it was my birthday, and a lot of people wished me well," he says. "My sister was going to bake me a cake, but, you know, I was in jail."

On a Friday in early May he was back on the street. A security guard shooed him away from the Bally's on Orleans, so Fly hobbled over to the front of a building on Institute Place and sat down on a low wrought-iron fence. "*StreetWise*," he called out to workers as they returned to the building after lunch.

A burly young man promised to give Fly something on his way out.

"I won't be here then," said Fly.

The man looked chastened and fished in his pockets. "I had lunch with my girlfriend, and she gave me nothing to take back to work," he said. "How's that for love? I got nothing for you."

Fly shoved his hands in his pockets and stared at the ground.

A police cruiser pulled up, and the officer rolled down her window. "They're complaining about you," she said. "Move on."

Fly rose from the fence and tottered back toward Bally's. ■

THE POWER OF THE KEYS

Lugging around that mass of cold, shiny metal helps Doug Jennings bear his more existential burdens.

Sloppiness is a trait that rubs Doug Jennings the wrong way, so he stopped me one morning near the corner of Eightieth and Ashland.

"Your jacket collar is tucked into your shirt," he said. I fixed myself up, thanked the stranger for his thoughtfulness, and watched him amble off. I couldn't help noticing the thick chain holding dozens of keys slung over his right shoulder, reflecting swirling bits of sunlight onto his green Michigan State Spartans jacket.

"What's with the keys?" I asked him.

"I collect 'em," he said. "They're the keys to my broken heart."

Jennings headed into a dollar store to bum a cigarette, not having any of the cheap roll-your-own kind he prefers. Rebuffed by a clerk, he continued his quest. Briefly he took the keys off his shoulder, swung them in the air, then put them back where they'd been. At the gas station at Seventy-ninth a friend on crutches gave him a smoke. Jennings entered the Rothschild Liquor Mart and purchased a fifth of Richards Wild Irish Rose, his beverage of choice since he was a teenager. He just turned fifty-five.

"Usually I have a drink when I start walking someplace," Jennings says. "With the keys I forget about drinking until I get where I'm going. They make me feel comfortable."

Jennings has been amassing keys since 1983. "I was going with this lady named Peggy Brown, and her father, who worked for a moving company, had a bunch of

Doug Jennings

skeleton keys," he says. "He asked if I wanted them, and I said yeah. I hooked them together and started carrying them around."

The keys are acquired all over. "Somebody'll go into a grocery store and leave their keys on the counter," Jennings says. "They won't come back, and the owner'll give me the keys. Other keys I find on the street. I don't steal any of them or nothing." His chain contains bike, gas-tank, locket, luggage, and jewel-box keys, plus plenty of keys to automobiles, principally from American manufacturers. "I don't even know how to drive," he says.

He totes the keys from March or April until November, when the chain becomes too cold to carry. Then he stows that year's supply in the basement of the bungalow he shares with his sister and her family on South Justine. He never reuses a chain. He can identify past sets from their adornments: 1997's chain has a bullet and some handcuff keys that he found on the pavement; 1998's has an old-fashioned sink fixture; 2003's has a brass belt buckle. None of the chains has any plastic. "I don't like plastic," Jennings says. "Everything I have has to shine."

Jennings, a slim man with a mustache and goatee, is a fixture on the South Side, walking about slowly. "What's the point of hurrying?" he says. He prefers the alleys to the streets. "You meet good people in the alleys," he says. "They'll be sitting down, drinking and talking. And you don't have to step on anybody's toes like you do on streets." On the blocks near his sister's apartment people know Jennings as Uncle Doug, but farther afield he's called the Key Man or simply Keys.

"I'm stopped every hour or so," he says. "Teenagers try to pick a fight with me. 'I bet you can't beat my ass with those keys,' they say, but I put my head down and keep on walking. My keys aren't a weapon. I'd never use them for that. Never had to.

"Lots of times it is little kids on the bus who speak up. 'Oh, Mom, look,' the kids will say, and then I let them hold the keys. But I been kicked off a bus because of the keys, too, when this woman driver got scared and called the cops. Usually the police are no problem. They pull me over, check me out, and I'm off again."

Jennings tells some curious people that when he went to jail he got tired of hailing the turnkey. "I'm looking for a chastity-belt key," he'll say to others. "Now if I find a woman, I'll have to find that key." If that one falls flat, there's always the crack about the keys being to his broken heart. "That's how I meet women," Jennings says. "'I wouldn't break your heart,' the girls say, and we get to talking." The relationships that result are fleeting, he says, just for sex. "I don't want no more girlfriends. They're a headache."

The son of two railroad workers, Jennings grew up on the West Side. He was twelve when he first ran afoul of the law. "They said I pulled up a lady's dress in

Douglas Park," he says. "They took me to the Audy Home and then, because they didn't know what to do with me, to Chicago State [now Chicago Read] mental hospital. I was in the nuthouse for four years."

When he emerged, Jennings married a young woman named Lucinda he'd met at the hospital. They had four children. They're still married. "We don't believe in divorce," he says. "Till death do us part, and all that means. She's my best friend. But I don't know where she is." He'd later have one more child with Peggy Brown.

Jennings held a number of jobs—picking up paper for the Park District, doing janitorial work at John Marshall Law School, toiling at an envelope company— while maintaining a sideline of snatching purses. "I was good at that," he says. "I got away with most of the purses, but then I got caught." It wasn't until 1973, after his fourth turn behind bars, that he gave it up.

He worked for a cousin who ran a taco stand, then took up house painting, the steady nature of which the cousin thought would discourage Jennings from drinking. He did maintenance on some Northwest Side buildings and manned a paper stand owned by a son-in-law. He developed a trade helping women with their gardens and chores. Lately he's been house-sitting for rehabbers who want to make sure they aren't ripped off at night. His current gig, which pays $150 a month, has him sleeping at a two-flat in Englewood. "I got a little mattress there, some blankets, a TV, and a radio," he says. "When they turn the gas on, I'll be able to cook up something to eat."

In 1996 Jennings's son Douglas Jr. died of AIDS; later that year so did his best friend, Willie Christler, who went by the nickname Napoleon. "Doug and Napoleon were inseparable, like Siamese twins," says their mutual friend Art Conley. "When you'd see one, you'd see the other. They lived together for a time. Doug had been collecting keys all along, but since Napoleon passed, they have become an obsession. It takes his mind off the loss, I think."

His employers all notice the keys, but don't seem to mind. "If Doug wants to burden his shoulder with those keys, that's up to him," says Dorothea Campbell, an elderly West Pullman resident for whom Jennings paints, moves furniture, and does yard work. "Doug is not nasty or messy, but very nice. When he comes to me he sets his keys down by the house and gets to work."

Eno Ekong, a real estate investor and rehabber who has employed Jennings in the past, is bothered not by the keys but by Jennings's behavior. Ekong says Jennings drinks too much, fails to obey instructions, and attracts undesirables. Jennings doesn't much care, especially about the drinking. When he tried sobriety in 1989, he says, he ended up taking his clothes off in a forest preserve and the police had to be summoned. "If I gave up drinking now I'd probably die," he says. "I'm not giving up no kind of habit that I got."

Off the Beaten Path

READER

FRIDAY, JANUARY 21, 2000 | VOLUME 29, NUMBER 16 | CHICAGO'S FREE WEEKLY

Bosom Buddies

Robin and Katie are men, they're women, and they're best friends.

BY GRANT PICK

PHOTOGRAPHS BY KATHY RICHLAND

CONTINUED ON PAGE 16

READER
CHICAGO'S FREE WEEKLY

Bigot for Hire

Nobody likes a Nazi, but Art Jones has found his niche.

A SCHOLAR TREKS THE WASTELAND

C. Ranlet Lincoln's *Perspectives* is the city's least watched TV
program at 6:30 A.M.

elevision does not take lovingly to academic types. They are usually the
last guests on the *Tonight Show,* if they get on at all, and they are almost invariably relegated to Kup's final panel of the night. Prime time, unless the academic
in question is involved in a sex scandal or running for political office, or both, is
out of the question. And it doesn't take an intellectual to figure out why: eggheads
suffer from a malady that, in the eyes of the TV producers, is worse even than
tousled hair, smeared lipstick, or an unzippered fly—they are boring.

By all rights, it shouldn't be this way, because academics know so much more
than the rest of us. But their regular endeavors—teaching, research—are based
on logic and content, not style, and style is the substance of television. Academics are bred for the classroom and the laboratory, where what counts is the
meaning of a philosopher's words or the form a bacteria takes on the slide. At the
university, the cognitive is king, and a joke—rather than being the core of a hit-
or-die act—is simply a bit of comic relief in the midst of a discussion on alpha
rays or something equally esoteric. Put an academic on television, away from his
habitat, and you have a hippo in the mountains.

The exceptions to this rule have adapted; they have moxie. Truman Capote
is popular because he gossips, William F. Buckley because he attacks with his
rapier of a tongue, Daniel Patrick Moynihan because he is also a gay blade and
street politician.

C. Ranlet Lincoln

The highest brow on local TV is the dean of the University of Chicago extension division, C. Ranlet Lincoln, and he does not adapt himself to TV one iota. On his panel discussion program, *Perspectives,* which has been on the air for eight years now, Lincoln insists on teaching and refuses to entertain. This makes his program knowledgeable, couth, but duller than most people can tolerate, a show for graduate students and cats with insomnia. But follow him to his home ground, the Midway, and he performs swimmingly amid the traditions of the U of C.

The usual slot for academics on TV, Chicago included, is dawn, and by 6:30 A.M. most of our local channels have abandoned intellectualism and settled into their daily routines. On Channel 2, pert Mary Jane Hayes is cooing as Chef Louis concocts the Continental dish of the day. On Channel 5, Jerry G. Bishop snappily guides some author through the main points of his latest book for thirty minutes, then closes down the show with, "Stay calm and try to adjust"; the author puts his eyes to the floor, wondering if the advice had been meant for him or for the viewer. A farm report is on Channel 9. Channel 11 isn't even up yet.

But on Channel 7, the intellectual ghetto continues with *Perspectives.* Scholarly guests discuss everything from the electron microscope to the ancient Assyrian language to the plight of middle-aged Jewish women. The program is produced for the station by the U of C, which guarantees high-level chatter. What cinches it is host Lincoln, a lanky, patrician man of fifty-one.

Lincoln doesn't necessarily know a lot about the topic at hand, but the panel, which always includes at least one U of C figure, does. Lincoln puts himself in the classic role of Socrates: what he doesn't know, he asks. "Instead of research and preparation," he explains, "it puts me in the spot of listening hard and well."

The material Lincoln listens to is dry enough—what *is* going on at the Argonne National Laboratories?—but the audience is parched more than it need be by Lincoln's own questions and summarizing statements, which usually come together. They are arching, complex, and longer than long, with parenthetical remarks and prepositional phrases flying off them like streamers from a wedding car. "I think Ran can always come up with a question, which is terrific," says one cerebral U of C faculty member, "but often he takes so long to ask a question the listener forgets what he's been asked."

On a fall Sunday, Lincoln is to tape three shows on the problems of the handicapped. In WLS-TV's twelfth-floor green room, he meets his guests: Marianne Hammet, the thirtyish mother of an eight-year-old retarded girl; Rami Rabby, thirty-four, the blind program chairman for an upcoming conference on the handicapped; and Israel Goldiamond, fifty-six, a paraplegic and psychiatry professor at the U of C. Lincoln is very tall—six feet, four and a half inches—with a lilting gait and arms and legs that seem to extend endlessly. "You have to watch out for the coffee cups," he cautions himself more than his guests as he seats them on the set's blue-cushioned chairs, which are across the studio, ironically, from the Eyewitness News desk.

The strains of Shostakovich, the voice of announcer Mike Rapchak, and photos of university quadrangles introduce the show. The panelists, as Lincoln would have it, are well informed and articulate. Dr. Goldiamond points out that the disabled are often talked to in "all those tones with which one addresses a child"; Rabby chides the Chicago school system for refusing to hire the handicapped as teachers before 1969; Mrs. Hammet beseeches the public to see her daughter "as a positive, not a negative" and admits that as a parent of a retarded child, "You mourn your whole life." The talk is civilized, if less than stirring, larded liberally with rarefied language and uninterrupted by commercials.

The conversation is nudged along by Lincoln, now summarizing, now asking. The nudge, however, often turns into a body carry. This, a statement-question on the handicapped show, is typical: "So I take it there would be in that sense a connection between these two topics: one, the relationship of the handicapped person to the society at large, and two, that these particular agencies of society are supposed to provide services to the handicapped; and the connection between these two major issues is that, I would understand, that because of the relationship of the handicapped person in the society at large, namely that they are kept out in various ways, their ability to have some degree of control or influence over the character of the program or agencies is minimal. Do I have it right?"

As Lincoln winds through the statement, the eyes of Mrs. Hammet, the mother, seem to roll back into her head.

The conversation on the problems of the handicapped will be packaged into three twenty-five-minute shows and aired a week later, but few will see them—or want to. The TV audience at 6:30 A.M. is piddling; to hold last place in this slot—as *Perspectives* did during a recent, monthlong Nielsen survey, with only four thousand homes a morning—is sorrier still. (The Channel 9 farm report, *Top 'o the Morning*, ran away with the time period, at thirty-three thousand homes.) Lincoln, who finds most other talk shows "inane," doesn't consult the ratings. His chief concern is producing what he considers good discourse. The station concedes that *Perspectives* is a good show to have on its log when the Federal Communications Commission asks to see public service programming.

The show does seem popular among its participants, though. "It's so conversational," exults Rami Rabby, the blind handicapped conference leader, back in the green room after his appearance. "You get into an issue. On normal shows about the blind, they'll ask you how your Braille watch works—they never really

talk about the problems of the blind." Subrahmanyan Chandrasekhar, a "super-star" astrophysicist at the U of C, also seems to approve. Although he denies it, it is said of him that when the *New York Times* called to ask for a copy of a com-mencement speech he'd given, he sniffed, "What do I need with the *New York Times*?" He allows that he keeps the news media at arm's length, but found his appearance on *Perspectives* in 1971 "quite pleasant."

If the style of *Perspectives* doesn't fit comfortably into the television format, it nonetheless exemplifies the University of Chicago, as if it, like the atomic bomb, were perfected at Stagg Field. Watching the show, one can't help but be reminded of the U of C academic style that was crystallized by Robert M. Hutchins, univer-sity president from 1929 to 1946. Under Hutchins, study of grammar, rhetoric, logic, math, and philosophy were mandatory for U of C undergraduates; students earned credit toward graduation only by passing tough, comprehensive exams, and they were urged to read one hundred "great books."

The years have winnowed away Hutchins's rigid curriculum on campus, but the emphasis on discussion (as opposed to lecture) in class, the other hallmark of the tradition, is as strong as ever. "It's certainly the way I conduct my classes," says humanities professor Marvin Mirsky, "and most of my colleagues do the same." "Ran is looked upon as a good spokesman," explains Virginia Wright Wexman, *Reader* film critic who produced *Perspectives* while a graduate student at Chicago. "This whole idea of discussion is so ingrained at the U of C—they are wedded to discussion. You have on *Perspectives* the quintessential U of C style."

Ranlet Lincoln didn't reach the U of C until middle age, but as a young man he found the next-best collegiate substitute: St. John's College in Annapolis, Mary-land, a small school that in 1937 began a Hutchinsesque curriculum with no electives or majors, no lecture classes or textbooks, and no endeavor held more important than the rigorous pursuit of classical subjects. "My intellectual bag-gage goes back to St. John's," observes Lincoln. "The pattern of teaching is so similar to the U of C—you read worthwhile texts and try to understand them."

The Lincolns are old New Englanders, not on Abe's lineage. Ran was born in Brooklyn and named for his maternal grandfather, Charles Ranlet, a barbed-wire manufacturer. His father, a stockbroker, went to work as a midlevel financial an-alyst for a string of federal agencies, and the family finally landed in Washington. His parents were divorced when Ran was fifteen. He dropped out of high school, did a tour on a destroyer during World War II, then tested into St. John's.

While there, he worked at a small radio station in Annapolis. He would open the station up in the morning and close it down at dusk. He read the news, played records, and fell in love with broadcasting. Once out of college—he had married following his freshman year, and he and his wife today have two children—he signed on with the Voice of America (VOA) and ended up a radio officer in India in the early fifties, the height of the McCarthy years.

"I'd been in India three or four months," he remembers. "The secretary of state [John Foster Dulles] came to India on an official visit. I was considerably involved in PR, and I arranged for him to make a national speech on radio, among other things. I wrote a friend of mine at VOA in New York, describing the visit of John Foster Dulles in negative terms and Dulles, if I remember, as the most repellent man I had ever met.

"Sometime later one of Joe McCarthy's henchmen was snooping around my friend's desk. He didn't find anything on my friend, but he found the letter. Excerpts were broadcast by Walter Winchell." And Lincoln was fired, ending his two-pronged dream to join the Foreign Service and/or become a successful broadcaster.

He bounced around, working as an admissions officer at St. John's, a producer for a St. Louis educational TV station, the vice president of a PR firm, an administrative aide at the Missouri Botanical Garden and then at the U of C Laboratory School. In the midsixties, he was lured to the university proper as alumni director and in 1968 became dean of the extension; with the deanship came the TV show, which Channel 7 had proposed.

Bearing only a bachelor's degree, Lincoln admits his position is a high one at Chicago, where even janitors are reputed to have Ph.D.s. Still, the university extension he heads, like *Perspectives,* is hard and fast in the Chicago tradition. Many colleges, finding students hard to come by in the post–baby boom years, have spun off low-cost extensions with noncredit courses of every stripe, from citizens band radio to how to cope with wife swapping. Not the U of C. "We're determinedly intellectual," shrugs Lincoln. "We don't go in for encounter-group kinds of stuff, first because there's so much of it, and I don't think you need a university context for them." Most exemplary of the extension is its Basic Program, a two-year, noncredit regimen in which adults study the works of Plato, Freud, Nietzsche, and others. A comedy festival that brought Dave Garroway and The Second City alumni to campus this fall was a radical departure.

An associate professor in the undergraduate college, Lincoln has for some years taught a humanities course to freshmen. He is tough in class; he wants preparation and reasoned discussion. What he gets is similar in some ways to his TV show, except that if his panelists stray from the topic here, they flunk.

On the rainy Tuesday following the show on the handicapped, Lincoln strides into his classroom in Cobb Hall on Ellis Avenue and makes for his seat at the end of a rectangle made of tables; he is conservatively dressed in a corduroy sport coat, checked shirt, striped tie, gray flannels, and loafers. He requires the students to post cardboard signs at their places for identification. "I know they're tedious," he sighs as he doffs his trench coat, "but they enable me to feel less rude"; he has a terrible time with names.

The work to be examined today is Plato's *Apology*. It is the defense mounted by Socrates in 339 B.C. at his trial for corrupting the young men of Athens, for making them question. Lincoln spies a hardcover edition of Plato's collected works and informs its owner, "There's scarcely an investment you will make that will be more worthwhile." "I ripped it off from my roommate," the student confesses. Lincoln smiles wanly.

The discussion begins in earnest. Students try to explain why Socrates is mounting his defense: is it to save his life or to have his say before certain conviction? Lincoln furrows his brow, cups his chin, moves his arms around like tendrils; rarely does he take a student's point without digesting it, finding it somehow lacking, then throwing it back with another question attached: "Why, why is it then that Socrates presses in the manner of defense he knows all along would fail?" agonizes Lincoln, whose great-grandfather taught classes at Brown University. He calls each student "Mr." or "Miss" and encourages likewise, feeling that the practice instills respect.

"When these kids come to class in the fall," he will say later, "most have the opinion they learned in high school: that what's meant by discussion is that everyone expresses his opinion. Then they think they've discharged their responsibility. But the reason we exchange opinion is not because it's democratic, but because someone's opinion might be more valuable than another."

The arguments about what Socrates was up to grow hard to follow, even for U of C students, but the most emboldened try and try again to win Lincoln's nod that, yes, they have found Socrates' purpose. Miss Goldfarb, a pretty young woman in a turtleneck, comes up with more answers than an oracle, but none satisfies Lincoln, who instructs the class in the end, "Think about these things for Thursday."

Ran takes some coffee after class in the basement of Cobb Hall. He meets Miss Goldfarb on the way out. "You seemed well prepared today," he tells her, then pushes past through the door with his right arm.

Miss Goldfarb looks pleased enough to have just won the Nobel Prize. Some forty U of C graduates, teachers, and researchers have won it, including Saul Bellow and economist Milton Friedman just this fall. She could someday, too. She will be brilliant and exacting by then, but ponderous, and Johnny Carson would sooner book a talking snake on his show. She will just be growing ripe for *Perspectives*.

BIGOT
FOR HIRE

Nobody likes a Nazi, but Art Jones has found his niche.

On the third weekend of April, Art Jones went to Washington.

Jones, a Southwest Side salesman who is chairman of a group called the America First Committee, drove to the capital to observe the first anniversary of the U.S. Holocaust Memorial Museum. One year before, President Clinton had joined Ted Koppel, author Elie Wiesel, and Israeli president Chaim Herzog in dedicating the austere brick structure. "The Holocaust reminds us foremost that knowledge divorced from values can only serve to deepen the human nightmare," said Clinton, "that a head without a heart is not humanity."

Jones has no use for such rhetoric. Joining members of the Committee for Open Debate on the Holocaust in greeting tourists and school groups at the museum, Jones was dressed in a gray shirt, a navy blue tie, and a black garrison hat. His chest brimmed with campaign ribbons. The gray shirt is the uniform of the America First Committee's "defense corps," and is to be distinguished—says Jones—from the brown shirt worn by Hitler's original storm troopers, the SA. "I consider my committee a white patriotic nationalist organization," he says. "We're social nationalists as opposed to National Socialists."

Jones and his associates carried signs. "We don't buy the Holocaust lie," read one placard. "Holocaust survivors—a list of swindlers," said another, playing on *Schindler's List*. The signs enormously offended the tourists, but Jones was unperturbed by their shouts. "Jews can be very irrational," he says. "I just

Art Jones

maintained military discipline, but they continued to yell and scream and give me the finger. And they grabbed at their crotches. Tell me, why do Jews always grab at their crotches?"

It's not easy being a bigot in the United States today. The Holocaust Museum opened to acclaim. Steven Spielberg won prestige and a sizable box office with *Schindler's List*. On the fiftieth anniversary of D-Day, the triumph of American good over Nazi evil was retold in every medium.

Yet white supremacists like Art Jones persist. Some neo-Nazis resort to violence, but although Jones has had his share of altercations and gets blustery with ease, he's basically a propagandist. He puts out a newspaper, maintains a hotline, participates in demonstrations, and appears on TV talk shows. "I'd be a fool if I didn't take every opportunity to get my ideas before the people," he says.

Art Jones is forty-six years old. He's a sandy-haired, bespectacled man who usually dresses in a sport coat and tie and removes the glasses before he goes on television. He's loquacious, with a tendency to bore in on a topic and work it endlessly. Michael Sandberg, Midwest civil rights director of the Anti-Defamation League (ADL), puts it differently: "Jones is a blowhard, really, loose-tongued and indiscreet."

For a living Jones sells unspecified home-improvement items for a company he'd prefer not to name. "It's a well-paying job," he says, "and I don't want to lose it." On the side he peddles health insurance. "Whenever I make a sale on one of my items, I turn around and ask, 'Say, how's your health insurance?' Often I make two sales in one." Many of his customers are blacks in the projects, and when he's talking business he keeps his politics to himself.

Jones believes in what he calls "revolutionary pan-Aryanism," a creed whose premise is the desirability of overarching white power. "It's an international white movement," explains Jones. "Our aim is to establish a white-run world. The world would be better off with the white man in charge of everything. There'd be light where there is now darkness, knowledge where there is ignorance, law where there is anarchy, food where there is famine." At the point where you get the idea, Jones still goes on and on.

Jones's goal is political power by constitutional means. "The white race has got to do something, and fast," he says, "because unfortunately we're facing extinction if we sit back and do nothing." If politics fails the white-power movement, he hints that matters could get rough: "If we can't get anywhere through the ballot box, we'll have to resort to the cartridge box."

Jones believes society suffers mightily from the presence of its darker and hook-nosed elements. He says the average black person has an IQ fifteen to twenty

points below that of an average white person and is seven times as likely to have
retarded offspring. "There are also certain differences in the central nervous system and the endocrine system that make blacks prone to violence," he adds.
"They learn basically by rote because they aren't too hot with abstract memory."
Blacks are superior in athletics, Jones acknowledges, especially in running.

"Homosexuals are a sign of the decay of our society," he says. "They are
creatures from a different world who are to be pitied, especially in this time of
AIDS." Jones concedes that "intellectually" Asians are advantaged. "But cultur-
ally they are primitive. They're dog eaters, after all."

This is not to ignore Jews. "As a group," he says, "Jews are the most dangerous, subversive, treacherous, sick-minded people on the face of the earth,
overall. They're Communists and con artists. They're the biggest slumlords in
the city of Chicago, the biggest pornographers in the country. They put trash on
television. As commodities brokers they rip off the gentle farmers, who make
a pittance while the Jews make a killing. The man who sold us on Vietnam—
Kissinger—is a Jew, and he ought to be shot. To my mind the conduct of the Jews
has earned them the deepest hole in hell."

Jones is particularly offended by makers of consumer goods who post a symbol, usually a *u* in a circle or in parentheses, on their products to indicate they
are officially kosher. To earn a symbol, Jones contends, a company has to employ
a rabbi to bless its output, thereby hiking the price of the merchandise. "That's
a religious tax," he argues.

Lots of companies *do* employ rabbis to ensure that their goods are produced
according to Jewish law, says Rabbi Yosef Wikler, editor of *Kashrus,* a magazine
on kosher practices published in Brooklyn. Wikler says manufacturers indulge
in overkill. Food products such as ketchup require rabbinical review, he says,
but items like tinfoil, paper cups, and bottled water don't; companies are simply
tagging on the symbol "to give them one-upmanship over the other company in
the marketplace." Yet to employ a rabbi-inspector adds very little to the retail
price. "You're talking maybe one penny on a can of tuna," says Wikler. "Is that
highway robbery?"

Jones thinks so: "When I tell people about the religious tax, it's the easiest
way to win converts."

Jones draws his information about rabbi-inspectors directly from Wikler's
magazine. He is remarkably well read, especially on Jewish subjects, relying
on periodicals and on a two-thousand-volume home library that contains any
number of works on the Holocaust.

The Holocaust never took place, Jones has concluded, and it stuns him that
the public seems to think it did. "I'm impressed by the bullshit gullible people

will swallow," he says. As proof he cites inconsistencies in accounts of the period. Take Elie Wiesel's *Night*, his recollection of life at Auschwitz and Buchenwald as a child. "Now Wiesel writes that on one night in the dead of winter he ran forty-two miles. That's impossible! Yet Wiesel said he did it." (In *Night*, Wiesel describes a forced march. The next morning a commandant announced the prisoners had covered forty-two miles.) Jones concluded there were no gas chambers. As to where all those millions of Jews, political dissidents, gypsies, and homosexuals evaporated to, Jones says, "A lot of them just changed names. Other people migrated to Australia or they came to this country, and many died fighting in the Red Army on the eastern front."

He blames the Soviets for murdering millions in purges of their own. "But all I hear are six million Jews, six million Jews, six million Jews."

The future for Jews, blacks, and gays will not be rosy once Art Jones rules the world. "With the Jews I would be merciful," he says. "They've got their synagogues, their Stars of David—it would be nothing to scoop them up and throw them out of the country. With blacks, realistically, you couldn't do that because there are too many of them. You should give them part of the country and say, 'It's your turf, your territory—run it like you'd like.' We could deal with sympathetic black leaders like Farrakhan and work out the whole thing. Homosexuals would be rounded up and isolated from the rest of the country, in camps or in some remote region of Alaska. They couldn't be allowed to circulate."

The America First Committee, the vehicle for Jones's activities, takes its name from a short-lived group established by General Robert E. Wood, then chairman of Sears, Roebuck and Company, and R. Douglas Stuart, a scion of the Quaker Oats founding family, to oppose U.S. entry into World War II. The original America First Committee acquired a bigoted tinge from the beliefs of Charles Lindbergh, its most celebrated spokesman. Lindbergh considered the war in Europe a spat among like-minded white nations, while the real danger to western civilization lay in Asia. Rather than fight among themselves, Lindbergh said Germany, France, and Britain should unite to build "a western wall of race and arms which can hold back either a Genghis Khan or the infiltration of inferior blood." In an address in Des Moines in 1940, Lindbergh rued the persecution of Jews in Germany, but criticized Jewish organizations for sounding a drumbeat for entry into the war. If America entered the conflict, Jews "would be among the first to feel its consequences. Tolerance is a virtue that depends upon peace and strength. History shows it cannot stand war and devastation."

Jones is certain Lindbergh would have been pleased if Germany had defeated the Allies. "The worst thing that would have happened if Germany had won is that I'd be speaking German now and eating sauerbraten instead of hamburger," he says. "At least the white race would prevail on this continent."

The present-day America First Committee functions from a cramped apartment in the Chicago Lawn neighborhood that Jones shares with his wife, Patricia, a professional tutor. Jones refuses to say how many members the committee has, but all its activities seem to involve him. When you call the committee, you hear his voice on the line execrating racial minorities and hailing "white Christian patriots." Staying timely, a message putting down D-Day is followed by another commenting on O. J. Simpson. What most troubles Jones about the Simpson case is neither murder nor wife abuse but miscegenation.

Having no children, and no hobby besides Nintendo, Jones feels free to go off on weekend excursions whenever he pleases. This spring, for instance, he picketed in Washington and traveled to Appleton, Wisconsin, for a dinner honoring Senator Joseph McCarthy. "I just happen to think Joe McCarthy was one of the great patriots of all time," Jones says. These trips can be perilous—last July at a rally in Pennsylvania a skinhead busted Jones in the head with a bottle.

He edits the *War Eagle*, a quarterly newspaper with a circulation of ten thousand. The publisher is John McLaughlin, a farmer from Champaign who is a little more temperate in his views than Jones. "I'm prowhite," says McLaughlin, "but it remains to be seen if the white race is superior. You can pick out some real scummy white people." Recently, McLaughlin made use of a mailing list that had belonged to David Duke, the former Ku Klux Klan grand dragon and onetime candidate for governor of Louisiana, to distribute fifty thousand copies of a newsletter edited by Jones. "And I've been talking to some skinheads in Missouri about putting together a special skinhead edition," McLaughlin says.

The *Eagle* carries articles written by Jones that are scholarly in appearance down to the source notes, but whose contents mirror the headlines: "The Non-White Face of Crime" and "Martin Luther King: Traitor and Hypocrite." The pages are enlivened by drawings of fierce, big-lipped blacks and sinister Jews. In the *Eagle* you can find listings of other white-power groups, not to mention "America's only pro-White law firm," all seemingly based out of post-office boxes in sparsely populated areas of the country. You can find out how to order not only Hitler's *Mein Kampf* but also *Michael*, a novel by Hitler's information minister, Joseph Goebbels, that not even Jones has read.

A highlight of the latest edition is Jones's review of *Schindler's List.* Jones acknowledges Spielberg's cinematic skills, but he tells me, "I didn't think I was going to see something so hackneyed and clichéd. The only thing Spielberg didn't show was a lamp shade made of human skin. At some parts I felt like laughing, but I couldn't, because I was surrounded by Jews."

The review locates a wealth of Holocaust bromides—from a rabbi getting his sidelocks cut by Nazi henchmen to Dr. Josef Mengele making his infamous selections at Auschwitz. "To make this movie, Spielberg must have read every tale of woe and misfortune spun by the so-called 'survivors' of the mythical 'Holocaust,'" Jones writes. He was particularly offended by the most affecting image in the movie—a young boy hiding out half-submerged in the excrement of a latrine. The scene reflects "the Jewish obsession with human waste that appears over and over again in their 'Holocaust' literature," Jones states. He calls Schindler a traitor to Germany and dismisses the movie as "a fine piece of Jewish hate propaganda."

Jones's romance with white supremacy began when he was a boy. Playing soldiers in his neighborhood of Beloit, Wisconsin, he was taken with the Nazis, the characters most kids took as the villains. "The Nazis looked so cool and sharp and spit-shined," Jones recalls enthusiastically. He began to collect German war memorabilia from friends whose fathers, like his own, had served in World War II—swastika armbands, Mauser rifles, hand grenades. In high school he looked up material on the John Birch Society at the local library.

Jones held various jobs—factory worker, busboy, door-to-door magazine salesman—before being drafted in 1969. When he shipped out to Vietnam he took along his copy of *Mein Kampf*. An infantryman and a mortar man in the central highlands, he studied the book—by now underlined, with certain passages starred—during the quiet moments between firefights.

"I took a trip back into Hitler's world," Jones says. "I could see what had taken place in Germany in the twenties was taking place in America in the sixties. Hitler had this keen insight into human nature, into the psyche of the masses. He saw the weakness of the average person, as opposed to the superiority some individuals have over everyone else. I saw that what he was saying about the decline of morals and the proper respect you should show your cultural and ethnic heritage was absolutely true." To this day Jones wholly admires everything about Hitler, from his talent as an artist to his plans to rebuild Germany. If the führer had a shortcoming, says Jones, "it's that he was too kind—he let the British escape at Dunkirk."

A civilian again, Jones enrolled at the University of Wisconsin–Whitewater, where he joined the Young Republicans but then was drawn to other organizations. Although the Klan interested him briefly, he was repulsed by "crude and vulgar remarks made about blacks feeling up white girls." When he happened upon *White Power*, the newspaper of the Virginia-based National Socialist White People's Party (NSWPP), he was sufficiently taken by the organization George Lincoln Rockwell had founded in 1958 to join up.

Jones's convictions troubled his divorced parents. Lillian Jones, an evangelical Sunday-school teacher, opposed her son on religious grounds. "My mom's church says not to mess with the people of the Book, the Jews," says Jones. He describes his father, a factory worker, as "apolitical—all he wanted to do was hunt and fish and trap." And yet his son's behavior got to him. After dropping out of college, Art Jones returned to Beloit, took a factory job, and founded a local NSWPP unit. One day he was leading a party demonstration when Art Jones Sr., having a drink in a nearby tavern, was so offended by the sight of Nazis walking by that he bounded into the street with his fists cocked. The sight of his son leading the way stunned him. "Dad, don't push me," Art told his father. "I don't want to fight you." Art Jones Sr. walked away in tears.

("He got into that Nazi mess in college," says Art Sr., now retired in Alabama. "It ain't worth a damn. I fought those goose-stepping rascals during World War II. Everybody can have their beliefs, but I don't believe like he does." Lillian Jones, who remains in Beloit, says of her son, "He was brought up in the church, but he kind of got away from it. He shouldn't have. I'm praying for him all the time, that he will change.")

Blacks protested Jones's demonstration in Beloit, and Jones's union steward told him to clean out his locker. He moved to Milwaukee, where he worked in a foundry and then for an electronics company. In time, though, he became a full-time organizer for the NSWPP, a position bankrolled by weekly collections from "the comrades"—as Jones describes his party associates. In 1976 he ran as the NSWPP candidate for mayor of Milwaukee and placed third in a field of seven. Afterward, he mounted an antibusing campaign on behalf of two women running for the school board who were defeated.

In 1977 Jones migrated to Chicago to open an NSWPP branch in Cicero. It was a period when neo-Nazism was becoming equated with Chicago: in a notorious legal battle, Frank Collin, head of the rival National Socialist Party of America, was jockeying to win the right to march in Skokie. Jones couldn't stomach Collin once he'd learned the man was half-Jewish—his father, Max Simon Cohn, had survived Dachau. Jones says, "I come from a very strong solid white line on both sides. My dad, when he's wanted to get under my skin, has hinted around that there may be some Indian blood in the family. But he's just kidding."

Jones takes pride in the fact that although Collin called off his march after winning the right to make it, the NSWPP—called the Cicero Nazis—actually did show up in Skokie. "We got in our white-power van and drove out there," he recalls. "We stood on the main street and sold *White Power.* Some people were supportive—it's not a totally Jewish town, you know." Later, producers of a made-for-TV movie on Collin and Skokie approached the NSWPP for

Nazi paraphernalia. Jones was good enough to offer what he had for above-market prices.

The Collin years invigorated Jones. "It was a dangerous time," he remembers. "You had those nutcakes in the JDL [the Jewish Defense League] planting bombs. But it gave you a sense of mission. You felt you were part of history, part of a revolutionary movement that the average Joe shied away from, if not out of physical fear then out of fear for his pocketbook."

Soon the NSWPP split internally over Iran and the Ayatollah Khomeini. Jones says Commander Matt Koehl felt the party should support the ayatollah because he was an enemy of Israel. "But the ayatollah was just a big asshole," says Jones, "and every patriotic American, no matter his color, hated his guts." Koehl also wanted to shelve party demonstrations for three years, says Jones, "because we weren't enlisting high-quality people anymore, but street thugs with a uniform fetish." Jones, who was convinced that the street displays built up the party organization, decided in 1979 to take a breather from white-power politics and return to Beloit.

Within a year his wife-to-be, Patricia, persuaded Jones to return to Chicago and help Collin's successor, Mike Allen, rejuvenate the National Socialists. Jones didn't like Allen, and he was put off by the filth at Rockwell Hall, the party's Seventy-first Street offices ("One night I was upstairs, and here comes this big-ass cockroach, yea big"), and he soon left to form the America First Committee with a National Socialist cohort named Richard Wendorf, who's since left Chicago. The committee laid down ten guiding principles, the most significant of which states, "The Natural Law governing all Human Life is based on the maintenance of Racial Integrity and genetic heredity."

After a year in Oak Park, the committee set up headquarters in a two-story building in Brighton Park. The committee was based there three years, until the landlord, troubled by his tenants' activities, canceled their lease. Since then Jones has operated the committee out of his apartment, but the loss of a real headquarters continues to rile him: "Ours was the last headquarters of a right-wing group in the city of Chicago. Farrakhan has a headquarters. The queers have their places and bookstores all over the place. But not us."

In 1984 Jones ran for Congress in the Republican primary. He ran for Thirteenth Ward alderman three years later and in 1988 was a Republican candidate for mayor, although GOP operatives knocked him off the ticket for filing faulty petitions. The city missed some novel ideas. As mayor he would have introduced a "matching funds ordinance" requiring Chicago's Jews to contribute a dollar to municipal coffers for every dollar they gave to Israel and a "neighborhood amendment" permitting any neighborhood where a majority of the residents so petitioned to ban black migration. The last time Jones campaigned for Congress,

1992, he called for ditching affirmative action, testing doctors annually for competence, and awarding a public-aid bonus to "all new-born children of legitimate origin whose parents are American citizens and [are] gainfully employed."

To support himself, Jones has held sales jobs, mostly for insurance companies. For five years he sold insurance, doing well enough to earn an agent of the year award in 1985 for a unit selling high-risk health policies. His boss, Jerry, was Jewish, and Jones kept his Nazi affiliation hidden until the day Jerry retired. "Why, Art?" he wondered. "Why the Nazis?" Jones answered with a discourse on Zionism and Communist Jews.

"Jerry and I parted friends," says Jones. "He was married to a Catholic woman, and he had a son who was retarded. If he walked in this place today, I'd say, 'Hey, Jerry, sit down.' He was a fair and decent human being, even though he was a Jew."

My conversations with Art Jones took place at T. J. Michael's restaurant, a coffee shop at Fifty-ninth and Kedzie where we'd occupy a booth and talk for a couple of hours. In time we'd notice whoever occupied the next booth craning to study us. Jones appeared unruffled by the attention.

At the end of our first talk he asked me a question.

"I was wondering," he began tentatively, giving my face an especially long look, "what's your ethnic background?" When I confirmed what he suspected, that I was Jewish, he said we could continue our dialogue so long as I'd be fair in my reporting. I said I'd try.

Some weeks later we were at the end of another long conversation. I was finishing a piece of blueberry pie—for some reason Jones always made me hungry for pie—when I asked him what I should do.

"What do you mean?"

"Well," I said, "Jews are inherently inferior, vicious, mean, and scheming."

"So?" he said.

"I'm Jewish," I reiterated.

"On both sides?" he inquired.

Afraid so, I said.

Jones nodded soberly.

"How do I get out of the hereditary bind I'm in?" I wanted to know. "How can I redeem myself?"

"Pray to whatever God you believe in to save you from what's coming," he said. "You don't want to be a Jew or a black when we come to power. This thing could bust wide open. There could be a lot of violence and death."

But I'm Jewish, I reminded him, coded irretrievably to my fate.

"I am capable of making a distinction on the basis of individuals," he said. "But even though I might like you personally—and I do—if it came to a question of making an exception for you, I wouldn't, because what if everybody had his own favorite Jew or favorite black? Like Goebbels said, if everyone had a favorite Jew, we wouldn't get rid of anyone. If you're lucky you'll get kicked out of the country. If you're not lucky you'll end up dead. But you'll pay in hell, anyway."

So there's no recourse for me?

"Your solution lies in working with your own people to reform them, to stop them from what they have done in country after country. Your best bet is to get hold of all those fallen Jews, to make them sit up and fly right. But it's almost impossible. It's like getting Dracula not to suck blood. But personally, again, I have nothing against you. I hope you live to be a gray-haired old man—in Israel."

In recent years neo-Nazis have been prosecuted for violent behavior in Germany, and so too have white supremacists in this country. Ten members of the Order, a clandestine group based in the western states, were sentenced to lengthy prison terms after being convicted of criminal racketeering in Seattle in 1985, and two years later two Order members were convicted in the killing of Alan Berg, a Denver talk show host. According to the ADL, from mid-1990 to mid-1993 neo-Nazi skinheads killed at least twenty-two people across the country, compared to six over the previous three years. Last August a self-proclaimed neo-Nazi named Jonathan Haynes shot to death a Wilmette plastic surgeon for giving patients "fake Aryan beauty." This spring Judge Earl Strayhorn found Haynes guilty and sentenced him to death. Now Haynes faces murder charges in the shooting of a prominent San Francisco hairdresser. The alleged motive was the same.

Jones is a gentler sort. He says he's been in his share of street brawls, "but lately I've been the victim. I don't want you to paint me as a cream puff, but my personal approach is to deal through legal channels to take the country back." Jones says of Haynes, "He's a nut, and I don't support what he did." He believes skinheads are "undisciplined," but he concedes his misgivings may relate to his being of an older generation.

The ADL's Michael Sandberg thinks the danger in Jones is that his verbiage may give license: "Skinheads who are seventeen look to the older generation to give them an ideology, and propagandists like Jones furnish it." Says John McLaughlin, Jones's most committed follower: "We have a lot of people, particularly young people, who are alienated by what's happening in this country and are looking for answers. Art's a Johnny Appleseed, trying to educate them."

To gain a rostrum, white hate groups have turned increasingly to television. Tom Metzger, a California TV repairman who leads a group called the White

Aryan Resistance, has become familiar to millions of viewers. While Art Jones isn't at that level, he loves the exposure game.

Jones says that in 1989, when David Duke, then a Louisiana state representative, addressed the convention of the Populist Party at Chicago's Bismarck Hotel, he was brought in to handle security. After Duke spoke, Channel 2 reporter Mike Kirsch asked whether he knew of Jones's party affiliations, and Duke replied that he'd never met Jones nor had any connection with him or his organization. Then, Jones says, "I gave Kirsch a shove, and as he was walking out I grabbed for his tie. I went into a tirade of hatred against the media, and I got the loudest round of applause from those people who were looking on." A mention of the incident showed up in the *Tribune* and in Kirsch's report.

To white supremacists a talk show constitutes a higher kingdom than spot news, with the Valhalla arguably *Geraldo*. *Geraldo* used to feature white-power activists with great regularity; in 1989 a neo-Nazi skinhead guest broke host Geraldo Rivera's nose. "We've been living in politically correct times, and people are afraid to mention the wrong word, to say 'girl' instead of woman," says Bill Lancaster, a *Geraldo* producer who mounts programs on racism. "So when people are channel surfing and all of a sudden they hit a show and somebody's saying, 'you nigger bastard' or 'you Jew kike,' they'll stop and they'll watch. They [such shows] are guaranteed numbers, or they used to be."

During the summer of 1992 Lancaster learned that several white-supremacist groups intended to rally in Janesville, Wisconsin, at the behest of Klan leader Ken Petersen (who has since denounced the Klan). "Usually when these guys get together, you're talking about thirty-five people at a rally, but they were expecting more than that and we wanted to check it out," says Lancaster. Rivera himself traveled to Janesville to report, and Jones, contacted in advance about an interview, remembers thinking, "If Geraldo Rivera wants me on his show, who am I to deny the great man?"

He didn't. But after taping an interview with Jones in Janesville, Rivera slipped past a police line onto Petersen's property. According to Lancaster, John McLaughlin approached Rivera, who's of Jewish and Hispanic descent, and said, "You're a Jew and a spic and you're not welcome here." McLaughlin says Rivera was pressing him for an interview and it angered him and "I did call him names." He also tossed a cup of melted ice at Rivera and knocked away his microphone. A scuffle ensued. "They were both swinging at each other and rolling around on the ground," recalls Lancaster. "The Janesville police jumped in and separated them. They promptly arrested Geraldo, which is the most asinine thing. They hauled him off to jail, and we stopped filming."

When Rivera arrived at the jail, Jones was already there; he'd been charged with hitting a pregnant woman at a rally earlier in the day. Spotting Rivera, Jones expected a second interview, "but to my astonishment they put him in the cell next to me." Jones says Rivera, apparently not realizing the identity of his jail mate, moaned, "I got busted for fighting a fucking Nazi. Boy, my wife is really going to give it to me." Back on the streets, Rivera talked tough about his encounter with McLaughlin. "He came and violated my space," he told the *New York Post*. "I just wasn't going to let this racist punk get away with it."

Perry Folts, then the Rock County district attorney, decided not to prosecute Rivera. "We reviewed the videotapes, and we thought his behavior was either self-defense or that he'd had adequate provocation," says Folts. McLaughlin was charged with disorderly conduct and Jones with battery, and after both men missed court appearances, warrants were issued for their arrest, warrants that are still outstanding. "I didn't see any sense in going further," remarks Jones, who denies ever hitting the pregnant woman. "This is just a kosher kangaroo court."

The episode wore out Jones's welcome with Geraldo. But he found another talk show home. He says he became an "unofficial adviser" to the *Jerry Springer Show,* hosted in Chicago by the former mayor of Cincinnati. His job, he says, was to round up panelists who'd make sparks fly by denouncing other panelists, such as teenagers into drugs and teen transvestites. Jones himself appeared on a program that focused on whites who act like blacks, and vice versa. "I said the worst aspects of black culture rub off on whites when we are forced to live with them," Jones recalls.

In May 1993 Jones was back on a show devoted to racial extremists. Other guests were Tom Metzger, his son John, and Michael McGee, a former Milwaukee alderman and commander of that city's Black Panther Militia. Recently the Metzgers had achieved a kind of martyred star status among supremacists—first a civil court returned a $12.5 million verdict against them for inciting Portland skinheads to kill an Ethiopian immigrant, and then a misdemeanor court in Los Angeles found them guilty of participating in a cross burning. But on this particular *Springer* program they were merely bystanders.

McGee set the tone by advocating sniper attacks and assassinations if whites didn't make reparations to blacks for enslaving them. "The black people are getting more primitive, more and more violent, more and more ignorant," Jones declared. When a black member of the studio audience asked how Jones explained a Jeffrey Dahmer, Jones took umbrage: "For every Jeffrey Dahmer we produce, you produce ten thousand rapists, murderers, robbers, thugs, dope addicts, pimps, and whores. Now that's a fact. Those are the crime statistics of the FBI." McGee responded, "I do not take insults, and so if you sit here and continue to insult and you use that word about whores, we'll start a war right now."

Indeed, McGee jumped Jones there on the stage. During a twenty-minute break, Springer got everyone to agree to behave, and the taping resumed. Jones shook McGee's hand in a gesture of peace. Much to Jones's displeasure the police never charged McGee, and last September Jones sued McGee, Springer, and Springer's executive producer and syndication company for two million dollars in damages. "I doubt I'll ever be on the *Jerry Springer Show* again," Jones figures.

"I'm not sure we'd go to him again," says Springer. "You kind of learn your lessons." Yet Springer goes to others, continuing to mount twenty programs a year with racists, sometimes with unfortunate consequences: in April five Nazi skinheads who'd just appeared on *Springer* spray-painted racial epithets on the restroom walls of a Ninety-fifth Street Wendy's and attacked two employees.

Springer, whose Jewish parents fled Germany for England before the war, justifies these programs as enlightening. "We need to be aware that these groups exist," he says. "They are most dangerous when we ignore them. What destroys them is the light, and what TV is great at is throwing light, in exposing evil in the world. These groups can't stand the exposure. If we had had TV in the 1940s, there's no way we'd have had the Holocaust we did. The civil rights movement thrived when the cameras opened up on Bull Connor. That's not to say there won't be evil, like in Bosnia, but with television at least the world's paying attention."

Bill Lancaster says Geraldo airs programs with racists to serve the public's right to know, not to popularize the abhorrent. "If these groups [of racists] are on the rise, yes, TV may have had some part in it," he says, "but there's no way it can all be credited to an appearance on a talk show. In tough economic times these people need scapegoats, and they find them in other racial groups."

Oprah Winfrey used to feature racists. In 1987 she faced off against a sampling of the population of Forsyth County, Georgia, a locale where no black person had dared live in seventy-two years, and a year later a skinhead called her "a monkey" on the air. Souring on these programs, Winfrey soon dropped them (though she has since performed with reformed hate-group members). "At first Oprah thought she was making people aware of these groups, but she learned she was empowering them," says her spokesman Colleen Raleigh. "Oprah will no longer provide a forum for hatred." Similarly, the ADL refuses to share the stage with white racists. To do so, says Michael Sandberg, implies that there is a respectable alternative to tolerance, "and there just isn't one."

Lancaster says the profusion of TV talk shows has diminished the number of hate-group programs Geraldo airs. "Because talk shows are so ubiquitous, they aren't being watched so much anymore," he says, and now he demands a "news hook." "Racism has no effect on our numbers," Springer reports, "not like sex does. You put on naked people, and the ratings go up."

Jones retains some bitterness toward Springer: "I basically built his ratings, but the only compensation I ever got was one time they paid for my parking." Yet hope springs eternal. "I got a call from the *Montel Williams Show* the other day," says Jones. "They wanted young people in their twenties to respond to *Schindler's List*. I found the people, but they didn't want to travel to New York."

Jones has gotten into television himself. He's excited that a segment featuring him is part of the college TV course *Dealing with Diversity* that is being aired on PBS stations. And Jones recently filmed four videos—on South Africa, the Holocaust, nonwhite crime, and his neighborhood amendment—that he's forwarded to cable access stations around the country. He expects a liberal airing.

On the surface Jones may seem to be moderating. A "Pat Buchanan for President" sticker graces the bumper of his small blue car. But no one should think Jones is trimming his racial ideas. "I wonder about everyone's interest in someone like Michael Jordan switching from basketball to baseball," he tells me one afternoon at T. J. Michael's as I dig into some banana cream pie. "He's just a big tall dumb nigger. If I was as tall as he was, I'd be a basketball star, too. Say, is that pie good?"

MORNING
MOUTH

Mancow Muller's Animal House of the Air.

Mancow Muller, the frenetic morning disc jockey at WRCX-FM, only arrived in Chicago last July. Yet according to the latest Arbitron ratings, his time slot has moved from nineteenth in the metropolitan market to fifth among all teenage and adult listeners. And among eighteen to thirty-four-year-olds, a coveted demographic among advertisers, he has soared to first, besting Tom Joyner at WGCI-AM and sending Kevin Matthews at WLUP-FM from second to third place. Nearly 20 percent of men aged eighteen to twenty-four in the Chicago area prefer Muller to his competitors.

"You come into a market the size of Chicago, nobody should know the name Mancow for at least another year," says Muller. "The fact that you know my name—and that I'm headed to number one—is an amazing thing."

For the first six months the twenty-seven-year-old Muller was here, only three billboards announced his presence, among them an ad along the Kennedy that read "O.J. thinks Mancow's killer." Evergreen Media Corporation, which owns the station, ran TV ads for WRCX, but only recently did it begin running a commercial strictly for *Mancow's Morning Madhouse.* "The really amazing thing is that so far he's succeeding mostly by word of mouth," says WRCX's general manager, Mike Fowler.

It's not quite that simple. In part, points out Robert Feder, radio and TV columnist at the *Sun-Times,* the growing command *Madhouse* has in the ratings

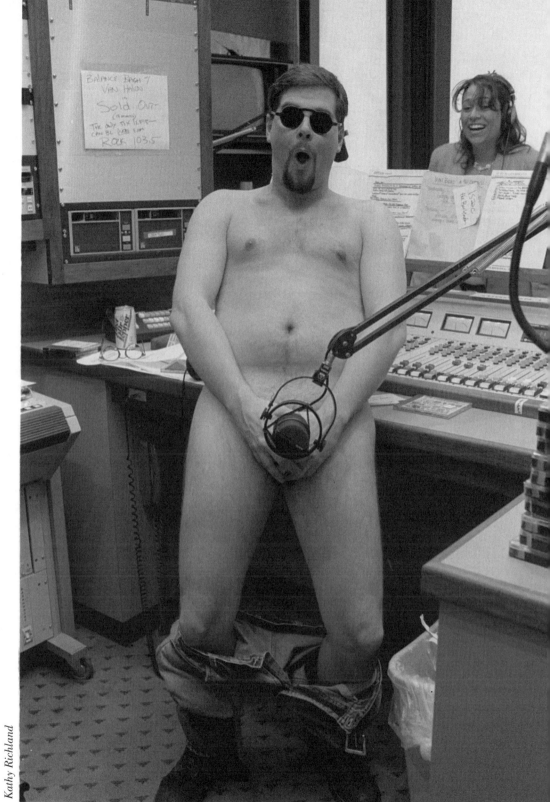

Mancow Muller

is the result of uncertainty at other stations, where old hosts (including the outrageous Ed Volkman and Jo Bohannon at WBBM-FM) have been quitting or getting fired and new hosts have been coming on.

Muller is also a remarkable self-promoter. He'll make a personal appearance anywhere. At car shows and bar parties he mugs shamelessly and usually lingers with his fans long past the appointed departure time, signing autographs and dispensing T-shirts. He's happy to raise money for charity; in September he spent two nights in a bark coffin at the Hard Rock Cafe, raising nine thousand dollars to fight spinal muscular atrophy. And he's been moonlighting with the World Wrestling Federation and on *Downey*.

Clearly he clicks with his fans. Before a recent *Downey* taping, filmed at studios on the Near West Side, Muller advised his listeners to get tickets, and they showed up. "The Cow's nuts," said Kim Buczek, a data-entry clerk, as she waited to be seated for the show, a beauty contest featuring women and female impersonators. "Mancow's stunts, the phone calls—it all makes you laugh." Shouts of "Mancow! Mancow!" reverberated through the studio as an assistant tried to warm up the audience. Morton Downey Jr. walking in was a distinct anticlimax.

In 1992 Evergreen Media, which also owns WLUP-AM and -FM and radio stations in other major markets, acquired the Blaze, the heavy-metal station WWBZ-FM, for twenty-eight million dollars. Evergreen had styled the Loop around lippy talk jockeys like Jonathon Brandmeier, Steve Dahl, Garry Meier, Kevin Matthews, and Danny Bonaduce, and it had just changed the AM signal to WMVP, a sports channel (now Dahl's home in the morning). Evergreen was positioning its Chicago stations to be a predominantly male province—"the testosterone network," the company calls it in its latest annual report. The Blaze would be recast to capture the youngest listeners, those in the eighteen-to-thirty-four bracket.

Jim de Castro, Evergreen's president, was the one who imported Brandmeier from Arizona to Chicago, and he wanted to work the same magic again. He didn't have to look far. Among the stations Evergreen owned was KMEL-FM, a Top 40 outlet in San Francisco that was a rival of KYLD, the station Muller had made the fourth-most-listened-to station in the market and the first among eighteen-to-thirty-four-year-olds. In part Muller had accomplished that by hectoring KMEL. His sidekick, Chewy Gomez, once perched atop a cherry picker and taped Federal Express envelopes to KMEL's office windows, encouraging disillusioned staffers to stick their résumés inside. De Castro came courting, intent on knocking off the competition in San Francisco and bolstering his Chicago property in one stroke.

"Every time I went to San Francisco I would look up Mancow," says de Castro.

"We had beers together and dinner. I wanted to get to know him." When de Castro asked Muller whether he might be interested in coming to Chicago, the nation's third-largest radio market, Muller played it cool. "I like the weather here," he said. "A straight white guy in this town has it pretty good."

De Castro, who dispenses one-dollar bills as a sign of affection, sent Muller a letter enclosing a dollar. "I've got a million more of these if you come work for my company," he wrote. In January 1994 back came a letter from Muller with a ten-dollar bill inside. "Your sales will increase one hundred times one of these if I come to work for you," he wrote. He ended the letter by asking whether de Castro wore boxer shorts or briefs. "I could not work for a man who wears boxers unless the price is right."

He gets it, de Castro thought, then sent Muller a one-hundred-dollar bill along with two first-class plane tickets to fly to Chicago for the weekend. Soon they were negotiating. Muller was making something in the low six figures in San Francisco; de Castro offered more—guesses range up to three hundred thousand dollars a year—and allowed him to hire or recommend key staff. "De Castro wanted to keep Mancow happy," says Irma Blanco, who was Muller's news-person in San Francisco and followed him here. Muller also hired Allan Fee, who'd been the program director of a station in Cheyenne, Wyoming, as his producer and sports reporter.

"There are ten radio talents in the country, and Mancow's among them," says de Castro. "Evergreen has changed the face of radio in this market, and we're doing it again with Mancow, who's as good as anyone who came before." Early on he told Muller, "Do whatever you want to do—just entertain, have fun."

"It's a dream come true," says Muller, who got his start in radio when he was at school in Missouri. "I had had offers in LA and New York, but I'd turned them down. I wanted to be back in the Midwest, and Chicago has such good radio. They've given me a program director who keeps out of my face. I have complete freedom."

Mancow's Morning Madhouse features sex talk, sexist innuendo, racial and ethnic stereotyping, rude phone calls, news, sports, and put-downs of rival disc jockeys, as well as outlandish street stunts by a beefy fellow with a thick South Side accent who goes by the name of Turd. The goings-on are punctuated by calls from listeners, who usually begin by telling Muller "Love you, love your show," and by rock sets from the last decade or so—Stevie Nicks, Billy Idol, Stone Temple Pilots, Pearl Jam.

Holding it all together is Muller, who defines himself as "a left-wing, conservative, Bible-thumping radical who curses. I believe in God and in capital punishment. Abortion is murder—but I'm not a woman, so it's none of my business.

I'm radical about animal rights. I have no problem with color or race. It doesn't matter to me who you sleep with or what color you are. I could care less." Yet on the air he's constantly belittling Asians, women, blacks, Hispanics, midgets, homosexuals, the retarded, the disabled—all of which he says is intended simply as humor.

"Mancow, love you, love your show," says Nicole, a caller from Carol Stream.

"Hey Nicole, what can I do for you?" says Muller, headphones on, pacing the floor of the studio on the thirty-seventh floor of the Hancock Center.

"I want that plastic surgery you've been talking about this morning—for my boobs."

"What size are you talking about? Around here we go from phone girl to Irma, from Tater Tots to 'Oh, my gawd!' Hey Irma, is it hard to find clothing that you enjoy?"

"I don't want to be small-chested anymore," says Nicole, not waiting for Blanco to answer.

"My girlfriend's Asian," Muller says, "but in a male-dominated society we judge a woman by the size of her hoots. And I do like a sizable set."

After Nicole hangs up Muller briefly directs his attention to Turd, whose real name is Jeff Renzetti. Yesterday Turd stopped at Superb Video, an adult-film parlor in Kenosha. Tom Peters, the manager, listens to Mancow even though he often thinks he's "disgusting." Turd walked among the booths, handing patrons tokens that showed a naked woman from the waist up on one side and a naked woman from the waist down on the other. "Heads you win," read the token. "Tails you win."

"So yesterday, Turd, you were going into the booths and cluing our listeners in on what's happening in Kenosha," Muller says. "Sort of a blow-by-blow."

Muller moves on to the first guest of the morning, Charles Pixley from Rochester, New York, who's pushing an anticancer medicine made from camphor. "My dad's so sick with cancer," Muller informs Pixley. "He's desperate." Pixley excoriates the medical establishment and the FDA, which has refused to OK the medicine, but Muller decides to ditch him. "This is a fascinating area, but this guy's so boring," Muller says off-mike. "I'm just trying to find anything I can to save my dad."

Dave Adler, a studio musician who's trying out today to be an ongoing character on the show—a homeless piano player—improvises some music while Muller throws out suggestions for names of a band he's trying to organize. "How about Mancow's Blow Daddies?" He then describes how after yesterday's show he and Turd rode around with a large plastic phallus Turd had bought in Kenosha until the police pulled them over and ticketed them for riding without seat belts.

Off the air Adler frets that his contributions are bland. "You're great," Muller says. "Relax."

Soon Muller's serenading his listeners: "I love it when you lick me down there. I love it when you lick my pubic hair."

Next up is Laura Steele, a New York–based psychic who writes for the *National Enquirer* and has popularized a blue dot that's printed in the paper for readers to meditate on. "It brings you love and health and makes you feel better," she tells Muller, who's more interested in hearing some forecasts. She predicts that O. J. Simpson is going to plead insanity, that Newt Gingrich will develop public relations problems, and that Muller should be focusing more on his love life.

"I'm not investing the time I should in my personal life," Muller admits, "but as long as there's hand gel and some magazines you don't have to. Say, Laura, do you really believe that blue-spot stuff? You've got all this white trash running around saying, 'I got to rub that blue spot.'"

Steele gone, Muller moves to the fate of Matthew Coppens, a Mancow fan and emergency-services volunteer who was directing traffic outside a basketball tournament in suburban Richton Park in December when he was struck from behind by a car. He lost both of his legs, and Muller has been promising to do a benefit concert for him. "I don't even want my name mentioned," Muller says, still on the air. "This Matthew Coppens is a guy with a great heart."

But off the air Muller later ridicules Rachel Barton, the violinist who lost part of her legs in a Metra accident in January. "I think she's a helluva musician, but big deal—she can still play the violin. If she'd have lost her chin I'd feel bad. I'm more upset that she has a mustache. A mustached girl with one leg—she's not going to get laid."

Blanco does more news, Allan Fee gives the sports as a character named Gump, and then there's more rock music.

Muller asks Adler to play some television-show themes, but when he comes through with the music from *Cannon*, the crime drama that starred William Conrad, Muller says, "Give me a break, piano boy. Not some show about a fat ass that nobody ever saw."

At eight forty-five Richard Preston, author of *The Hot Zone*, the real-life thriller about the spread of deadly viruses, is welcomed aboard. "Tell the stuff about the black vomit," Muller suggests. Preston obliges.

Dave Richards, WRCX's program director, waltzes into the studio. Richards, an upbeat balding man Muller often refers to as "Sergeant Hair Club for Men," lavishes praise on Adler. "You're a funny sonofabitch," he says. Muller starts complaining to him that David Perl, a promotion man for A and M Records who's bringing two members of Extreme to the studio to plug their new album, is treating him high-handedly.

Shortly after this, in walk Pat Badger, Extreme's bass player, and Gary Cherone, their vocalist. Badger charms Muller by saying, "Love you, love your show." The interview starts off friendly.

Muller says he isn't going to ask about the meaning of Extreme's new single, "Hip Today," since history has taught him such questions are immaterial. "They once asked John Lennon, 'What does this song mean?' And he said, 'I took a dump and I wrote it.'"

Cherone sings a poignant a cappella version of "My Funny Valentine," observing afterward, "We're all just lounge singers. This is my future—everybody ends up in Vegas."

Muller then introduces Turd, a big Extreme fan. "Yesterday Turd was going door-to-door in a porno bookshop," Muller informs the musicians. "Have you ever masturbated in one of those booths?"

Badger shakes his head no, and he and Cherone start reminiscing about the lowlife in Amsterdam.

"You don't care if we don't play your wussy-wussy music," says Muller later, referring to the group's big hit, "More Than Words." Cherone blanches.

Badger has already left, pulled away by Perl to be a guest with WLUP's Kevin Matthews, one of Muller's favorite targets. "Mancow wanted exclusivity, but we couldn't do that," Perl explains later. "Kev has been very good to us, and we owe him." When the *Madhouse* goes off the air at ten o'clock Muller is still fuming.

The young, white, male, blue-collar Chicagoans Muller appeals to are "people who want to be entertained, to have fun, and get laid," in the words of one WRCX executive. "My people are passionate," says Muller. "There's a cult thing going on here—something like Letterman must have had in his early years. A feeling of *la familia,* as Irma would say. A real connection."

Muller, Blanco, and Fee are all twenty-seven. Turd is twenty-five. "Everyone here is the same age as the audience we're going after," says Fee. "We think about the same things. We think the same things are funny."

The *Madhouse* is really a fraternity-house romp, a form pioneered by Scott Shannon when he was a DJ on WRBQ in Tampa, Florida. "We started out in 1979," says Shannon. "We wanted to be the *Tonight Show* combined with *Saturday Night Live,* with heavy listener involvement, parody songs, and biting-satire skits." When Shannon took what he called his "morning zoo" to New York in 1983, he captured number-one ratings in a record seventy-two days. Many markets subsequently developed zoos, most of them cheap imitations. Chicago had a short-lived one with Paul Barsky on WYTZ-FM (now WLS) in 1986, and some people think the early Jonathon Brandmeier offered another. Shannon, who's still on radio in New York, is a fan of the *Madhouse* and calls it "a cross between a zoo and Howard Stern."

If Muller's mind too often reverts to the toilet or dwells on the libido, he makes no apologies. "People take a shit in the morning, and they talk about sex. I do too, and I discuss it all." Each morning he engages in risqué badinage with Blanco. "In the beginning I was shocked at all Mancow's T-and-A jokes," Blanco says. "But then I thought to myself, 'He knows what he's doing.' Now I'm used to it, though when he crosses the line I let him know." Crossing the line includes implying on the air that she masturbates when she's said she doesn't.

Muller often manages to get in a brutal dig at his better-known rivals, notably Kevin Matthews and Patti Haze, the morning DJ on WCKG-FM. Muller dismisses Haze, an eighteen-year radio veteran, as "an old rock hag"; he once flew a banner mocking her ("Listen to Mancow on Rock 103.5. Don't Listen to Sea Hag") over a concert where she was making a personal appearance. Matthews, says Muller, "is tired. He's always talking about his Mercedes-Benz, his superstar friends, and about playing golf." Jimmy Shorts, Matthews's sports-reporter character, "is some bullshit voice out of a psychopath's head."

Muller uses plenty of prewritten bits, including Top 5 lists and musical parodies, such as a version of Bette Midler's "The Rose" that Muller wrote after Rose Kennedy died: "Some say Rose / She's real dead now." Many of the parodies are lushly produced by Rusty Humphries, Muller's best friend and the creative director of a radio-jingle company, TM Century, located in Dallas. TM Century also sells WRCX all-purpose comedy satires and send-ups of popular songs.

Muller also tapes in advance what he calls "phone scams," calls he makes to sperm banks or 7-Elevens or whatever. "They were having a 'beaver feed' at a restaurant in Butte, Montana, and so I called. What man doesn't love eating beaver except for those damn homos?" He's called a tuxedo store in the suburbs to ask about bringing in a corpse that needed to be dressed up for a funeral, and he's phoned a series of auto-body shops to ask if they had a "sphincter."

He has a knack for snaring big celebrities as guests. "I have a friend in law enforcement, and I can get about any number," he boasts. "There is nobody in town who can beat us up on guests." Fee books the stars, and he does well. Since landing in Chicago Muller has interviewed on the air Arnold Schwarzenegger, Kevin Costner, Jack Nicholson, Bruce Willis, and David Letterman. But Brad Kava, a radio columnist for the *San Jose Mercury-News* who's followed Muller's rise, cautions that Muller isn't above having an actor mimic a celebrity when he's in a bind. "I basically stopped believing many of his guests," says Kava. "But it's great theater."

Muller is slavish with rock performers and often impolite to mainline nota-bles, especially those who bore him. "When you have some guy going on and on you have to cut him off," he says. "Ed Asner was the absolute worst. He just rambled on endlessly about his TV show, and I started playing songs right over him. When you're on to sell a book and you give your phone number too much I cut you off. If I'm rude I'm sorry. But you're welcome to be rude in return."

Sometimes celebrities are. A representative of Marianne Williamson, the new age psychology counselor, had warned that questions about a reported meeting between her, other gurus, and President Clinton were off-limits. Muller brought it up immediately, and Williamson slammed down the phone. When Muller talk-ed up "Gerbil Love," his perverse variation on the Captain and Tennille's vintage hit "Muskrat Love," the Captain stayed on the line, but not Tennille.

Muller pestered Kevin Bacon with calls to his home in Connecticut, but never got beyond his wife, actress Kyra Sedgwick, who hung up. Richard Moll, who played the bailiff on *Night Court*, got so sick of Muller's calls that whenever he phoned the actor would yell "fuck" into the receiver, ensuring that the segment couldn't be aired.

But when Muller's smarty-pants interviews work, he and his troops are thrilled. "Where there's tension on the air, that's such great radio," says Fee. Although even Muller can be shaken up by his own shenanigans. "Al Gore was in town, and I was hanging out in the Hyatt Regency near where I live. Some guys gave me a phone number that was great, the best. I felt I would be cheating people if I didn't call it." He says he tested out the number over the weekend and on the Monday celebrating Martin Luther King's birthday put a listener named Mike up to dialing it. A phone rang somewhere in the White House.

"Yes," said President Clinton.

"Yes. Bill, President," said Mike.

"Yes."

"Yes. How ya doing, sir? I'm a voter from the Midwest here, and I wanted to know what were you going to do to celebrate Martin Luther King's birthday."

"I'm sorry, who's this?" inquired Clinton, irritation creeping in.

"This is Mike. I'm just a concerned voter out from the Midwest, and I came across this phone number. I wanted to call and see how you were going to cel-ebrate Martin Luther King's birthday today, sir."

"I'm sorry, but this is a secure line. I don't know how you got through here."

"I don't know, sir. I must have got a wrong number then. I'm not really sure how I got it myself. I just came across it. And here you are—and I wanted to know how you were going to celebrate Martin Luther King's birthday."

"And your name is Mike?"

"Yes, sir."

"From where, Mike?"

"From the Midwest, sir. I really love you. I love what you're trying to do out there, and we really support you. We were just kind of curious how you are going to celebrate Martin Luther King's birthday today."

"Hold on a second please, Mike," said Clinton, disappearing.

("I think we oughta hang up," you could hear Muller say into a mike only listeners, not Mike, could hear.)

Suddenly Clinton was on. "Honestly, I don't know how you got this line. I'm going to have to have it traced, because this is a secure line."

"I didn't know that," said Mike, feigning ignorance.

"I'm going to ask you to give me your last name."

("Hang up, hang up," said Muller, sounding frightened.)

"I don't really want to get in no trouble," said Mike. "I mean, I don't want to create no problems, especially on this line."

"This is a secure government-executive phone line, and I do not know how you got this phone number."

("It's been nice working in Chicago," said Muller. "Good-bye, everybody.")

"Sir, believe me, I didn't know that anything like that was being taken care of at this point."

"I don't mind talking to you at all."

"Like I said, I'm really sorry. I didn't know that there was any problem with this line."

"I do need to know how you got this phone number."

"Is this really Bill Clinton, Mr. President?"

"Yes, sir, it is."

"I really don't even have the number myself, sir. It was, like, kind of call-forwarded for me through another person."

("He's going to sell us out.")

"Do you understand what's going on here? I mean I'm happy to talk to you. I wish you a very happy Martin Luther King day."

"I called for no disrespect."

("Oh, God, I hope he doesn't say our name.")

"I just want you to understand. This is a secure line. Very few people are authorized to use this line. The vice president . . ."

("I don't think he's being nice at all," said Muller. "I think he's being a jerk. Mike, Mike, hang up.")

". . . the secretary of state."

"OK, sir, I'm very sorry."

"All right. Have a good day now."

The line went dead. The Secret Service did arrange to come visit, says program manager Dave Richards, but no one ever showed up.

Muller says he wasn't sorry he'd bothered the president. "I would say that if it had been Reagan or Bush I would have been a little intimidated in doing this. But Bubba? I don't know. He doesn't command much respect."

Muller's mouth sometimes gets him in more serious trouble. According to a lawsuit filed in Cook County Circuit Court by former Chicago Bear Keith Van Horne, when it was reported in November that Van Horne was accused of accosting a woman at a gas station, Muller made some disparaging remarks about him on the *Madhouse*. Muller claimed on a later broadcast that Van Horne, then a talk-show host on WLUP, was infuriated and had waited for him at the Hancock Center elevator bank, chased him down the hall, and threatened to kill him. "The man is an extremely violent, troublesome individual, and I feel, personally, that he should be put in jail immediately," Muller told his listeners. "He is out of control. He is gonna hurt somebody. It may not be me, but he is a danger to society." Muller discussed Van Horne in similar terms throughout his show, and Blanco made the alleged threat part of her newscast.

Within three weeks Van Horne, denying he ever stalked or threatened Muller, had sued him, Blanco, Evergreen Media, and WRCX for defamation, asking five million dollars in punitive damages from each party. The case is still pending. WLUP canceled Van Horne's short-lived show, although de Castro says it wasn't because of the suit.

Muller has always worked hard at radio—Les Isralow, manager of a station in California where Muller once worked, remembers him sleeping only four hours a night—and he's kept up the pace in Chicago. He rises at 3 A.M. and writes material on a yellow pad while taking a bath. He's in the studio by 5 A.M. and starts the show at 5:30. After it's over he returns to the downtown apartment he shares with a woman he met in San Francisco who's currently working in insurance telemarketing. The apartment is decorated with toys. "The stuff makes me smile," says Muller. Once home, he has lunch and watches "a little trash TV," particularly *Jerry Springer*. He says he reads "like crazy," claiming he subscribes to one hundred magazines, and once a year rereads *All the King's Men*, Robert Penn Warren's novelization of Huey Long's political career. He naps in the late afternoon, then writes scripts and commercials, some of which he sells nationally, on into the night.

He also makes time for friends and family, especially his ailing father. He's constantly phoning them, his voice barking over the wire, and sending them mail. "You get candy, Led Zeppelin memorabilia, or a picture of him doing something stupid, like walking down the street with a hard roll over his pecker," says his brother Mark.

A couple of weeks before Muller was set to start in Chicago he came for a visit and ended up in Paulie's Pub in South Chicago Heights, where Jeff Renzetti was working as a bartender. "Paulie's is a neighborhood beer-and-shot joint," says Renzetti. "Mancow started messing around, and out of the blue he asked me if I wanted a job."

Renzetti was loud, and he cracked Muller up. That was enough. "He didn't know shit about radio," says Muller.

On the *Madhouse* Renzetti's role is to perform one stunt each morning and translate it on the air, each appearance preceded by a drumbeat and the chant "Turd, Turd, here comes da Turd." Virtually all of the stunts are Muller's idea. Usually he tells Renzetti what he's supposed to do that morning, although if it involves a costume he'll tell him the night before. Renzetti happens to excel at his assignments. "The guy will do anything," says Muller.

Turd has dressed up like a chicken and complained to the breakfast crowd at a North Side Golden Nugget, "You're eating my babies." He set up shop in front of the house of a reputed Nazi in Skokie. "We had a Jewish fest, handing out lox, bagels, and kosher pickles." He staked out city hall and succeeded in slapping his arms around the mayor ("He was the nicest guy in the world, though he's pretty short"). And on Martin Luther King's birthday passersby at Thirty-fifth and King Drive were invited to hug him ("Hug whitey").

Once he cleaned the house of a woman in Hammond, naked except for some Mancow stickers covering his privates. "I did her dishes, her windows," he reports. He conducted a cheap wine tasting for winos on the Near West Side, complete with free cheese. He slammed a Geo Metro into a wall going sixty-two miles an hour to test the airbag and survived without injury, but he hurt his shoulder in a snowmobiling stunt in Antioch in February.

On Ash Wednesday he was in Comiskey Park having his body coated with sticky cinnamon-roll gunk to test the theory, proposed in a study by a local foundation, that cinnamon rolls have a significant impact on penile blood flow. A day or two later a listener at a trailer park in Hegewisch invited Turd in to get his hair "swirled" in the toilet bowl. The stunt attracted hordes of beer-drinking listeners, angering the other trailer-park residents, including one man who came outside wielding a crossbow.

Turd did his most infamous stunts last September. He declared one day "Roadkill Tuesday" and invited people to schlep dead animals to a shopping center in south-suburban Frankfort. Within hours the site, next to a Burger King, was strewn with thirty carcasses, among them a beaver, a possum, a skunk, a German shepherd, and a two-hundred-pound deer. "It was a very hot day," says Renzetti. "The road kill was maggot-infested and gross. To tell you the truth, it was all pretty disgusting." As he does with most stunts, Turd awarded the person who made the best offering of the morning $103.50 to match the frequency of WRCX. The dead deer won hands down.

"We were really upset," says Tom Bartnik, Frankfort's director of building and zoning. "With all those dead animals outside a restaurant we were concerned about disease, about parvo, salmonella, and rabies." A fire truck took away the animals, and the site was cleaned with bleach. Renzetti was given a five-hundred-dollar ticket and charged an equal amount for the cleanup. "I was going to write a letter to the FCC," says Bartnik. "A prank is one thing, but this was a sick prank."

Shortly after this Turd positioned himself on the overpass at North Avenue and Lake Shore Drive with a naked inflatable female doll. Then he threatened to drop a cinder block on any car that flashed its lights and sounded its horn. He was quickly surrounded by squad cars. "They handcuffed me and put me in a paddy wagon," he says. Police also invaded the studio, telling Muller to turn off the tape of the cinder-block routine. "Officers, we're live," Muller informed them. Renzetti was fined eight hundred dollars and ordered to perform 120 hours of community service. "Gee," he says, "the cinder blocks I had were fake."

Well before 7 A.M. on Valentine's Day Renzetti is driving south on the Dan Ryan in what's called "Mancow Mobile One," a white Dodge Caravan painted with black cow spots. Kurt Goodwin, a doorman at the Hard Rock Cafe, is acting as assistant. The stunt of the day is to have Turd meet up with a listener named Randy and his girlfriend at the Frankfort location of the romantic motel Sybaris. Turd is supposed to instruct the couple on coital technique.

Meanwhile Muller has a male listener call his girlfriend, who happens to be married to someone else, at home, promising him a prize if he gets the woman to say "I love you." "The husband might answer," Muller warns. The coast is clear, but the woman becomes suspicious about her boyfriend's sweet-talking and doesn't offer the required endearment. As the boyfriend presses his case, Blanco starts to play his lover in the background, "Come back to bed, honey," she purrs.

Back at the Sybaris Randy and his girlfriend are nowhere in sight, and all the rooms are booked anyway. Turd tries to persuade the manager, Tim Reed, to make some accommodation, but Reed thinks Turd wants to interview his guests in the throes of love. "I didn't think that would have been appropriate," Reed says later.

As Turd tries to decide what to do next a long-haired man pulls up in a beater. "I hear Mancow's looking for a place to play with his band," he says. "God, I love Mancow. I'm on home confinement, and there's no better place for his band to jam than at my house."

Turd drives over to the Holiday Inn in Matteson to find a substitute love nest. On the way he hears Muller ring up Harry Caray at home in San Diego, where the broadcaster is having breakfast. "What are you eating?" Muller asks. "Hey, what's your name?" responds an irked Caray. "I think we've had enough conversation."

At the Holiday Inn Turd is delighted to discover a waterfall in the lobby that might double on radio as a bubbling whirlpool. "I'm saved!" he says. Through Muller he issues a call for a new willing couple.

First to arrive are Scottie, twenty-three, and his girlfriend Gina, twenty. Second are a woman and the young man who delivered the dead beaver on Road-kill Tuesday.

Scottie, a mechanic, is a Mancow superfan. He was so excited to hear Muller's call for lovers that he woke up Gina and raced down from Mokena with frost on his windows. "Brandmeier used to be big, but Mancow is *the* shit now," Scottie says. "From the click of the radio he's nonstop humor." Scottie and Gina had attended a promotional party featuring Muller held at a bar in DeKalb several weeks before. "Mancow was in a toga," says Scottie. "It was totally awesome." Scottie, Gina, and Gina's sister all had their photos taken with him.

"This is just radical," says Scottie. "Turd is the best. We'll be at work with the radio on, and the Turd will do something dumb as hell—and we'll stop and listen. I can't believe I'm sitting around with Turd. It must be in my genes."

"Look," Turd tells Scottie and Gina, "you're going to have to act this out. Pretend the waterfall is by your bed. We're going to do a little theater."

At 8:20 Scottie and Gina go on with Muller. "Love you, love your show," says Scottie. He and Gina are fully dressed, but Turd says Scottie's wearing boxer shorts and Gina's luscious in a black negligee. "We'll be opening up some oils, some lotions," Turd says.

"Make sure you look at Turd when you're on top of Gina," says Muller.

Over the next hour and a half Gina and Scottie periodically go on the air with Muller. Gina is monosyllabic, but Scottie shows a certain verve. "Oh man, this is beautiful," says Turd. "Gina's gorgeous. She has a shape like an hour-glass. Unbelievable. Unbelievable." Later he declares, "They're getting frisky. They've started fellatio"—deliberately mispronouncing the last word with an eye to FCC regulations. He feels sure Muller and the folks back at WRCX will think the two have actually been making whoopie. "Oh God," he says, "this is radio as it's supposed to be. I know how Orson Welles must have felt when he did *War of the Worlds.*"

Mancow Muller started in radio in 1985, when he was an eighteen-year-old student at Central Missouri State University in Warrensburg. He worked at KOKO-AM doing the station breaks from midnight to dawn and making sure the feed from Larry King was coming in all right. At the end of his shift he started to talk with the morning man, and the station manager, Marion Woods, liked him enough to put him on in the afternoon.

"Right away he started doing weird and crazy stuff—at least weird and crazy for this market," says Woods, who's still at KOKO. "I was constantly being told by my higher-ups to get him to cut it out. So I'd tell him, and he always had this funny little smirk on his face, like he was thinking, Well, I got away with *that* one." Things came to a head after Muller claimed Paul Newman, then filming the movie *Mr. and Mrs. Bridge* in Kansas City, had purchased Old Drum, a cherished statue of a dog on the local courthouse lawn. "He said a crew was coming to take Old Drum away, and he went so far as to call up the mayor to talk about it," remembers Woods. "The mayor called me later and said, 'If that guy ever calls me again there'll be hell to pay.'"

Muller—whose real first name is Mathew, although for a while he went by his middle name, Erich—grew up outside Kansas City, the youngest son of John and Dawn Muller. "He was a good boy, and he never caused me any trouble—although he was a little screwbally," says John.

For a time Muller attended a Christian high school with the ambition of becoming a minister. He played juvenile roles at local dinner theaters and later, as a freshman at Central Missouri State, starred in Arthur Miller's *The Crucible* and did a solo performance in Christopher Durang's *The Actor's Nightmare.* His theater professor, Edward See, says, "Erich could have done a good job as an actor, but an actor is more of an interpretive artist. Erich is more creative. His mind is rather free. He's a little bit of a rebel, you might say."

Muller's personal life wasn't going quite as well. "I was involved with this nice little girl, the first woman I ever slept with, and she comes home and says she's pregnant. But as it turned out she didn't know if it was my baby. She's thirty, and she ends up marrying a sixteen-year-old guy and having an abortion. This devastated me. I'm nineteen years old, making five thousand dollars and totally disillusioned."

But radio sustained him, and soon he was angling for a job in Kansas City. "I'm waiting in station lobbies in Kansas City with my tapes, but nobody would listen to them," he says. But college degree in hand, he was hired to be a promotions aide at a now-defunct station in Kansas City, then as the sidekick to Randy

Miller, the morning jock of KBEQ-FM, a Top 40 outlet. Miller presided over a zany program featuring phone scams, street stunts, and off-color remarks. "Erich Muller was a goofball," says Miller. "He wasn't particularly talented, but you could see a lot of energy in him. He was very hungry to get out and do things."

Muller became a Turd. He covered himself in barbecue sauce and became a human sparerib. He interviewed shoeshine men to see how much they'd been drinking, and at Christmas he rang doorbells and said, "Show me your balls." People who invited him in won a prize.

Miller says he gave Muller his Mancow stage moniker. Muller insists it's from a "part man, part cow" bit he did back at KOKO that was inspired by the work of radio humorist Stan Freberg. But then there are bad feelings between the two men. Miller, now thirty-five, still does mornings in Kansas City and claims the *Madhouse* is a copy of his show. "It's the same thing," he says, "and it irritates me a little bit. Mancow wants to be me—to the point where it's an obsession with the guy. I grew a goatee, and he grew one. I don't feel resentment so much as I wish the guy would use his own stuff. You can only feed off someone for so long."

"I had grown up listening to Randy," says Muller. "When I got to him he was already an old talent who had lost his edge. I made him sound hip to a teenage audience. I was away from him for five years when I grew a goatee—I don't even know what his facial hair is now. If I stole my act from him, why is he still sitting there in Kansas City? He's tried to take his act on the road to other cities, but he's failed. And now he's the joke of the industry."

On the basis of a tape of his work he sent through the mail, Muller was hired in October 1990 by KDON-FM, a black urban station in the Monterey Bay area in California. His salary went from around fifteen thousand dollars to forty thousand dollars a year, according to Les Isralow, then the KDON manager. That market, seventy-fifth largest in the nation, is generally Catholic and conservative, and Muller made quite an impression. He ridiculed the mayor, who was running for reelection, for his polyester suits, hounding him by spinning the Kinks's "Dedicated Follower of Fashion." The mayor lost. "Mancow's big thing was sex," recalls Isralow. "'I have a pickle in my pants,' he'd say, 'and it's getting bigger all the time.'" Isralow loved Muller. "He made it exciting to go to work in the morning. But KDON's owner was afraid Muller would drive away advertisers. Around Christmas in 1991 Muller made a crack about Rudolph the Red-Nosed Reindeer 'licking Santa's ass,'" and Isralow was forced to fire him.

"I'd been a good boy, and I'd gotten totally fucked," says Muller. "From then on I lost all fear."

"We listened to his tape, and it was clear he was extremely talented," says Scott Fey, then general manager of KOSL-FM in San Francisco, where Muller worked next. The station, which started out urban but turned more contemporary after its call letters changed to KYLD, appealed to a female audience, and Muller toned himself down. "We talked about panty liners and how to take care of children. I was more sensitive, or I tried to be. Sure there were cracks about gays, but nothing mean-spirited. Someone would say, 'Guys should hold their sweethearts more after sex.' I'd say, 'No, I don't want to talk after sex. I want to go to sleep. There doesn't always have to be this emotional goo going on.'"

His guests included Pee-wee Herman, in a phone interview the morning after his arrest in Florida for exposing himself, and John Wayne Bobbitt, who was joined by a guy in an Oscar Mayer wiener outfit. But the event that made his reputation occurred in May 1993, after Christophe, the Beverly Hills hairdresser, had held up traffic for an hour at the LA airport while he cut President Clinton's hair. Muller had his sidekick, Chewy Gomez, get his hair trimmed on the Bay Bridge between San Francisco and Oakland. "We were out there for about thirty seconds," says Muller. "We had semis turning across four lanes to see the haircut. It became a four-hour mess." It was a slow news day, and the stunt played big. Muller luxuriated in the exposure, but says, "I had to do one hundred hours of community service in an orange monkey suit picking up trash."

It was around this time that Jim de Castro began courting Muller.

Muller is now getting television offers from people who want him to be another Morton Downey. But he insists he wants to stay in radio. "It's immediate, it's spontaneous, it's fun—there's nothing like radio. I'm not capable of doing anything else. I'm a professional smartass, and you don't see ads in the paper saying, 'Smartass wanted at Jewel [grocery store].' So it's radio for me. I want everybody to simulcast me. As long as someone else has a listener that I can get I want him."

He's still getting them, although this week he got some new competition when WCKG started running Howard Stern's New York show in Patti Haze's current slot.

So far the criticism of Muller and his show has been fairly muted, although most days WRCX does get complaints about the show's content. "A lot of things get taken out of context by somebody driving along and hearing only part of a routine," says program director Dave Richards.

Radio veterans complain that Muller is being petty when he attacks his competitors. "What he's doing is the oldest trick in the book—coming into town and going after the established players," says one prominent disc jockey who preferred not to be named. "Steve and Garry did it when they savaged Wally [Phillips] and Larry [Lujack]. It helped them, but where are they now?" Even Evergreen president Jim de Castro wishes Muller would end his diatribes against other DJs, especially Kevin Matthews. "We don't think it's in Mancow's best interests to ridicule and attack our own people. Can't we all get along is what I say. We're all talented here."

Muller gets mixed reviews from media critics. "I deplore this guy's use of ethnic and racial stereotypes and the prurient subject matter, but I'm able to separate that from his talent and his intelligence," says the *Sun-Times*'s Robert Feder. "He does possess an inherent charm, even when he's being naughty." Steve Nidetz, media writer at the *Tribune*, says, "To me he's not funny. He typifies the worst of the zoo genre. But then I'm older, and I'll give him credit. He came here to get ratings for his station, and he's done it." Radio columnist Brad Kava says, "The people who are making it now in radio, from Rush Limbaugh to Howard Stern, are appealing to the lowest common denominator, to the people in the cheap seats. Moderation and thought doesn't sell, except on NPR. Beavis and Butt-head does and now you're talking Mancow."

"Look, it's a radio show," says Muller. "People will step over crack babies and whacked-out, acid-tripped people who are in real trouble to put a letter in a mailbox to say how hideous I am. I'm the least of this world's problems. Laugh a little." ▪

BOSOM BUDDIES

Robin and Kate are men, they're women, and they're best friends.

The sassy young waitress at Father and Son Pizza in Jefferson Park distributes the dinner menus and soon returns to take drink orders. Katie, who's blond, statuesque, and wears a floral print dress with a lace collar, asks for decaf. "That'll be decaf—for Betty White," jokes the waitress, reminded of the old sitcom star. Robin, Lynne, and Carole laugh heartily.

There's a pause. "They say that I look like a matron schoolteacher," says Robin. Robin's tall, with russet hair and bangs, and is wearing a black blouse and jeans.

Betty White and the schoolteacher exchange a knowing glance and a giggle.

They're a lot alike. Professionals in late middle age, they've married, raised their children, and today, as empty nesters, have decided to live exactly the way they want to.

Each is the other's best friend. "There's tremendous worth in their bond," says Barbra McCoy Getz, a social worker who has been seeing Robin clinically. "It's the concept of here's another human being in the world who understands you, who can see you for who you are."

Now Lynne is saying, "A year ago a teacher at Lake Forest High School had an operation to become a woman. The district wrote a letter to the parents, and it was OK."

Carole mentions a teacher switching sexes at another high school.

Robin Hunt and Katie Thomas

"It's a shame all those parts can't be donated somewhere," cracks Katie.

Lynne turns to Robin. "If you're not a teacher, what do you do for work?"

"I'm a vice president for a picture frame company," says Robin, slowly smoothing the side of the red leatherette booth.

Lynne, who's in marketing, wears a dark teased wig and black eyeliner and resembles the late British actress Hermione Gingold.

"We're the greatest actresses," she says. "To present an image, we need to be on all the time."

The waitress returns with two sausage pizzas. Robin admires Carole's blouse. "It's not silk but polyester," says Carole. Lynne and Katie reminisce about the leisure suits they wore back in the seventies. Everyone agrees that Father and Son is a much more pleasant place for pizza than Chuck E. Cheese. "Oh, God, I hate Chuck E. Cheese," Katie says. "If the pope would spend a Saturday at a Chuck E. Cheese, he'd change his views on birth control."

"So how are you holding up?" Katie whispers to Robin between bites. "Have you heard from your daughter?" Robin's daughter lived with her father for two months after he moved out of the house to begin life as a woman. But now the daughter and her fiancé are living in Florida. "We talked on the phone last Monday," Robin tells Katie. "Thanks for asking."

At seven thirty the occupants of the red booth leave Father and Son and walk across Milwaukee Avenue to the Stardust banquet hall. They're headed to the monthly business meeting of the Chicago Gender Society, a support group. There's barely a glance from passersby. They're taken for what they want to be: four women out for a night of fun.

"Some of us, like Robin, are what's called primary transsexuals, and they want nothing more than to be girls," Katie explains. Katie, on the other hand, calls herself "a secondary transsexual." She dresses in women's clothing several times a week, yet enjoys coming home to a supportive wife. "When I was a kid, cross-dressing would have gone over like a lead balloon with my parents, obviously," she says. "For years I had a pastime on the side. But I've raised my kids, and now it's my turn. That's really what this comes down to."

Katie Thomas (not her real name) is a retired salesman who lives in a western suburb. When she first began cross-dressing in public a year and a half ago, she named herself after Kathy Levine, a QVC Home Shopping Network host. "Kathy Levine epitomizes my idea of a feminine woman," she explains. But she met so many Kathys at the Chicago Gender Society and at the Society for the Second Self, or Tri-Ess—a group for heterosexual cross-dressers—that in the end she settled on Katie.

Two or three days a week Katie, who's in her early sixties, goes out as a woman. Some effort is required. She shaves her beard with a Gillette Mach3 razor. She also shaves her legs and upper chest and tweezes her eyebrows. To create a bust, says Katie, "you can use anything from sweat socks to old panty hose—just so it won't be rock hard when somebody bumps into you." She favors silicone forms designed for women who have had mastectomies—she's found they pick up the warmth of the body.

It takes Katie about an hour to get ready. There are nails to attach ("Contact cement works best as the adhesive"), makeup to apply, and a woman's watch, a crystal-encrusted tennis bracelet, rhinestone wedding bands, and a fluffy blond wig to put on.

The clothing comes from Field's, Carson's, and Nordstrom's. The shoes are from Payless ShoeSource and DSW Shoe Warehouse. "I believe in sales," says Katie. "In my business life, I never paid a thousand dollars for a suit. I made sure I grabbed one for three hundred dollars. It's the same today. Paying more just isn't necessary."

She favors slacks, blouses, and blazers, having noticed on a visit to the mall that women out for the day generally avoid dresses. When she does wear a dress it's a size 14. For special occasions she has five sequined cocktail frocks and a full-length nutria fur. All told, she guesses she has four thousand dollars worth of women's clothing in her closet and spends one hundred dollars a month to maintain herself as a woman.

"This is not a cheap hobby," says Katie.

Leaving the house, she gets into her late-model sedan, which is parked either in the attached garage or out on the driveway. "If the neighbors know, they know," she says. "Now I assume that the lady across the street must have an inkling, but what are you going to do? I made up my mind that I'm not hiding anything. If a neighbor came up to me and asked I'd say, 'Yes—it's me. This is the way I am.' Actually, I'm fairly sure the old lady does know. She's a sweet lady. I'd love to have lunch with her."

To Katie, nothing much beats a chatty conversation over a light meal. "What interests me are personalities and relationships. To talk about the Bears, and who's up for a trade, bores the hell out of me. The only thing that separates me in personality from a natural-born woman are my genitalia."

On her days out, Katie hits the suburban malls, does lunch, and sees a movie. So far as she knows she's never been recognized as her male self or even picked out as a cross-dresser. She's worked hard to adopt feminine traits—mincing steps, fluttery hand motions. It also helps that she's not especially tall. "With heels on I'm still under six feet," she says. And she avoids one common mistake—the thick makeup, high hair, and short skirts that make some transsexuals look trashy. She learned her lesson the time she pulled into a gas station wearing a tight blue blouse over a leopard-skin skirt. A galoot came on to her. "He said he wanted to talk," says Katie, "when all I wanted to do was get to the ladies' room."

As a man, she applied for a credit card in the name Katherine, supposedly a daughter. Along with a driver's license that pictures a pleasant-faced bald man, she keeps an identification card with a photograph of herself and an explanation on the back: "Katherine A. Thomas is a male-to-female transgendered person who presents as a female. This is a natural expression of her personality and a requirement of her ongoing transgender therapy."

She's never had to show the card. For that matter, she's never had any therapy. "For one hundred bucks an hour, I can buy an awful nice outfit," she says.

"Am I lucky?" she says one noontime that finds her attired in gold hoop earrings, a yellow plaid blazer, white blouse, and slacks as she downs an omelet in a coffee shop. "I don't know. I'm of the mind-set that I'm not doing anything wrong. No one has the right to judge me. I'm not hurting anyone, I'm not embarrassing anyone, and when I'm dressed as a woman I feel like the real me. If you get your nose out of joint, so be it."

She grew up in a Catholic household on the South Side. "As far back as I can remember, when I was a little bitty kid, I was interested in being like a girl," Katie says. "I would dress up in secret. To my knowledge my father, who was a cop, was never aware that I did it, although once when I was thirteen my mother caught me. After that there were no more instances, as far as she knew— I got smarter."

She says, "I can't tell you why I was born this way, whether it's physical or psychological." Katie's wife, Roberta (not her real name), thinks it goes back to her husband's relationship with his mother. "He always admired her," says Roberta. "She was a beautiful woman with beautiful manners, and he wanted to be like her."

They married barely out of their teens. Dressing up as a woman for a Halloween party, Roberta's husband confessed to her how much pleasure it gave him. "I guess I loved him enough," says Roberta, "and it was something he wanted to do. It didn't hurt anybody. People think it's bad, but I never have."

"Roberta has been wonderfully, wonderfully understanding over all these years," says her husband. "This has never been brought up as an issue, or thrown in my face during an argument."

Roberta has bought Katie bras and other articles of clothing. When Katie retired last year, Roberta gave her the tennis bracelet she now wears. In August she and her husband actually purchased the same outfit, a skirt and sweater combination, at JC Penney.

"If I were a woman," Katie muses, "maybe I'd be attracted to a man. But as it is I love women, and I always have. In having sex, sexuality takes over and you enjoy it—though sex has diminished with age, like everything else." She and Roberta maintain an active social life. They love movies, favoring comedies and love stories.

While they raised their three children, Roberta's husband would don women's clothes when the kids were away, or late at night when everyone was asleep, or in his hotel room when he was on the road selling. Once the kids were gone, he focused on Friday nights. "I would sit around the house and watch TV in drag," Katie says.

He hit sixty and realized this wasn't enough. Two years ago he spotted an ad for a Tri-Ess meeting in the "Woman News" section of the *Tribune*, and with Roberta's permission decided to attend. When Katie drove up to a Holiday Inn in a western suburb, "I was very, very scared," she says. "Terrified would be the better word. Remember, I had never been out in public before."

Tri-Ess meetings draw fifty or more people (including some wives) for an evening of socializing, panel discussions, and presentations on electrolysis, cosmetics, and false hair. Wig and corset shops display their wares. Katie arrived early and headed to the newcomers' table. Immediately she felt embraced. "Everyone talked about themselves, about how they came out, and I did too," says Katie. "It was quite nonthreatening, and I stayed for the rest of the evening."

The next month Katie attended a Chicago Gender Society meeting at the Stardust. Seated at a round table in the mirrored banquet hall, she noticed Robin, who was wearing a smart black skirt and sweater outfit. They got to talking. "We were just chatting back and forth, and a nice connection was made," says Katie.

In August of 2000 Robin and Katie met again at Tri-Ess. That night a couple renewed their wedding vows—"except the groom was a cross-dresser," says Katie, "and he came all dolled up in a wedding gown. His wife was the bridesmaid. A Jesuit priest officiated at a Mass, complete with communion. The DJ said, 'They never covered this in disc-jockey school.'"

Katie and Robin fell into an intense conversation. "After that we were back and forth on the phone," says Robin, who's in her midfifties. "I used to have 'Robin Tuesday,' when I became Robin, not Bob. I wouldn't go to work, but would sit in the park and read or else go shopping. On one of those Tuesdays Katie called, and she joined me."

They met for lunch in front of the Field's store in Woodfield Mall, Bob in drag and Katie in "drab"—argot for "dressed as a boy." They sat on a bench for two

hours and never got around to lunch. "We talked about our lives—my story, his story—and how we felt when we were kids," says Robin. Robin persuaded Katie to come with her that night to a CGS social gathering at Temptations, a lesbian club in Franklin Park known for its pool and darts. Even though Katie doesn't drink, she went home, changed into women's attire, and hit the club.

Robin grew up in Rochester, New York, as Bob Heinzman. "My mother owned a dress shop," says Robin. "As a kid I was responsible for cleaning up. When I was ten or twelve, I would go in on Sundays to run the vacuum, and I would put on dresses. At that time and in that environment—in the fifties—I didn't know what it was. But by high school I figured something was going on. I wasn't all that attracted to women. Oh, I took a girl to the prom, but mentally I couldn't get into it. Whereas another guy might lust for a woman, I admired women. For me it was a study—I looked at what they wore and how they lived. But though I had mixed feelings about my gender, the safest place to be was as a boy. To have been anything else back then would have been unacceptable."

It was 1952 when George Jorgensen, a former soldier from New York City, announced in Denmark that he'd undergone hormone therapy and a series of operations to become a woman. BRONX "BOY" IS NOW A GIRL, headlined the *New York Times*, as the concept of switching sexes entered the general consciousness. Jorgensen returned to the United States as Christine Jorgensen, where she was ridiculed by the public and condemned by mainline physicians. She went on to a life of lectures and nightclub appearances.

After college and a tour as a military policeman in Vietnam, Bob Heinzman married a woman he'd met while playing billiards and then dated a year. "I wasn't conflicted about getting married," Robin says. "My hormones were raging, and sex is sex. Besides, my wife was a good kisser." Heinzman worked in accounting for Xerox and was transferred to Chicago in 1967. Five years later he left for a career as an information-technology consultant.

Unable to have children of their own, he and his wife adopted three youngsters. "I tried to be normal," says Robin. The Heinzmans settled into a wooded estate with a pool, a greenhouse, and a horse barn in Wayne, a town in western DuPage County. Bob became a Cub Scout and Pony Club leader. "We had a lot of good times together, but there was always something going on inside me," Robin says. "I felt shame. The feeling is, you're different, and you fear that if your friends and family find out you'll be rejected. I couldn't relate to the stereotypical male interests or activities. I didn't knit or crochet, but I was always more comfortable sitting around talking to the girls, who were more supportive and protective of each other."

Bob dressed up in secret. Fifteen years ago his wife found a stash of women's clothing in a bureau. She confronted him, and made him attend a sexual behavior consultation program at Johns Hopkins Hospital in Baltimore. "They said I was a transvestite, and that I should stop cross-dressing and become a normal man," says Robin.

He tried. But abstinence was immensely frustrating. About four years ago, when Bob's consulting work had him on the road a lot, he took to leaving home a man and changing clothes in the car. "One day I drove to the South Side and just kept on going, and by the afternoon I found myself in southern Illinois." The more depressed he became the more he stayed to himself, and the less he communicated with his wife.

He kept fighting his own nature. In 1999, after four months of not dressing up, he reached a point where "I couldn't stand it any longer. I started to do research on transgenderism, and by the end of December I'd had an epiphany. It occurred to me that the only way I could get rid of my urges was to change myself. Still, I knew there was lots to lose. You build your life, you develop more and more relationships, you've got kids and a better job. You're closer to retirement. Still, you know you're running out of time, and so you panic."

Bob called the Tri-Ess hotline, and over lunch a member of the group referred him to social worker Barbra Getz, whose office is in her home near Elgin. In February 2000 she opened her door to a balding, bespectacled, five-foot-ten man. "I'm a woman," Bob said. "I can't live like I am anymore."

According to the American Psychiatric Association's *Diagnostic and Statistical Manual of Mental Disorders*, fourth edition, people like Bob are suffering from "gender identity disorder." The transsexual community often uses the phrase "gender dysphoria." The idea of there being primary and secondary male transsexuals is credited to New York psychoanalysts Lionel Ovesey and Ethel Person. Getz, who has treated transgendered clients for twenty years, subscribes to it.

Ovesey and Person introduced their theory in the *American Journal of Psychotherapy* in 1974. Transsexualism, they wrote, arises from "an unconscious wish to merge with the mother in order to alleviate early separation anxiety." In a primary transsexual, the drive to become female is "insistent and progressive from the beginning and throughout the course of development." Secondary transsexuals are either homosexual or heterosexual transvestites. Their impulse to womanhood "may be either a transient symptom, or it may harden into a full-blown transsexual syndrome."

Getz also leans on the more recent work of Richard Docter, a psychology professor now retired from California State University, Northridge. In his 1988 book *Transvestites and Transsexuals,* Docter posited a continuum. On one end are periodic cross-dressers (such as Katie), who ally psychologically with females. "Theirs is the view that girls have it better in many ways," Docter wrote.

On the other end of the continuum are men who live as women out of a strong, persistent desire to become one. In these men—described in much the same way that Ovesey and Person described primary transsexuals—"the cross-gender self forces a reorganization of their self-system. A new (feminine) self takes charge."

In an interview, Docter says that 15 percent of periodic cross-dressers "seem to migrate into full-time living, whether they receive anatomical surgery or not." He ascribes hard-core transsexuality to "a neurological bias that takes place within the first twenty-four weeks of life." In 1995, Dutch researchers writing in the journal *Nature* linked transsexual tendencies to an enlargement in a region of the brain's hypothalamus. "Gender identity is determined by the brain, not by the genitals," says Randi Ettner, an Evanston psychologist who specializes in transsexuality.

No reliable data tell us how many Americans are transsexual, but figures from Europe cited in the *Diagnostic and Statistical Manual of Mental Disorders* indicate that one in thirty thousand adult males (and one in one hundred thousand adult women) seeks sex-reassignment surgery. Transsexualism may surface with age, says Randi Ettner: "Typically men get married and are locked into an existence. But when the children are gone, they say to themselves, 'It's now or never.' So a person who might have been able to put the condition on the back burner at twenty-five, at forty-two or fifty-eight can't wait any longer."

There's no consensus on what to do about it. "There are some doctors who think that you should get used to the gender with which you're born," says Dr. Jack Drescher, who chairs the committee on gay, lesbian, and bisexual issues for the American Psychiatric Association. "But the medical establishment hasn't come down with guidelines."

Professional opinions differ on the quality of transsexuals' lives. "It's getting easier now for people," says Richard Docter. "There are fewer laws against it, and there's less perception that this is a deviance." Barbra Getz thinks transsexuals today receive about as much respect as gays did in the 1960s. But Randi Ettner points to the movie *Boys Don't Cry,* about the real-life murder of a young woman who passed for a man. Ettner calls transsexuality "the most difficult obstacle a person can face."

"I invited him to tell me his story," says Barbra Getz. "I challenged him. 'You've been married a long time. You have kids. Do you realize you may lose your children, your marriage, and your job?' After a series of sessions with Robin, who came dressed as a woman, it was obvious that he was who he said he was. He was Robin, and Robin sought to be a woman, no matter the cost."

The late Dr. Harry Benjamin, a Berlin-born endocrinologist practicing in New York City, coined the term "transsexualism" and distinguished it from homosexuality. Benjamin helped pioneer sex surgery (he treated Christine Jorgensen), and he laid out widely accepted preoperative guidelines. These required Bob Heinzman to live one year as a woman, undergo hormone therapy, receive psychotherapy ("if required by a mental health professional"), and obtain letters recommending surgery from a social worker and a psychologist or a psychiatrist.

A few days before he met Getz, Bob had begun taking hormones he ordered over the Internet from overseas. She eventually referred him to Dr. Fred Ettner, an Evanston family practitioner (and Randi Ettner's husband), and last year Ettner prescribed Premarin, a popular estrogen supplement made from pregnant mares' urine, and an antiandrogen to suppress testosterone. This drug therapy softens the skin, develops the breasts, broadens the hips and thighs, decreases hair growth on the body and increases it on the head, reduces muscle mass in the upper body, and diminishes erections; furthermore, says Fred Ettner, it calms the person taking the drugs.

As he began to experience these effects, Bob, counseled by Getz, wrote his wife a letter. "I said that after talking with my counselor and doing research, there were conditions that I couldn't live with. I laid out my goal of being a woman for the remainder of my life."

A year ago Bob moved out of their house in Wayne and into a studio apartment on Chicago's Northwest Side. Today Bob and his wife are discussing divorce, primarily by e-mail.

"Some spouses can be horrendous," says Getz. "But you have to realize, their whole world has been turned upside down. They see their femininity being taken away from them. They fear their sexual identity is being attacked, that they'll be taken as a lesbian. Yet other people stay together. They just do. Their love is more profound than gender. Their closeness is just very deep."

Neither of Bob's two sons has found it easy to deal with what their father is going through. Bob's nineteen-year-old daughter has been more understanding. When Bob took his daughter and one of her brothers for a walk in the park and told them what was happening, she said she didn't care. "I was just glad he was happy," says the daughter, "and I gave him a hug." Robin has already been outfitted with a mother-of-the-bride dress for her wedding.

Bob's sister, a Washington lawyer, offered grudging support. "If this is OK with you," she said, "it's OK with me." Their father, an eighty-nine-year-old retired car salesman, and an older son who lives with him in Florida, were both puzzled.

"They have turned this into my being a homosexual," says Bob. In deference to his wife, he's broken off contact with their mutual friends.

So Robin's grateful for her relationship with Katie. For more than a year they've seen each other weekly for shopping or a movie. One typical day they parked in the Grant Park garage, strolled happily up Michigan Avenue to the Terra Museum (which intrigued them because of a bitter dispute then being waged within the museum's board), ate at a McDonald's, and ended up at Temptations. Before last June's Pride Parade, Mayor Daley hosted a reception at the Cultural Center, and Robin and Katie attended. "We showed up fairly early and so we went to Boudin Bakery on Michigan Avenue," says Katie. "We sat down as two women. I said to her, 'I think we're dead and gone to heaven.'"

Robin and Katie like to discuss politics. Both are moderately conservative Republicans. "I vote for Henry Hyde and Pate Philip, but then you have to in DuPage County—they check up on you," says Katie. "I believe you can't let people die in the streets, but we don't need a welfare program for everybody." She does stick up for transsexuals. Back in her salesman days, a customer joked that his hairdresser was going "from Angelo to Angel." Katie responded, "He'd be a brave person to be who he is." The customer conceded Angelo that much, and Katie felt a frisson of delight: "I'd put in a shot for our side."

Robin and Katie also talk a lot about clothes and makeup. "She tells me if something looks good on me, and vice versa," says Katie, although Robin insists that Katie's the one with the fashion sense. Katie perceives Robin's life to be a lot tougher than her own and is generous with personal advice. "I tell him, 'You should try this instead of that,'" says Katie. "I try to be sympathetic." Robin's grateful. "This condition we have can eat you up. You need someone to talk to you, a listening post, and here I've found Katie. She's my big sister."

"When I realized what my transitional goals would be, I knew I couldn't keep on consulting," says Robin. "I needed more stability." In April of 2000, Bob became materials director for Franklin Home, a small, 120-year-old manufacturer of mirrors, picture frames, and other wall decor in Irving Park. It's a firm where he'd consulted for two decades. He worked out a four-day workweek that allowed him his Robin Tuesdays.

But to comply with Harry Benjamin's preoperative guidelines, Bob needed to become Robin at work. Coming out on the job can be risky. According to It's Time, Illinois, a transgender lobbying group, the working rights of transsexuals are protected by law in this state only in Evanston, DeKalb, and Urbana-Champaign. Chicago's human rights ordinance doesn't cover transsexuals. A 1999 administrative judge's ruling does allow transsexuals to claim their condition as a disability under the Illinois Human Rights Act, but "few of us want to think of ourselves as handicapped," says Beth Plotner, the lawyer who chairs It's Time, Illinois.

"Often people who change their sex at work are let go," says Barbra Getz. "Oh, it's subtle. 'We'll talk about it,' a boss will say. 'We'll see.' Then the person is fired." Plotner estimates that half the people who come out as transsexuals at work lose their jobs, although last summer a friend of hers didn't. The principal of Marie Murphy Middle School in Wilmette changed gender, became Deanna Reed, and weathered the protests of some parents. "She has a contract, and to have let her go would have breached the contract," says Plotner.

Katie and Barbra Getz helped Robin map a strategy. In January, Bob made an appointment to see his superior, Franklin Home's president, Steven Kottler. Bob reviewed his performance at work. Oh, he's resigning, thought Kottler; I'll have to find another computer expert to run the materials department. Then he told Kottler about his divorce. "Steve said he was happy with the job I'd been doing, but was sad to hear I was getting divorced," says Robin. "Then I said that I also had a health problem."

He's sick and going to die, Kottler thought. Then Bob began talking about gender dysphoria. He gave Kottler some literature, asked his boss to help him become a woman at work, and left.

"I'm a pretty liberal person," says Kottler. "I was kind of shocked, but I wasn't stupefied, either. This is what somebody wanted to do with his life. Bob was a valued employee, and I thought we should give him support."

Kottler talked to Franklin Home's labor attorney, who explained the lack of employment protections for transsexuals, and he opened a Bob Heinzman file. "But then you'd do that with anybody who has a problem," Kottler says, "so the person can't come back later and say that you messed up."

He and Bob came up with a plan.

On March 16 Kottler convened his supervisors and office staff in the Franklin Home conference room. "I talked a little about where the company was business-wise," says Kottler. Then Bob stood and read a statement that Katie had gone over for typos and misused words.

Bob thanked Kottler for the chance to address the dozen or so people who were present. "I expect that this meeting will be very emotional for me," he began, "so I will be reading a statement rather than speaking from notes, to ensure that I cover everything that is important to say." At this point Bob began to sob, and his audience sat in bewildered silence.

"Does anybody have any questions?" Kottler joked.

"I suffer from a health condition called gender dysphoria," said Bob, when he could resume. "For those of you that know about this condition, it may shock you but will not surprise you. To be honest, I hope after I explain it to everyone, it won't surprise any of you."

He announced that he was becoming Robin Ann Hunt, and he said that Kottler had given him permission to be Robin at work. If anyone objected to his using the ladies' room, he said, he'd make other arrangements.

"In closing," Bob said, "I would like to say that I am extremely pleased that I can do this transition with people that I have grown to love for at least the last two years and for some of you as many as twenty years. You are a wonderful group of people, and I enjoy working with all of you." Then he introduced Barbra Getz, who had brought along a video on transsexualism.

"It was all very emotional," Robin remembers. "I'm crying all the way through. Some people got up and gave me a hug."

And some didn't. "Everyone was just astonished," says Deedee Davila, Robin's assistant, who knew what was coming. "Some of us were sympathetic, but others were mean and gave each other looks of disapproval." Davila says a certain manager who'd sparred with Robin over a new computer system smirked and made faces. Davila stood up for her boss. "I don't care where you pee," she told Bob for all to hear.

Robin called Katie afterward and told her, "It went great."

Bob announced that for the next two weeks he'd answer any question Franklin Home employees put to him. "Everybody asked him things," says Davila. "What about your marriage? Your children? Why are you doing this after all these years?" As the two weeks went by, Bob felt increasingly understood and accepted.

He emerged as Robin on March 30. "It was casual Friday," she recalls. "I arrived in jeans and a top and walked right in that morning. Of course, Deedee was overwhelmed because I didn't look anything like Bob. Gradually people came by my office to check me out." On her desk, Robin found a bouquet of flowers sent by the office.

"During the day there was a problem on the plant floor," says Robin. "I had to go out there, so I followed Deedee out to where they make the picture frames. I walked by twenty people. I talked to the foreman and then came back to my office. Then Deedee ran back to find out what everybody thought."

The August business meeting of the Chicago Gender Society at the Stardust begins with a social hour. Transsexuals from all points on Richard Docter's continuum mingle over drinks and conversation. Some are cross-dressers; others have already gone through sex-reassignment surgery. There are also a few male suitors, a couple of lesbians, and one unkempt man in black horn-rims who is assumed to be a curiosity seeker. In a corner are the Island Girls, a high-styled group from the Blue Island area who host parties at a bar in that suburb. At a table off to one side, Rachel's Wigs is doing steady business.

"I'll go to a wedding, and the women are in beautiful dresses," says Lynne, Robin and Katie's friend in marketing. "I'll come home tight as a drum, thinking that should have been me." At the bar, Connie, who's wearing an elegant cocktail sheath and a matching shawl, groans about how long it took her to change for the evening. "It was a two-hour time-waster." Marie, a shapely cross-dresser many years Connie's junior, celebrates a vacation in Toronto ("I was a total femme on the trip") and then laments her inability to explain herself to her father. "I can't tell my retired firefighter dad that I'm a girl who likes girls," she says, sweeping a hand in front of her face. "It's too complicated."

Founded in 1987, CGS now claims 170 members. President Olivia Connors says it offers transsexuals a harbor. "Here we find friendship and share our thoughts." Connors, who's fifty-four, is in insurance, and she also works at Transformations, a popular suburban boutique. She's had a rough moment or two—she describes being set upon and pummeled at Clark and Diversey in 1993—yet she seems comfortable with her life, about three-fifths of which she says she lives as a female.

"God, it's been a fast summer, and a wet one," says Connors, dressed in black checked slacks and a black blouse and wearing a swept-back wig the color of eggshells.

She likes to begin meetings by going around the hall asking for responses on some admittedly dumb topic. "Tonight I want you to tell us about something you've lost and something you've found," she says. Someone talks about weight loss, someone else about dropping and recovering a wedding ring on a beach. Robin pipes up, "What I found was sex. What I lost was my virginity."

An outlandish figure in a blond wig and red shorts volunteers "my ability to go into public looking like a Barbie doll." Someone else says, "What I lost was between my legs." The room chortles.

Fred Ettner is the evening's speaker. He began taking transsexual patients a decade ago, after a transsexual with a sinus infection who'd been refused treatment by other doctors came his way; now transsexuals account for 10 to 15 percent of his practice. "If a transsexual comes into my office and says, 'I have a problem with my gender,' that's enough for me," says Ettner. "But I can tell you, it's a tough haul for you to get a doctor to listen to you."

He talks about stem cell research ("Imagine if I could create ovarian tissue and put it inside you") and answers questions. How much does Premarin cost? Do I need cosmetic breasts? Will estrogen suffice?

Ettner speaks for forty minutes, and when he sits down at ten thirty, Connors calls a break. Robin and Katie quickly disappear out the door. In ten minutes,

Katie returns. She explains that she and Roberta had gathered up a fan, an old television, and some magazines, including *Cosmopolitan,* for Robin's new apartment, and that she and Robin were just moving it all to Robin's car. "She needs stuff, she doesn't have much money, and so I help her along," says Katie.

Various announcements—a beauty pageant, a Christmas party—take the meeting almost to midnight.

Drawing on her background in sales, Katie coordinates advertising for the CGS and Tri-Ess newsletters. She staffs the Tri-Ess hotline. She's begun giving informational talks at universities. After speaking at Loyola she was taken to lunch at Cy's Crab House on North Ashland. "I winked at the headwaiter," Katie says, "and the Loyola kids said, 'I love your shoes. Where'd you get them?'"

She took a couple of voice lessons from Lynette Venturella, a speech therapist with a transsexual clientele. The one-hundred-dollar-an-hour fee made Katie quit, but not before picking up one important tip: speak from the chest—not the belly—to raise your voice a level.

Lately Roberta has been joining Katie for shopping forays and lunch. "We go out and eat as missus and missus," says Roberta. "Sometimes you feel that people are looking, but it's none of their business." Roberta's friends don't know her husband cross-dresses, and if one of them spots her with Katie—it hasn't happened yet—she intends to introduce her husband as her cousin. In July Roberta and Katie attended the CGS garden show together, Katie in a denim skirt unbuttoned to allow some leg to show. A photograph of the occasion shows Roberta, seated, leaning back into Katie, the two of them smiling for the camera.

"I have a very happy life," says Katie. "I have no regrets. I'm in a committed relationship for more than forty years. There's no job anymore, so I'm not going to get fired, and nobody is going to throw me out of the house. I couldn't be happier to have the release of cross-dressing."

But she makes an admission. If something happened to Roberta, she allows, "I'd live more as a woman. I'd have to convince my kids that I hadn't gone crazy, but yes, I'd proceed down that path—though we're not talking about an operation at this point." Katie's children don't even know she cross-dresses.

Robin describes herself as "a heterosexual woman except without the plumbing." She's halfway through the obligatory year of living as a woman. When Bob set off on his man-to-woman odyssey, he drew up a two-year budget. On it he listed living expenses, hormone therapy, psychotherapy, electrolysis, voice lessons, clothes, wigs ("You've got to have five of them, 'cause they only last a few months," Robin says), breast implants, the legal costs of a name change and a divorce, feminizing facial surgery (that traditionally means an Adam's apple reduction or a procedure to soften the jawline), and the eventual operation to remove the penis and create a vagina. All this came to $97,599.

But expenses so far have been half what Robin expected. She lives simply. Her apartment contains a bed, desk, table, and television but neither a phone nor a stereo. "There are Franklin Home pictures on the wall," says Robin. "They're nice, but they look out of place." Insurance has helped pay for her hormone therapy. (It usually doesn't, says Ettner.) "I'm getting by without electrolysis," Robin says, "though sometimes I have to shave twice a day."

Like Katie, she went to Venturella for voice lessons until the cost made her quit. She gets by with a contrived falsetto that Venturella considers "abusive" because it can lead to nodules on the vocal cords.

On December 4 she legally changed her name to Robin Ann Hunt. Genital surgery is the big event still ahead. Getz urges her patients to choose a surgeon carefully. "They have to build a vagina," she says, "and that can be tricky because you want the equipment to be sensitive. You want a clitoris that has feeling. And some surgeons do better work than others."

Fred Ettner says genital surgery is a two-step process that most plastic and urological surgeons refuse to perform. It runs to twenty thousand dollars in the United States and to ten thousand dollars if done in Belgium, Thailand, or Montreal. Robin has earmarked $17,500 for her surgery. She hopes it'll be performed by a doctor in Neenah, Wisconsin, Ettner recommended.

Robin's frayed family ties have been a constant source of pain, but Christmas brought some relief. She visited her father and brother in South Carolina over the holidays, worrying particularly about her father's reaction. He surprised her. Returning from a hayride, he found Robin standing in her brother's living room. He studied her. "Gee, you've got great legs," he said.

After that, Robin says, "we had some great discussions." They centered on sex. "My dad's questions related to why I wanted my penis cut off," she says. "He was a ladies' man and he knows the value of the thing."

She's feeling more and more comfortable at Franklin Home. Kottler says he thinks of Robin primarily as a female. "What can I do for you, ma'am?" the company president said when Robin entered his office recently. "Thank you," said Robin. To her pleasure, Robin was promoted to vice president of manufacturing in August, even as Franklin Home was laying off half its factory workforce after its major client declared bankruptcy. To her added pleasure, the snickering manager was among the many who lost their jobs. Of the remaining forty employees at Franklin, Deedee Davila guesses that only a half dozen don't accept her boss. She says, "The younger generation doesn't bat an eye."

Robin has lost twenty-five pounds and a paunch she'd hated is gone. Her personality has also changed. "Bob Heinzman was very quiet," says Deedee Davila. "He didn't laugh or joke. He was serious and sad, very inward to himself. But as soon as Bob came in the door as Robin he's been lively, smiling, and joking. On Saturdays when Robin and I are alone at the office together, we check out the repairmen who come in and we put on music and dance."

Robin is exultant. "I'm outgoing and confident," she says. "It's like I've had a remission from cancer."

The friendship between Robin and Katie endures. "If she moved to South Carolina, say, that would affect our relationship," says Katie, "but I can't see anything else changing things, as we carry our conditions to our graves." Asked about Katie, Robin refers to the novel *Anne of Green Gables*, which she read last year. "Anne talks about being a kindred spirit to a friend. Katie is my kindred spirit for life."

Business

CAB SLEUTH

Cab sleuth "calls all cars" to retrieve lost goods.

On Saint Patrick's Day, two buddies pile into a cab downtown and ride out to a McDonald's in Jefferson Park. It being Saint Pat's Day, the friends apparently are feeling no pain, and when they alight, one of the fellows leaves behind his Pierre Cardin wallet, stuffed with $120.

The next afternoon, the wallet owner, sobered up and missing his cash, places a call to Christopher M. Kelly at the old Kraft building on Peshtigo Court near the Chicago River.

Officially titled a complaint and hearing officer for the city's Public Vehicle Commission, Mr. Kelly, a sixty-four-year-old man with graying reddish hair and glasses, is really a canny detective who locates articles lost in cabs.

"Was it a Checker cab you were in?" Mr. Kelly asks the wallet owner, who confirms the company but can't recall any details about the driver.

"OK," proceeds Mr. Kelly, "think about the cab again. Anything peculiar about it? Was there a scapular hanging from the rearview?"

The wallet owner says no about the Catholic devotional badge, but by the time Mr. Kelly hangs up, he has gleaned enough information to begin a search.

That search has a good chance of success, for Chris Kelly is a wizard at his craft.

Of 500 articles logged as lost in Chicago cabs last year, 169 were turned in voluntarily by the drivers. Of the remainder, an estimated 28 percent were recovered through the efforts of Mr. Kelly.

"He's a gem," asserts Mr. Kelly's supervisor, Tony Olivieri, deputy consumer service commissioner over public vehicle operations. "This man could find a needle in a haystack. Sometimes, what he does is just miraculous."

There exists an unending need for Mr. Kelly's skills. To start with, riders seldom remember much about the cabs in which they travel. While taxis carry their identification numbers in at least nine places, from the license plates to a spot facing passengers in the backseat, rarely are the numbers noted. Neither are the characteristics of the driver.

"People don't know if the guy was black, white, or Middle Eastern," observes Mr. Kelly, "or whether he had hair on his face."

Notwithstanding, the objects left behind—briefcases, wallets, umbrellas, suitcases, and even the occasional flute—matter to riders. When they finally talk to Mr. Kelly, likely as not, they are agitated over their loss.

But not for long. "I'm a helluva public relations man, what can I say?" relates Mr. Kelly. "I know how to talk to people, especially on the phone; I have savvy in un-upsetting them. If they've lost a wallet or a pair of gloves, I show them empathy, so when we are finished, we are almost friends."

Mr. Kelly's higher skill, however, is in ferreting out articles on the shreds of evidence he is given. There are 12,738 cabbies in Chicago, "and I know most of them," explains Mr. Kelly. "I'm acquainted with their modus operandi. Plus, the garage men at the cab companies are very cooperative. And hotel doormen are great—they have minds like traps."

Based on his contacts and familiarity with the drivers, Mr. Kelly launches his search by making phone calls. He approaches the search cynically, realizing that too many drivers are either unconcerned about lost goods or greedy enough to keep them.

One incentive: if articles are turned in but not retrieved within two months, the driver is the gainer. Currently, Mr. Kelly's office closet is home to cameras, jewelry, "and the wallet of some deadbeat"; all await claims by drivers.

More important, Mr. Kelly possesses extraordinary verbal skills.

"He has the gift of gab," remarks a supervisor of cabbies at O'Hare International Airport. "He simply talks the lost stuff out of the city." Mr. Kelly places his calls by day and by night, and he has occasionally cruised by the homes of drivers he thinks are harboring goods.

A case in point: recently, a San Francisco marketing executive who was staying at the Raphael Hotel exited a cab without the black appointment book that is her life. "If I don't get that book back," the woman told Mr. Kelly, "I'm dead." It wasn't long before Mr. Kelly had a phone number for the driver, only there was no one home.

"I called all day at work and then, when I got home, every ten minutes from 6 to 9:30," relates Mr. Kelly. "From 9:30 to 11, I kept calling. I had to pick up my wife from work, but when I got back, I called until 1 A.M."

Later that morning, Mr. Kelly had his breakfast and then swung by the driver's home address. It turned out the cabbie had moved, but Mr. Kelly finally reached him by phone at his new house. "I said to him, 'Where's the goddamn book?' Soon, I had it."

Out-of-Towner's Nightmare

Consider the fate of Ron Scarborough, regional sales manager for Millipore Corp., a fluid purification company based in Boston. In town for a meeting, Mr. Scarborough cabbed it from O'Hare to the Stouffer Hamilton Hotel in Itasca on March 14.

In a nightmare of nightmares, Mr. Scarborough, who was scheduled to make a presentation for the company president, left the briefcase containing his papers in the taxi's trunk, along with a small personal computer.

By the time he contacted Mr. Kelly the next day, recalls Mr. Scarborough, "I was pretty frustrated." He was also armed with a dearth of information. The vehicle number indicated he had been in a Checker cab, yet the identity of the driver eluded him. The man was of Pakistani or Greek origin, Mr. Scarborough felt sure. But one of his colleagues insisted the guy resembled Woody Allen.

With only the suggestion that the driver's name began with an *A*, Mr. Kelly set to work with his calls. Soon, he had pinpointed the driver (he was Greek), who brought in the briefcase and computer; both were promptly shipped off to the grateful executive at his Missouri office.

Mr. Scarborough was startled at Mr. Kelly's doggedness and sense of concern: "I travel all the time on my job. Now, I like Chicago as a city, but you don't expect to run into somebody that concerned in Chicago. Maybe in a small town, but not in Chicago."

Mr. Kelly inspires such praise even from people for whom he hasn't succeeded. A while back, when Mel Marks, a Chicago marketing consultant, lost a new sport jacket and a pair of trousers in a cab, he was referred to Mr. Kelly.

"To talk to this man, you'd think he was doing the most important thing in the world," relates Mr. Marks. "It's as if discovering an AIDS vaccine were nothing compared to finding something lost in a cab. His follow-through is incredible."

Although Mr. Kelly has so far come up dry in efforts to help Mr. Marks, he still checks in with phone calls and now wants the consultant to come in to screen mug shots of cabbies.

If Mr. Kelly himself doesn't persevere, sometimes, his reasoning does. Two police officers once called to report that a woman had taken a cab from the Chicago Marriott on Rush Street and left behind an attaché case containing eleven thousand dollars. Mr. Kelly promptly talked to the Marriott doorman, who said the woman had flagged a taxi on her own.

Playing on some doubt as to the woman's powers of recollection, Mr. Kelly suggested that the cops check out the coffee shop where she had eaten breakfast earlier. Sure enough, there on the counter lay the attaché case. "But there wasn't eleven thou inside," notes Mr. Kelly. "There was thirteen-five."

Craft also plays a role in Mr. Kelly's ability to establish ownership of items the cabbies turn in.

Years ago, an unmarked camera was given to Mr. Kelly. "Nobody had reported the thing as lost. What was I going to do? Well, I developed the film at my own expense, and there in the background of one picture was a license plate from Colorado. So I called out to Colorado, and that camera found its way home."

Just weeks ago, Mr. Kelly connected seventy-seven dollars worth of cosmetics with their St. Louis purchaser by following the lead of a Neiman-Marcus sales receipt.

One of eleven children born to Irish immigrant parents in the Bronx, Mr. Kelly dropped out of high school in his sophomore year. After a stint in the navy, he began a career with what is now Airwick Industries, the New Jersey–based maker of room deodorizers and air fresheners.

In the early 1970s, Airwick opened a new manufacturing plant in St. Peters, Missouri, where Mr. Kelly became plant superintendent. He retired in 1974, however, to spend more time with his children. Plus, he admits, "I didn't really cotton to the atmosphere" at the plant.

Back in Chicago, Mr. Kelly toiled in the political vineyards of John Merlo, Forty-fourth Ward Democratic committeeman. Connections secured him a job as a clerk in Cook County's Marriage License Bureau.

Within a year he had transferred to the public vehicle branch of the city Department of Consumer Services, where he was quickly elevated to the rank of hearing officer.

In 1985, he began a thirteen-month tour as acting branch chief, which he didn't like. "I can deal with cab companies and ordinances," Mr. Kelly looks back, "but not with petty things. Maybe I wasn't good at delegating. Anyway, I got sick of being the king."

As a mere functionary earning thirty thousand dollars a year, Mr. Kelly not only finds lost articles but has acted as a hearing officer on police citations and citizen complaints against drivers.

The hearings—over accusations of discourtesy, overcharging, and the refusal to take a fare to a requested destination—result in warnings, suspensions, or even license revocations. "Usually, some action is taken," says Mr. Kelly.

Who gripes? Everyone, it seems, including celebrities. Harry Caray once objected to fare gouging, and comedian Shecky Greene, so profane onstage, couldn't stomach a cabbie calling him a foul name. And Channel 7 newsman Jay Levine "didn't like that some guy treated him rudely," according to Mr. Kelly.

When Dan Rather got into a much-publicized tiff with a driver in November 1980, it was Mr. Kelly who took testimony from the CBS broadcaster.

Mr. Rather was riding to author Studs Terkel's Uptown apartment when he either was kidnapped (Mr. Rather's version) or refused to pay his fare (the driver's side). Columnist Mike Royko, then with the *Chicago Sun-Times*, championed the driver in print, but Mr. Kelly heard Mr. Rather's side and found it credible. However, the anchorman eventually dropped the matter.

Potential Outcome

Whether passenger complaints will be eased by the recently enacted taxi industry reforms Mr. Kelly can't predict. On the one hand, he thinks a relaxation of the near-monopoly held by the Yellow and Checker companies may be conducive to greater neighborhood service. Conversely he worries that the quality of drivers may fall. "The new ones had better cut the mustard," he warns.

Meanwhile, the lost-and-found work continues to energize Mr. Kelly. Despite more than a decade on the job, extensive heart surgery, and a hearing aid (the result of an old navy injury), he exhibits a boundless professional joy.

"What can I say?" remarks the grandfather of five. "I'm a real BS-er. I love to talk. This is being a detective, except no one gets hurt physically. You get such satisfaction when you find something for somebody."

SPEED WASH

A West Side business story.

The first arrivals push through the door of the Davis Speed Wash on Roosevelt Road just past five o'clock on a frigid February morning. They walk to the rear counter, where owner Hughzell Davis is dispensing cups of thin coffee for fifty cents. They settle comfortably into what seem to be their regular spots. Some sit on a row of colored plastic chairs, a couple slide onto folding tables, and others stand. They peer at the street through the windows' black metal grille, talking quietly as the sky lightens.

"There's a depression goin' on," says George Gray, a middle-aged man in a threadbare coat. "People think the new president has some kind of magic wand over the economy, but he doesn't. The Congress does. That's my thinking."

Gray has come out of the cold after walking the streets all night. He complains that his welfare has been cut to the bone. Gray had surgery recently, and while recuperating in a nursing home he was arrested for theft. "Supposedly I stole my roommate's wallet, but they really planted it in my drawer," Gray tells Glenn Dupree, the muscular fellow standing next to him.

"Lousy coffee," remarks Dupree, as he sips Hughzell Davis's brew. Dupree dropped his wife off at work and now he's at the Speed Wash. There's a five-dollar bill tucked into his hatband in case he needs it. "I'm a hustler," he explains. If he's lucky, he says, a friend will pick him up soon to do some jobs. "If the

Robert Drea

Hughzell Davis

guy stands me up, I'll go home to my son. He's eight, and his teeth should get brushed before he leaves for school."

Gray begins a rambling account of playing basketball in high school.

"All that basketball was a waste 'cause you never got no piece of paper," Dupree says. "A diploma counts for a lot. You need one to make money, and I'm about getting my GED and making money. All I need is a little luck."

"There ain't much of that around here," says Gray.

There isn't much in the way of a coffee shop either, which is why these men gather at the Speed Wash. This stretch of Roosevelt Road, between Kedzie and the city limits in Lawndale, was once the commercial heartbeat of Jewish Chicago. But the road has been down on its luck for decades. The strip is now distinguished by fast-food joints, liquor stores, churches, vacant lots, and Laundromats. There is no shopping in the grander sense, only small operations fishing off the bottom.

The Davis Speed Wash is a small oasis, not only a Laundromat but a notions store, coffeehouse, community center, and economic success. The residents of Lawndale find friendship, safe haven, and a measure of respect while drinking Speed Wash coffee and watching their dirty clothes hit the spin cycle.

Every day but Wednesday, John Franklin "Monk" Tucker, the morning clerk, opens up the Speed Wash. More important, he puts up a full-bodied coffee that the regulars much prefer to Hughzell Davis's. "They come from everywhere for my coffee, from Maywood and the South Side," boasts Tucker. "They're crazy about the stuff."

Besides the coffee, the Speed Wash offers four varieties of plastic-wrapped Danish, which the clientele can heat up in the microwave. A television, positioned high in a back corner, broadcasts the morning news shows, which will give way to diversions like Joan Rivers and the soaps; in the afternoon there's *Jeopardy.*

The morning conversations go off in the usual directions—politics, sports, women. Many of the regulars have known each other for years without establishing some of the basics. "I don't know names," says Frank Ware, who rolls out of bed each morning and over to the Speed Wash. "That guy over there is Rabbit. That fucker's Doc. Willie over there I've known for a long time. Don't know his last name, and whether Willie's his first name I couldn't say."

As the men talk, nibble pastry, and drink coffee, Tucker stands watch. "You got to keep your eyes open," he says. "I know who is who and what is what. I don't take no shit from nobody." The smallest infraction riles him. He will reprimand someone for sitting on the folding tables. Wash your hands in the sink in back that's only for washing and drying clothes and you're likely to be confronted by Tucker, talking tough and brandishing a small billy club.

Tucker acts from experience. "It's rough around here," he says. "I've seen twelve or thirteen people killed, most shot but some stabbed. Drugs are on all the streets—on Grenshaw, Fillmore, Independence, and Roosevelt. If it's midnight and you don't have a gun, you better not be out walking."

By the time Hughzell Davis arrives at eight thirty the men are drifting outside. Some walk east, past a shuttered store and onto a vacant lot where they will loiter away the day. Others buy a bottle of wine and a paper at Sunshine Food and Liquor, the Arab-owned grocery across the street. Shortly George's Music Room, a full-service record store and local bright spot, will open. Owner George Daniels puts speakers outside and blasts gospel music. "Gospel sets the morning mood on the block," says Daniels. "In the afternoon, anything goes."

The area's women enter the Speed Wash as soon as their kids leave for school. "They all have their schedules," says Davis. "We have Monday washers, Tuesday washers, and Sunday washers. Wednesday is usually slow for some reason. When the mailman brings the welfare checks the business just flows in."

Most women are carting dirty clothes and sheets, although a few who have washers in their buildings show up with articles dripping wet. "Folks also sometimes do their clothes in the bathtub," says Davis. No one has dryers, at least renters don't, since to run one requires an extra gas line or a 220-volt electrical line strung into a building, a cost Lawndale landlords won't bear.

The Speed Wash has twenty-two washers and eighteen dryers. "Bedspreads, blankets, comforters come cleaner here," claims a sign. Over the folding tables in front is a fish-eye security mirror.

Davis, a sweet-faced man of fifty-two, invariably wears the camouflage cap that came to him from a son who was in the army. His principal venue is the back counter, where he sells laundry soap, panty hose, barrettes, candy, pork rinds, aspirin, laundry bags, and pop, not to mention coffee. There is a bottle of hot sauce on the counter for those who like it on their potato chips.

Doing their wash, the women scuffle across the worn tile floor, heft wet clothes into carts, and make chit-chat with one another and with Tucker and his attendants. These are Delores Ruffin, Joe Greer, a self-styled "goodwill ambassador" who helps out voluntarily, and the Laundromat's tart-tongued fixture, Rose Coffee. "Honey, I been here twenty-two years," says Coffee. "I know everyone and everyone knows me. They can tease me and I don't get upset and if they want help I give it to 'em."

The camaraderie is one of the reasons many of the women are here. "This place is nice and homey," says Carolyn Jones, a young welfare mother with two kids. "I always get to jabbering with the other people." Patrice Henry, a young mother, processes five loads of wash every Saturday. "When you come up in here, you be having fun," says Henry, "getting together to do laundry, talk, and laugh. You catch up on what your girlfriends are doing."

Other customers use the Speed Wash more reluctantly. Robin Johnson, an office manager who has lived two blocks away since she was a girl, comes on Saturday to do wash for her husband O-Jay, their five-year-old son, and her niece. "I'm always praying the place is empty," says Johnson. "I put my stuff in the washer and come back later to put it all in the dryer. There are all these guys I don't like hanging out around. O-Jay used to tell me not to go, but Davis's place is so close to home. Besides, Monk is on the lookout, Rose has known me practically my whole life, and the coffee's good." Adrienne Smith, an assistant gas station manager, would rather patronize "the biggest, cleanest place I can find, but sometimes it's hard to get a ride. I use this [the Speed Wash] as a last ditch."

Davis tries to make his establishment comfortable. He addresses each customer as "mister" or "young lady," and as a rule they call him "Mr. Davis." He's a softie about making change to catch the bus. "I also take messages for people," says Davis. "Someone will have a mother living down south and the mother'll call here and I'll pass on the message. We've got several customers in their eighties who we pick up and bring over."

Young drug traffickers frequently spill in from the street, to buy candy and coffee with sugar. "If they can't get drugs they need sweet stuff," says Davis. "It pacifies them." Increasingly, unfortunates hawking one product or another—screwdrivers or hand cream—come inside to find buyers. The homeless slip inside to rest, and although Davis normally doesn't allow them to sit for long, or sleep, "if it's cold or raining I relax my ways," he says. He is most permissive early in the morning, with the men.

But it aggravates Davis to see someone arrive with food. "They leave their wrappings, or they want free napkins from me," he says. "Why should I have to clean up after them? I'm making no profit off them." When someone slams a washer in anger or is seen swilling a bottle of beer, Davis has a quiet word. "I never swear or holler," he says, "but I make clear that sort of behavior is out of line. I've had some fights, but whenever I see something I tell the people to settle their dispute outside."

Outside, Davis often finds drug dealers standing around. "They use my doorstep as a lookout point for police or for actual sales," he says. He politely shoos them away, and doesn't call the police. The dealers don't go far. A lookout is normally posted across the street, at the entrance of Sunshine Food and Liquor. The proprietors of Sunshine are more tolerant than Davis and refuse to trouble the lookouts. "You don't stick your nose in anything," says a Sunshine clerk. Actual sales occur behind the grocery.

The Speed Wash weathers its share of crime, such as the May break-in when an intruder stole the color television. But there have been no holdups or major brawls. "I've been fortunate," Davis reflects. "I haven't a clue about why, except that if I'd been a real snob or a bastard who knows what would have happened. I treat people as I'd like to be treated."

In the afternoon school kids come in with their mothers, and there's a particular feeling of community. One day this winter a girl from Marshall High was showing off her grades, first to Rose Coffee and then to Davis. There was one *D* on the report card, in math; Coffee and Davis praised the girl for her good marks yet encouraged her to pick up the *D*. A four-year-old girl who had graduated from preschool came in with her mother one afternoon in May and accepted congratulations all around.

Davis stocks penny candy for younger children. "You'd be surprised how many kids come in here with a dollar's worth of change in their pockets," says Davis. For teenagers he lays in fruit drinks and chips.

By six thirty the last loads go into the washers, and an hour and a half later the Speed Wash closes for the day. "If people aren't done, I don't put them out," says Davis. By eight o'clock, when Davis finally padlocks the door for the night, the Speed Wash will have brewed some 175 cups of coffee.

Millard and Deeker, a real estate firm, gave Lawndale its name in 1870 and began developing the area, which reaches west through mid-Chicago roughly from Western to the city limits. Lawndale first drew Dutch, Irish, and German families, then Bohemians. In the early 1900s came the Jews, most of Russian and eastern European origin, who occupied the two-flats that were erected in profusion during the period.

By 1930 the overwhelming majority of the population was Jewish, and Lawndale was known as "Chicago Jerusalem." It supported sixty synagogues and other quasi-religious institutions, notably the Jewish People's Institute, a large community center. Novelist Meyer Levin, who grew up in Lawndale, set his novel *The Old Bunch* there. Lawyer Elmer Gertz was reared in a Lawndale orphanage. As a young woman Golda Meir, the future prime minister of Israel, was a local librarian. The Twenty-fourth Ward Democratic machine became a legendary force in city affairs; in time Cook County party chairman Jacob Arvey, a former alderman, would launch the national political careers of Adlai Stevenson II and Paul Douglas.

Roosevelt Road was the shopping mecca. "A dense shopping area, the street was lined with every kind of store imaginable," native Beatrice Michaels Shapiro would recall in a monograph. "You name it, they had it. You wanted a sign painter, there was Primack; you wanted floor covering, there was Kramer; you wanted wine, there was Wexler's; you wanted high-fashion women's clothes, Milton Sacks and B. Nathan filled the bill. You could have a party or a wedding at Cafe Royale or the Blue Inn or a number of other places. There were ice-cream parlors and eateries, jewelry, furniture, and men's furnishings stores galore, and on and on."

Lawndale supported three banks and six movie theaters, which featured current films plus the top stage performers of the day—Sophie Tucker, Benny Goodman, the Marx Brothers. The great delicatessens included Silverstein's at St. Louis and Roosevelt, a locale favored for wedding showers. "A shower always attracted passersby, who could observe the doings from a window on the St. Louis Avenue side of the building," wrote Shapiro. "As kids, we'd peer through the window and watch wide-eyed as the bride-to-be would open her beautifully wrapped gifts, and *voilá!* from one of the boxes would sometimes emerge a pair of nylon stockings—a precious gift indeed during the war years."

As a Jewish commercial strip, Roosevelt Road had no equal. "Oh, there was Lawrence Avenue in Albany Park," says Irving Cutler, a retired geography professor and Lawndale historian, "and there were nice Jewish shopping strips in Humboldt Park and in South Shore. But there was nothing like Roosevelt Road." Many businesses that still grace Chicago—from Fluky's hot dogs to the Piser Weinstein and Weinstein Brothers mortuaries—have their roots on the street.

By 1950 blacks had started to move in and the Jews out, to the North Side and the suburbs. In 1960 Lawndale was 91 percent African American. Roosevelt Road went into decline, although a number of white merchants hung on into the sixties. Then came the Martin Luther King riots in 1968. "The stores were torn up bad," remembers Monk Tucker. "There wasn't too much left afterwards." Few merchants returned. "Either their businesses were destroyed and they got out, or else they were afraid and saw no future and got out," says Irving Cutler.

But black businessmen, ironically, now had access to Roosevelt Road. "The riots opened things up for us," says Ralph Moore, who at the time owned a Laundromat on Thirteenth Street. "SBA [Small Business Administration] loans were readily available, and the old owners were moving out from fear and intimidation."

A man named Leo Golsher had operated a Laundromat at 3860 West Roosevelt Road since 1951. But in 1969, after the riots, he sold out to Ralph Moore, who wanted to move to a main drag. For a time Moore ran both the Laundromat and a dry cleaners across the road, but eventually he combined these operations in the Laundromat.

Moore says the vicinity still supported many businesses. A tavern, a beauty shop, a furniture repair shop, a hardware store, and a five-and-dime were within easy reach, and also John's restaurant, where you could linger over a full meal or a cup of coffee. Another restaurant, known for its peach cobbler and banana pudding, stood where Sunshine Food and Liquor is today.

But off Roosevelt Road the housing was in decay. Every winter fires started by space heaters would gut a few more apartment buildings. "If the blacks owned the buildings, they couldn't afford to rebuild," says Moore. "If other nationalities owned them, they didn't want to." From 1960 to 1990, Lawndale would lose 48 percent of its housing units, according to the city's housing department; its population shrank from 125,000 to less than 50,000.

Worse yet, the area's large employers—General Foods, Coca-Cola, Western Electric, Sunbeam, Alden's—gradually took their leave. The largest employer was Sears, Roebuck and Company, whose national headquarters, bank, and retail store stood on a fifty-five-acre site at Homan and Arthington; but even Sears began to pull out in 1973. By 1987 the Sears site offered "some warehousing and very, very little else," according to a Sears spokesman.

Moore says many black shop owners on Roosevelt Road had a hard time of it. "They really didn't know how to manage a business. Many had trouble buying wholesale and setting prices. Others would make money fine, but then they'd blow it on cars or at the racetrack."

But Moore's Laundromat on Roosevelt Road thrived. So did two new Laundromats Moore opened across the Eisenhower Expressway on Madison Street, and "it all become kind of taxing for me. Then my wife, who used to help me out, got arthritis." In 1984 he put his place on Roosevelt Road up for sale, and Hughzell Davis offered to buy it.

Davis had grown up in the Mississippi Delta, the fourth of a farmer's ten children. After high school he briefly worked in a factory that made backing for carpets, then migrated north to Chicago. For five years he was a warehouse clerk at the Spiegel catalog house. "It was a job, but it didn't pay well enough," Davis says. He trained in computer accounting at a Loop trade school and soon began an eighteen-year stint in computer operations at the American National Bank, where he rose to shift manager.

In 1984 the First Chicago Corporation acquired American National and a new supervisor fired Davis. "It was tough and I was disappointed," he says, "but they made the right move. I was burned out by the rat race and the politics that you have to play. I was tired of going to school to keep up." A friend interested him in buying a Laundromat, and even though he knew nothing about the business ("I could turn on the machine, is all"), he made Ralph Moore an offer. They settled on a price of $49,000 for the building and the business; Davis put $10,000 down and has been paying Moore off since.

"When I first came over here I was concerned a lot," Davis says, "but I had kept all Moore's employees, and they knew people." Moore's washers and dryers were shot, so Davis installed new equipment. He put up new paneling and redid the ceiling. In went video games (which were discontinued after burglars stole the money out of them). Davis passed out key rings and calendars and for a couple of years revenues were respectable.

But in 1986 Mark Holstein opened a spanking new place at Roosevelt and Keeler. "My idea was to revitalize the neighborhood," says Holstein, a former paint salesman whose half-million-dollar facility, called the Clean Scene, offered double the Speed Wash's washers and dryers. (The Clean Scene is still the largest noninstitutional construction project in the Twenty-fourth Ward since the riots.)

"When I found out about Holstein opening down the street, my heart almost popped," says Davis. Yet Davis was determined not to be hostile. "He wasn't the enemy, and why should he be?" Davis says. He made it a point to have a sandwich with Holstein. "He and I sat down and shot the shit and got along fine," says Holstein.

Nonetheless, Davis found his sales dipping 20 percent, and he began to offer coffee, hair accessories, candy, and other items as a sideline. There had always been a Pepsi machine in the front of the store, but now Davis laid in five more kinds of pop in a back-office cooler.

Customers are encouraged to carry discount cards. Twenty visits to the Speed Wash and you have the option of taking a five-dollar premium or continuing to log benefits; two punched-out cards win you a laundry cart. "It keeps 'em coming back," says Davis. Not everything succeeds. During the past year Davis entered into a deal to sell beepers for a wholesaler, "but the guy went sour on me," says Davis, and he's abandoned the idea.

Sales have rebounded some. Today the Speed Wash grosses $160,000 a year. The average Laundromat in the United States takes in $96,000 annually, says Richard Torp, spokesman for the Chicagoland Coin Laundry Association. Torp says about Davis, "He's doing good business for a small store. It's commendable. Evidently he's pleasing his customers."

Glenn Dupree happens by the Speed Wash for coffee at about six o'clock almost every morning. Afterward, he's usually at his leisure. He used to assist his friend Ike, who specializes in hauling and gutting, "but Ike's a cheap motherfucker and that's why I stopped working for him," says Dupree. He says he runs a crew of his own, but mostly on weekends.

Dupree didn't finish his senior year at Crane High School. "This woman got pregnant with me," he says, "and, shit, I dropped out." Since 1979 he has lived on Fillmore two blocks from the Speed Wash, in a three-bedroom house owned first by his mother and since her death by himself. Early on he held a series of jobs, including six years as a short-order cook. "Wherever there was money to be made, there was Glenn," he says. But he wound up on General Assistance. Because GA is designed for single, employable adults and he was married, he was, he admits, not entitled to it.

Last July new budget cuts eliminated Dupree and thousands of others from General Assistance. Now all he receives is $111 a month in food stamps. Dupree passed up the new Earnfare Program, which offers a welfare check in return for part-time employment. "I have a heart murmur, and my right leg is crippled," he explains. "I get sick. It takes me a half hour to get out of bed in the morning." At the moment he is angling for Social Security disability benefits. Meanwhile, his wife has taken a factory job, packing cologne into boxes.

Dupree passes the days alongside an oil drum behind a three-flat near the Laundromat. The surroundings are sparse—no grass, two dead trees, a shopping cart, and several cars being worked on by Frank Ware, Dupree's friend from the Speed Wash and the street. Ware was ticketed once by the city for keeping a fire going in the oil drum, but the ticket failed to douse the flames. During the winter people come to warm their hands over the fire, and in every season the drum serves Dupree as an outdoor stove.

"People'll be out here working on their cars, and they can't wait to finish so they can eat my food," he says one spring morning that finds him resplendent in a black Bulls hat, deep purple sweatshirt, and bright blue jeans. There's a diamond stud in one ear. "I make pork or ribs, fish, and wieners."

Wieners and pork in a can are today's specialties. The oil drum, stuffed with burning timbers, has been turned on its side, and Dupree is preparing to be the chef. He slices some onion and sprinkles the bits on a half-dozen hot dogs positioned on tinfoil. Opening a can of processed pork, he sprinkles the contents with onion, pepper, and seasoned salt. "Don't forget to put in some Spanish fly," yells Ware from underneath the car he's tuning up. Dupree laughs. He places the pork can on the piping hot surface of the oil drum; the wieners also go atop the drum on a rusty grill.

"I'm Mr. Rogers," shouts Dupree to his audience, which includes Ware, a woman named Gayle, and several other men with time on their hands. "Soon you'all are gonna have some real good food."

"Hey, Glenn, you got your pimp clothes on today," jokes Gayle. Humorously, Dupree doffs his Bulls hat in Gayle's direction, revealing a scalp he has shaved clean. "Bald I don't have to worry about no brush or no comb," he says. One of the men announces he's off to Maywood to look for work. "I'm going to buy a lottery ticket," says another fellow, an announcement overwhelmed by the wail of a souped-up car driving by. Dupree knows the driver. "Hey, motherfucker, can you smell prime nigger cooking?" he yells.

When the food seems done, Dupree unwraps a loaf of Wonder bread. He deposits a hot dog on each piece of bread, then slops on some pork. Everyone grabs a sandwich and eats heartily, washing down lunch with beer. Ware, the exception, is drinking vodka and water. It's ten forty-five.

Soon Ware slips away. "He knows he's drunk, so he's going into his house," remarks Dupree. Ware, forty-eight, is the father of four children by various women. One daughter was raped and murdered at the age of fourteen, according to Ware, and he says he hasn't been the same since.

He carries the marks of a hard life. "I been shot five or six times," he says. "I take the bullets out myself or do nothin', so there you go." To prove his point, he displays a maimed part of his left hand where a knuckle used to be, and shows off a scar near his left eye. "Some guy shot at me," he explains, "but I didn't go to the doctor because I couldn't find my medical card." Cross Ware at your peril. In May he concluded a girlfriend had stolen a saw and sixty dollars in cash from him. "I plugged her up the side of the head with some of my tools," he says. He was charged with battery and hauled off to jail.

Ware lost his driver's license after a series of drunk-driving arrests, although he continues to drive a 1974 Oldsmobile. He's held "so many jobs I can't recall them all." He receives $155 a month in Illinois assistance that comes to persons presumed eligible—but not yet approved—for Social Security disability payments. He gets food stamps and makes some money repairing cars.

"Here's home," says Ware as he welcomes a visitor to the basement apartment he occupies in the three-flat; he lives for free in exchange for watching over the building, which was bought recently by someone in Maywood. The top three floors are empty and being renovated. "I go upstairs and check on things," Ware says. "I listen. I've run a few people out, and I hit one guy with an iron pipe."

Ware's apartment consists of four rooms, but only one is usable. He cooks fried chicken and pinto beans and ham hocks on a hot plate, sleeps on a box-spring mattress, and sits in a reclining chair afternoons and evenings watching *Gunsmoke, Bonanza,* and karate movies on a small television. There is no phone or water in the building. To use the toilet, Ware must fetch water from a nearby fire hydrant. When he wants to take a shower, he goes to his brother's house across the street.

From the oil drum Dupree can eye the drug dealers hanging at the corner of Grenshaw and Springfield. "Those little rodents," he remarks. "They're pathetic, out on the corner selling rock [crack cocaine] or blow [heroin]. They come out after the kids go to school, and they're out again in the afternoon once the kids get back. They'll walk through a crowd of kids giving out fucking candy." (The dealers on Grenshaw do more than that, says a neighbor: they throw a kids' block party during the summer and give away hams at Christmas.)

A cop car glides east along Roosevelt Road past Springfield. "Ready on the road," yells a lookout at Sunshine Food and Liquor, meaning the cops are driving by. Once the police car is out of sight, the lookout gives a second signal—"He's straight." A dozen persons suddenly materialize in a line behind the Sunshine grocery building, and a dealer makes his sales at high noon.

"Look at that shit," says Dupree disapprovingly. "I don't have anything to do with that shit."

Glenn Dupree doesn't drink coffee at the Speed Wash because he needs to. "I can make coffee my own damn self," he says. "The thing is, I like to have coffee and a roll and shoot the shit with the other fuckers who are hanging around. Plus, it's best to leave some money circulating in the neighborhood, and not with the drug dealers."

The neighborhood can use the help. Only a few employers remain. One of them is the Roscoe Company, an industrial laundry that's been a Lawndale fixture since 1927 and intends to stay. "People that work for us live in and around this area," says president Jim Buik. "We have a ready supply of labor." Not every employer feels so comfortable. "We had a sign on the building but we had to take it off because we don't want anyone to know we're here," says one small manufacturer. "It's not safe."

The mean annual household income in Lawndale is $18,336, according to the U.S. Census Bureau, about half the city average. About 40 percent of the neighborhood gets public assistance. A 1991 study for Chicago's Department of Economic Development reported 121 businesses along Roosevelt Road, but "there is a combined total of forty-nine vacant storefronts and vacant lots along the commercial strip, and pedestrian traffic is extremely shallow and widely dispersed. Apart from food and liquor establishments, there appears to be very little support for other businesses."

Most Speed Wash regulars leave the community for major purchases. Glenn Dupree goes to an Aldi for his canned and frozen goods, to Moo and Oink on the South Side for meat, "or wherever there's a sale." He buys rice at a church. "On Sunday we go to Jew town [the Maxwell Street shopping district], where we buy jumbo eggs with double yolks plus fruit," he says. North Riverside mall is his destination for most clothing, although he purchases neckties and jeans from a Goodwill store and other thrift shops.

Frank Ware drives his Oldsmobile beyond Lawndale for nearly all his needs. He favors a flea market at Twenty-sixth and Pulaski for clothes. "'Cepting suits," he remarks. "A woman I just dropped bought me some suits in Detroit. Nice ones. Basically, though, I don't need 'em, because I don't go to church and it's best to avoid funerals."

Robin Johnson, who lives a block from Dupree, shops for groceries at the Omni or the Aldi in Cicero, or at the Super Giant supermarket at Pulaski and Harrison. For clothes she heads to the Brickyard or North Riverside malls. Johnson frequents a Lawndale dry cleaner and Sunshine Food and Liquor, "to play the lottery and for two-liter pop."

"There's nothing to buy around here, except for gas, a clothes wash, and a can of pop," says Hughzell Davis. Davis acquires supplies for the Speed Wash from wholesalers and discount houses. He says he'd like to open an account at the Community Bank of Lawndale, owned by the neighborhood-based Pyramidwest Development Corporation, but he's heard negative comments about the small institution so he banks on the South Side.

Laundry turns out to be a major contributor to the economic health of Lawndale. Johnson's biggest local outlay is the ten to fifteen dollars she spends each Saturday at the Speed Wash. Ware takes his wash once or twice a week to the Speed Wash, jamming it all in one washer to limit his expenses. Dupree and his wife own a washer and dryer, but he sometimes does his laundry at the Speed Wash anyway "just to get out of the house."

The 1991 study for the Department of Economic Development found that the average Lawndale resident spends $54 a year along Roosevelt Road on clothing, $29 to dine out, $2.67 on furniture, and $2 on auto care. The largest outlay is for groceries—$698. The study didn't give a dollar figure, but it reported that after groceries residents spent more of their money on laundry than on anything else.

In recent years Lawndale has been the subject of several attempts to spur retailing. In 1988, Twenty-fourth Ward alderman William Henry helped start a chamber of commerce, which limped along for several years and finally died. Henry also tried to godfather a pact between Arab merchants and black community members, which came to naught after Henry was indicted on charges of extortion and mail fraud and was defeated for reelection. He died in May of 1992.

Plans by Wallace E. "Mickey" Johnson, a former Chicago Bull, to build a shopping center near Roosevelt and Homan have gone nowhere. And although Lawndale did participate in the Commercial Area Revitalization Effort (or CARE), a city program meant to spur retail development in declining neighborhoods, the principal benefits have been trash receptacles and street banners along Roosevelt.

A CARE banner flies from a pole outside the Speed Wash, and a trash receptacle is nearby. Recently the city installed a bicycle rack in front of Sunshine Food and Liquor, but no one can recall seeing a bike locked up there.

"You talk about all these programs that are supposed to revitalize this area, and nothing really works," says Hughzell Davis, who joined the chamber of commerce and participated in CARE. "What I see out here depresses me. All I see are black folks going no place. They're just in a rut. All my waking hours I spend in an environment where it's easy to get bad feelings, to think that what I see around here is life."

Davis has the most sympathy for his female customers on welfare. "The ladies are in a bad situation because, sure, they should work, but they have the responsibility for their kids.

"The men, though, they're looking for a handout. Nobody's going to give them anything to get them up the ladder, but that's what they expect. Each situation is different, I know that, but why don't they go home and figure out what to do, instead of just standing around on the street? They think if they stand out there long enough something's going to happen.

"They have only themselves to blame. I could be in the same place they are but I'm not. Even if they don't use drugs, they are addicted to standing on the corner with their buddies. They refuse to give up twenty-four hours a day of doing nothing, afraid that if they get a job they won't be able to stand out there anymore, that they'll miss something.

"Clinton gets blamed over the economy, like he could change things in Lawndale in the city of Chicago. Clinton's only going to do what Congress allows him to do, and Congress seems to be fighting him. If the whole economy improves maybe then things will change, but not before.

"My best advice to the men would be to move away. Go clean, with new friends and a new neighborhood. That's the only way to break the cycle."

Davis is seldom approached for advice, although he is free with it. A few do consider him a role model. "I talked to him several times about getting into my own business, and he encouraged me," recalls Ann Marie Parker, a laboratory assistant at Malcolm X who's a Speed Wash customer and wants to run her own pharmacy one day. "To find a black businessman like him around here is a rarity."

The idea of being considered an example perplexes Davis. "I can't say what I am," he says. "You'd have to ask somebody else."

He continues to draw satisfaction from the Speed Wash. Last year Davis and his brother-in-law opened a Laundromat on Clybourn on the North Side, but Davis is content to let his brother-in-law handle the other place. "I never say to myself that I don't want to go to work," he says. "I come every day and look forward to coming here because it's mine. The boss is me. I don't go on vacation really, three or four days at most but nothing more. I'm not ready to get out yet. Maybe in ten or twelve years, but if my health holds up and I don't burn out I'll probably stay around."

DINNER
IS SERVED

Getting started in the restaurant business was hard work for
Wendy Gilbert. Staying in it is no picnic either.

They say the restaurant business is tough, and it is. For every new eatery
that gets glowing reviews and has tightly packed tables on Saturday night, another one sinks into oblivion. Yet there's always someone crazy enough or passionate enough to tempt the odds. Including Wendy Gilbert, who recently opened
the Savoy Truffle in West Town.

Located two blocks south of North Avenue at 1466 North Ashland, on a block
with a church, a corner grocery, and Tina's Beauty Salon, the Savoy Truffle has a
limited menu and no liquor license. It has only eight tables and only twenty-four
seats—barely enough for a respectable game of musical chairs. Gilbert functions
as owner, cook, food buyer, and majordomo. Her sister decorated the interior.

Wicker Park and Bucktown are crammed with dinky, moderately priced, homey restaurants, many run by women. But Gilbert considers her modest little place
a personal statement, a high plateau in her life in food. "So many restaurants are
this: Bam, bam, bam—you come, you eat, you leave. But coming to me should be
different, an experience where, I hope, you remember the time you had as much
as the food. I want you to feel like you're a friend eating in the kitchen of my
house—and the one having the most fun is me."

The sounds of Afro pop are wafting through the Savoy Truffle, and Gilbert, who
likes to dance to salsa music in her spare time, pivots in her sandals on her way

Photograph by Mike Tappin courtesy of Melinda Morrissey

Wendy Gilbert

to the stove in the kitchen. Her multicolored bracelets jangle, and she lets out a whoop. It's just after 9 A.M. on an August Wednesday. Gilbert was out late the night before at the Jazz Showcase, but now she's all energy. "I only need four hours of sleep. This thing about people being tired makes me nuts. What's the point of being tired? Tired translates to depressed in my book."

Gilbert, who's about to turn thirty-eight, is loaded down with jewelry—the bracelets, several rings, large gold loop earrings, and a weighty pendant that looks like a brass tooth. Actually it's the top of a large bullet that one of her sisters gave her, a piece she wears like a talisman.

She and Adolfo Perales, her dishwasher and cooking assistant, start preparing many of the dishes that will be served through the weekend. "Adolfo, chop up some onions, peel the carrots, and give me some lemon juice," she says. "And when you peel the potatoes leave two for me."

She busies herself readying a salad of smoked turkey, Granny Smith apples, and roasted pine nuts, squirting in balsamic vinaigrette from a squeeze bottle. "Today anything goes in restaurants," she says. "The more outrageous, the better. But the outrageous doesn't always taste good. I never break the rules. There's a way to do things—the way I was taught."

All morning long she moves between the stove and a center island, cooking, talking, occasionally shimmying to the music. Perales, a soft-spoken man in a green T-shirt, is off by the sink, waiting for Gilbert to hand him dirty pans, bowls, and containers. He scrubs them clean when he isn't fetching her this and that from the large commercial refrigerator.

Moving down a list, Gilbert steams up zucchini and carrots. She quarters some shiitake mushrooms, then sautés them in sherry and chicken stock to produce a mushroom ragout. She makes potato chips, seasoning slivers of potato with garlic, olive oil, salt, and pepper and sticking them in the oven. Perales hands her bars of white chocolate, which she decorates with purple food coloring and cuts into triangles that will adorn hot-fudge-and-caramel sundaes.

The skin of a tomato becomes a tomato rose for the bruschetta appetizer, an adornment Gilbert borrowed from Brennan's in New Orleans. Sections of baby eggplant bake while she concocts a stuffing from goat cheese, egg, mushrooms, and onions.

"Now I'm making tomato *concassé*," she says. "That's tomato, white-wine vinegar, sugar, onion, and garlic that's cooked forever. It's a French sauce that I put over couscous."

The back door to the kitchen is open, and Gilbert catches a boy watching her and goes off to have a word with him. He lives in a rear apartment with his siblings and his parents, a family that's often the subject of conversation.

"We talk all day," says Gilbert when she comes back. "Adolfo is a very smart man, and on a day-to-day basis he's a pleasure to be around. He's very calming, where I am just the opposite. But he does a couple things that piss me off. He squeezes the lemon juice and doesn't strain it, and he's late for work a lot. But he's *my* Adolfo, so what can I say? I don't know how he feels about me."

"Whatever she wants me to do, I do," Perales says later, then shrugs. "If I don't do something right she makes me do it over, and she gets mad, excited. But she's not getting mad directly at me."

At midday a deliveryman from Wild Game, a company owned by Kay Kharasch, a close friend of Gilbert's, drops off an order of mushrooms and smoked meats. Gilbert pays the bill immediately by check. "I don't believe in credit," she says. Then she resumes her kitchen tasks. She takes out eggs, sugar, and milk to make crème anglaise, a custard sauce for berries. "This is one of those things I hate to do. Any time you deal with eggs as a thickening agent it gets touchy."

In walks Leo Witkowski, an air-conditioning repairman. The Savoy Truffle is surviving the summer heat with a window air conditioner that operates poorly or not at all. For three days the restaurant was closed, a note of apology posted on the door. Witkowski has told Gilbert that the unit, located high underneath the canopy over the front door, is in the wrong place to work efficiently, but when he suggested moving it or cutting away the canopy she barked at him.

"Actually, she screamed to high heaven," says Witkowski later. "All I do now is make the unit work a little better." So today he just washes out the filter. "Wendy, after you've made your first million, I'll put a compressor in the basement for you. That way it will be pleasant in here."

"Don't be put off by appearances," Gilbert says, laughing. "Leo is a very intelligent man. He overcharges, and he has a bad reputation all over town—but I still use him. What else can I do? I hate it when the air-conditioning breaks."

"How's business?" Witkowski asks her.

"Good," says Gilbert. "But Leo, you haven't eaten here."

"There's no valet," he says and laughs.

"Leo, there's free parking at the car shop across the street! You know what this guy's favorite restaurant is? The Busy Bee—with all that Polish sausage. I cross the street when I walk by I'm so afraid all that fat will rub off on me."

"How's your leek soup?" says Witkowski.

"Leo, it's *tomato*-leek soup—and it's wonderful." She's fiddling with some sesame noodles in a bowl. "*Everything* here is wonderful."

When Gilbert was barely twenty, it suddenly came to her that she wanted to become a chef. She still can't fathom why. "A Jewish girl from Skokie—who knows a *chef*?"

Her mother was not the inspiration. When Gilbert was a girl her mother piled the family dinner table with standard fifties fare—a roast, stewed vegetables, potatoes. "Oh, I cooked," says her mother. "But no one would ever have called me a *cook*." Gilbert remembers not her mother's skills but that her father loved to eat out at Chicago's modest bunch of ethnic restaurants.

And it took a while before Gilbert even started cooking. She gave the University of Wisconsin three days to interest her and dropped out. She stuck around Madison for a year or two, then spent six months traveling in Mexico with an older sister. After that she got a job at a bookstore in Evanston.

But then in the midseventies she wangled a job as an apprentice to John Snowden, a renowned chef who ran the Dumas Père l'Ecole de la Cuisine Français, located in a building near the Glenview train station. Snowden, heavyset and in his sixties, had a teaching kitchen with a dozen stoves, where he imparted classic techniques with memorable hauteur. "He was a crusty old man who cared a lot about what he taught you," recalls Robert Gordon, a former student. "But if you did something he considered stupid he'd bust your butt—he could be very sarcastic." More than a few North Shore matrons wept under the strain.

For a year Gilbert lived in a spare room behind the school and toiled for Snowden seven days a week. He lived at the school too, in a big bedroom filled with ancient suits and stacks of gourmet magazines. He also had Afghan hounds that slept with Gilbert. "I walked the dogs, did the laundry, and cleaned the stoves," she says. Every Saturday night she put on white gloves to wait on students and other patrons who paid thirty-six dollars a person for the privilege of eating a meal put together by Snowden.

"I can't say he was nice to me," she says. "He was drinking heavily, and he was scary a lot. But I was young, and I learned from him. He was a mentor. One day he went into the hospital for spinal surgery, and he left me in charge. Part of my job was to visit him in the hospital every day and to sneak in a fifth of Martell. That's when I split and never came back." She never saw him again. She remembers that he died around 1980.

Next she enrolled in the chef's training program at the Washburne Trade School at Thirty-first and Kedzie, then run by the Chicago Board of Education. There she entered a different world. "The other students were basically blue collar—line cooks and grill cooks from the West and South sides without sophisticated palates. I was one of the few women." Gilbert is remembered by her instructors for her talent and her passion. "She was always concerned how this or that was made," says Ron Martin, who taught an introductory course on French cooking. "It seemed she was really fascinated with food."

During her second year she was on a team that entered a National Restaurant

Association competition at McCormick Place and took the gold medal. She was also hired as a cook at Cafe Provencal in Evanston and at Gordon in River North. She didn't like the snotty waiters at Gordon Sinclair's temple to nouvelle cuisine, but she appreciates how much she learned under chef John Terczak.

But by the time she finished at Washburne, in 1980, she was tired of cooking. She took time off to travel, then joined the family business, manufacturing boxes that fit on vending trucks and chrome plating truck parts. She helped set up warehouses in the Midwest to sell replacement doors and hoods to truckers. She also got married for a year and a half, something she doesn't like to talk about.

She says her business venture was successful, but after four years she again felt the urge to move on. So she started a catering company out of her house and named it Savoy Truffle after a John Lennon song on the Beatles' *White Album*. She catered some big parties but specialized in business lunches. Her steadiest customers were some stock traders at Paine Webber; she'd personally deliver them sloppy joes and other delicacies ("I drew the line at macaroni and cheese"). But when the traders had to cut back on expenses, Gilbert decided to become footloose again. "I hadn't had a vacation in three years. I'd gone through a divorce, and my dad had died. I went to India."

Gilbert arrived in 1991 and spent several months toying with the idea of setting up a business there. She flew to Chicago, then returned to India, expecting to settle in Delhi. But she wound up in Udaipur, a city surrounded by mountains north of Bombay. "I was sitting in a hotel garden in Udaipur surrounded by palm trees, and it was so unbelievably romantic that I said to myself, this is where I should be." She rented the garden and turned it into a small restaurant serving mostly comfort food for westerners—omelets, potato pancakes with applesauce, stuffed baby eggplant.

But from the outset there were difficulties. In December 1992 Hindu fanatics bombed an ancient Muslim mosque in the state of Uttar Pradesh, spurring riots all over India. The day Gilbert opened her restaurant Udaipur was under military curfew. "I had a full house, and I was clean out of food. When I ran out for milk and eggs, soldiers trailed me down the street." She also had unwelcome visitors: "Monkeys would waltz into the kitchen to steal my tomatoes."

The Indian women were fairly subservient, and some locals became suspicious of the brassy Gilbert. She relied increasingly on a rickshaw driver named Harish. "Harish could tell Wendy the way things were," says Jean-Marc Giboux, a French-born photographer who was on assignment in Udaipur and fell in love with Gilbert.

When the restaurant began to prosper Gilbert leased a small inn on Udaipur's picturesque Lake Pichola. She installed a tandoor oven and operated both the restaurant and the guest rooms, the bulk of her customers continuing to be foreigners. "To those unaccustomed to the country it can get intense, with the crowds and all the poverty," says Giboux. "Wendy'd take charge, playing the hostess. Harish would go get guests from the bus and train stations, and later he'd take them around to see the sights. We called the place Club W." Giboux remembers with enormous pleasure the holiday season of 1993, when all the guests holed up at Club W spent Christmas together. "We became like family. We exchanged gifts and had New Year's Eve under the stars overlooking the lake, with a big spread of food."

"In a sense I was very happy in Udaipur," says Gilbert. "I was cooking, meeting people from all over the world, and hearing stories you wouldn't believe. But I'm a very social person, and I missed everybody. Nobody ever came to visit me. My friend Kay got married. My other best friend had a baby. It came time to return home, and so I did." Giboux had also been reassigned to LA.

After the air-conditioning repairman leaves, Gilbert walks outside, nodding to a man in his undershirt sitting on a milk crate. She gets in her small, dusty Toyota and sets off to buy ingredients. It's early afternoon and the traffic is light, so she makes good time on Ashland. At Richard's Packing Company, a meat wholesaler on Paulina near Diversey, she buys almost a hundred dollars' worth of chicken, pork, and beef.

"Richard's deals with all the big boys," she explains. "They're reputable, and they're nice to me. Not everyone is. When I first opened there was this one company on South Water Market that was going to supply me with produce, milk, and cheese. So the first delivery arrives, and I notice that a carton of milk I ordered is sweating. It's been on the truck too long—any fool could see that. 'Get this out of here,' I said. 'What do you take me for, an imbecile?' Half the other orders were wrong too—and they were overcharging for the baby eggplant."

She switched to Stanley's Fruits and Vegetables, on the corner of Elston and North Avenue. Today she moves quickly down that store's aisles, foraging for arugula, endive, watercress, and basil. She has a congenial word with the retail manager and pushes through the checkout line, where she gets a 10 percent discount.

The next stop is D'Amato's Bakery on Grand near Racine. "Bread and coffee are the most important elements in any restaurant. They are the first and last impressions a diner is going to have. I don't care how good a meal is—you won't forget bad coffee or bad bread." The owner, Nick D'Amato, slips Gilbert's loaves into a bag. She asks him when he's going to eat at the Truffle, and he laughs. "I couldn't come until late," he says. "My wife makes me go shopping." Gilbert retorts, "Cheap excuse."

Back at the restaurant she's amazed that her coffee order hasn't arrived. "When are you *coming*?" she barks into the company's answering machine. At two forty-five she walks briefly to her house, just around the corner from the Savoy Truffle, but she's soon back in the kitchen, browning skinless chicken and rolling pork tenderloin in black peppercorn. "I can't stay home for long. I get too antsy there."

There are two phone calls all day. One's from her sister, who's leaving for vacation. They start arguing. "Gail, I know you're leaving for London but don't be mad," says Gilbert before the conversation ends abruptly. The second is from Giboux, who's come from Los Angeles several times to visit her and now is moving to Chicago to live with her.

No one calls to make reservations. "Bad sign," says Gilbert. But late that afternoon a Mr. Goodman calls to ask if Gilbert will be in the restaurant tonight. "Oh, Mr. Goodman, I'm here every night we're open," she says. "Are you coming in? . . . Oh, good, good. . . . See you at six then." Then she calls her mother to find out if, as she suspects, Goodman is a friend of hers. Her mother is out, so Gilbert leaves a message on her machine.

At four thirty in walks Richard Freeman, a friend who doubles as Gilbert's waiter. "Should I punch in, boss?" he asks irreverently. A thirty-five-year-old Ph.D. candidate in anthropology who holds a day job as a photo assistant, Freeman is wearing a T-shirt that reads "I get my drugs at Cosmos." Gilbert is not amused. "Richard, your T-shirt isn't going to cut it. I told you that you need a white shirt." Freeman slips on a plain T-shirt, puts some jazz CDs on, and sets the tables.

Gilbert prefers the flatware in the regular left-to-right order but lumped together on a napkin on the right, with the napkin opening like a book. She also insists that Freeman serve beverages off a tray and that each drink have a straw with a bit of paper covering the end. "Wendy's finicky," says Freeman.

"Adolfo, wash this," says Gilbert, handing Perales a dirty bowl. At last the coffee arrives, and Gilbert sighs.

"Tell me about that *concassé* again, Wendy," says Freeman. "Everybody wants to know what the hell it is."

Last December Gilbert was walking Giboux's dog down Ashland when she noticed a for-rent sign in a storefront. It had been a harrowing time for her—she'd been hospitalized for two months with a severe case of pancreatitis brought on by a gallbladder attack upon her return from India.

The space was tiny—only 750 square feet—but it had a fully equipped kitchen. She'd always hoped to someday open a restaurant in her hometown. "In the moments it took me to walk that dog home I knew I wanted the place. Sure it was small, but I was used to that from India. The size was a plus—I wanted a place where I could be in charge, where I'd cook the food and tell the waiter just how to put the watercress on the plate. It was a control issue with me."

She rented the storefront in February for what she describes as an "unbelievably cheap" rate. But when she gave her sisters a tour of the premises they were horrified. "Wendy, there's nothing redeeming here," said Gail, president of a family car-parts firm as well as an interior decorator. "This is so dingy. What's wrong with you?"

Gilbert felt sick when Gail's husband knocked on the low ceiling and discovered it was false, but when she saw that above it was a pressed-tin ceiling she burst out, "We've got character!"

Over the next few months Gail helped her sister make the most of the storefront. The tin ceiling and the walls were painted gold. The speckled linoleum floor was replaced with squares of red, purple, mustard, and turquoise. Fabric rectangles with a fruit motif went up inside the windows. Usama Haddad, a hairdresser by day, put his pastels and acrylics on the walls. The bathroom was painted purple, and framed postcards, mirrors, and candleholders were hung on its walls. Gilbert found white plates and flatware at auctions. An awning company picked from the yellow pages put up "what looked like a giant saddle shoe," according to Gilbert; a second try produced a simpler awning that pleased her.

Meanwhile Gilbert was crafting a business plan. "I laid out a work schedule, including how many hours each task would take me, how many customers I'd need, and how much they would have to spend." She lined up purveyors. The menu she came up with had hints of the exotic—smoked scallops and wild-rice salad over *gomae,* steamed and marinated spinach. But she wanted the dishes to be understandable to the average person. She wound up with only five entrées and six appetizers, counting the house salad, all of it relatively cheap and easy for her to get to the table.

In April Gilbert's landlord threatened to evict her because she'd billed the woman for stove, glass, and radiator repairs. Gilbert ate the expense. "It wasn't worth a fight," she says. In total she spent about ten thousand dollars—a pittance for a restaurant start-up.

She lined up friends like Freeman and Amy Wasserman, a sometime pastry chef employed at the Board of Trade, to be waiters. Perales was working for the painting and drywall contractor, and Gilbert offered him the kitchen job at one dollar more an hour than he was making. "I think she realized that I was a good worker and that I'd obey her," says Perales. Now forty-seven, he'd been a steelworker and a school maintenance man but had never worked in a restaurant.

The Savoy Truffle officially opened on June 8. "Ten minutes before opening I was on the floor hyperventilating," says Gilbert. "It was the moment of truth.

It was, well, Wendy, let's see what you can do. That first night some girls I knew from high school came in, and my mother's accountant brought in a group. This man I knew from salsa dancing was driving by, and he says he wants to stop by. 'By all means,' I said. 'Stop by, stop by.' Still, I gave away more food than I sold that night."

And so the Savoy Truffle joined 4,579 other restaurants in the Chicago area.

"I'm Seymour Goodman," says an older, bald, prosperous-looking man as he steps into the Savoy Truffle promptly at six o'clock, accompanied by his wife and a neighbor.

Gilbert appears dressed in a white chef's coat, an apron, black jeans, and boots. "I think you know my mom, but I don't know you—at least not yet," she says.

"Oh, that's OK," says Goodman. "Can I sit anyplace?"

"Why not this lovely spot over here?" says Gilbert, guiding them to a table in front.

Gilbert regularly comes out into the dining room. "I bow to every customer. I'm the most appreciative businessperson you ever met. Nobody leaves this place without knowing me." But she adds, "You welcome people and then leave them alone to eat. You only sit down after they are done. Otherwise it's rude."

As soon as the diners are seated, Freeman moves in, distributing menus, taking drink orders—water, iced tea, or noncaffeinated sodas that Gilbert calls "hippie pops." Freeman sets out the bread from a big basket with an iron grip shaped like a fish. ("I hate this basket," he says later. "It makes me feel like an idiot.") He describes the evening's special, angel-hair pasta with pesto, then vanishes.

Goodman appears in the kitchen, wanting to use the facilities. "Oh, Mr. Goodman, you've heard about my bathroom," says Gilbert, who's standing by the stove.

He's heading back to the dining room when Gilbert calls out "Great bathroom, huh, Mr. Goodman?" Goodman nods, then asks for a price list for the prints on the restaurant walls. Gilbert has had a falling-out with the artist and tells Goodman she thinks the work is overpriced.

The phone in the kitchen rings. "Is Seymour Goodman there?" says a sharp voice. "This is Wendy's mother. Tell her Seymour Goodman is one of my stockbrokers."

Freeman takes the orders: a plate of sesame noodles with vegetables, an order of the eggplant, the turkey salad, and an appetizer. Gilbert assembles the dishes, steaming the hot orders.

Toward seven o'clock the restaurant starts to fill with other patrons. Two young women and a man appear, carrying a six-pack of ale, which Freeman sticks in the refrigerator. (Gilbert can't get a liquor license because she has only one bathroom.) A local art-gallery owner and her boyfriend stop in.

The door is open to Ashland. It's muggy, but cool enough to leave the air-conditioning off. Gilbert notices a man standing alone in the entryway looking inside, and she goes out to talk to him. He's Polish and lives on her street. She urges him to come inside for dinner, but he declines.

Gilbert steps inside to sell the Goodman table on dessert. She says only 20 percent of restaurant customers buy dessert, but her salesmanship can raise the rate to 75 percent. Yet she talks them into only one *pot de crème*.

Lionel Hampton is on the stereo. "Get rid of that stuff," she tells Freeman. "It sounds like people are supposed to take their clothes off." Then she upbraids Perales for being too slow getting chicken from the refrigerator. "Come on, Adolfo, what are you *doing*?" And she cooks, sautéing pork tenderloin and heating up the chicken.

Goodman sticks his head through the window.

"Oh, Mr. Goodman," she says. "Thank you so much for coming. Have a card." Goodman takes a handful of business cards, and Gilbert gives his wife the sesame-noodle recipe. On their way out the Goodmans write some effusive comments in the guest book ("Great! Great! Great! Seymour and Norma Goodman"). Gilbert is delighted. "The Goodmans are happy. They will give my mother a good report."

The tables slowly empty. Freed up, Gilbert sits with her customers, gabbing with the gallery owner and the young salesman who lives across the street and eats at the Savoy Truffle once a week. "It's convenient," he says. "I don't cook much, and Wendy has a lot of neighborhood gossip—which is no surprise, because she talks so much."

Gilbert, Perales, and Freeman close up at ten o'clock. Gilbert's going salsa dancing with Freeman's sister.

In 1994 the nation's full-service restaurants saw their real sales, with inflation factored out, increase 4 percent to eighty-four billion dollars a year, according to Technomic, a Chicago-based restaurant and food-service consultancy. This year real sales are running at nearly the same brisk pace. "Business is booming," says Colleen McShane, executive director of the Illinois Restaurant Association, rattling off a list of established Chicago operators who've launched new places in the last few months.

Launching a restaurant as a newcomer is always hazardous, says Dennis Lombardi, Technomic's executive vice president. "If you're an independent, the risks are high. You have no brand equity. You're an unknown commodity. Will you speak to the consumer? Maybe your site is bad, or your menu is targeted wrong, or your prices are off. Your staff may be poorly trained. Or there's too much competition. Or you're undercapitalized. If you're a skilled operator you can reduce these risk factors, but it's no wonder that one out of two restaurants fails after three or four years."

One way to cut the risk is to open small and keep the quality high, a strategy that's exemplified by the operators who are filling Bucktown, Wicker Park, and their environs with modest, inexpensive places along the lines of the Savoy Truffle. "These closet-size, counterculture restaurants—except with better offerings—with women in charge are a trend now," says *Chicago* magazine reviewer Jill Rohde. Observers say the trend has its roots in the needs of the young, well-educated, health-conscious neighborhood residents. "People there don't want to spend a lot of money or travel far for good food," says Erwin Drechsler, the chef and co-owner of Erwin on North Halsted.

In 1989 Sheila McCoy, an IBM computer trainer, turned Leo's Lunchroom, an old breakfast place on West Division, into a popular hangout for the hip, building in part on the skills of the night cook, Donna Knezek. Last year Knezek split and launched her own place, the Bite Cafe, at 1039 North Western. Jane's, owned by hostess Arden Nelson and chef Jeff Auld, opened in Bucktown, at 1655 West Cortland, in June 1994. This June a thirty-two-year-old chef named Katherine August, a veteran of a couple tony downtown restaurants, established Wildfire down the street from Leo's, at 1924 West Division.

Arguably the most successful of the bunch is Wishbone. In 1990 Joel Nickson, a longtime hotel cook, raised thirty thousand dollars from friends and family and made over what he describes as "a little greasy spoon" at 1800 West Grand. Within a year, partly on the basis of positive reviews of the economical southern-style cuisine, Wishbone receipts jumped from $4,800 to $19,000 a week. In 1992 Nickson started a second, 180-seat restaurant across from Oprah's Harpo studios on West Washington that has been an even bigger success.

Such rewards don't come easily, if at all. "You work your buns off in these places, and you don't make much money," says *Chicago* magazine's Rohde. "You have to love it." Donna Knezek, whose Bite Cafe is the same size as the Savoy Truffle, says, "Someone who does this has a masochistic tendency, because you're talking a seventy- or eighty-hour week. But there's no work in corporate America anymore. Why not a restaurant? It's yours, and you can open up for less than ten thousand dollars."

"Eventually all chefs want to start something of their own," says Wildfire's August. "With large companies you get lost in the system. For myself one driving motivation was to have the freedom to change the menu without summoning twenty people to a tasting. I know I'm a fabulous chef. Now I have the freedom to be creative." She also thinks women are better at running a small house. "We're better able to deal with the long hours, the personalities, and the stress of it all."

Gilbert recoils at the suggestion that more women choosing to operate little restaurants in marginal Chicago neighborhoods constitutes some sort of trend. "There are more women everywhere—in business, in fashion, in film. What's the big deal here?" It also riles her that she's being lumped in a category with other Near Northwest Side restaurants. "I don't do buffalo wings," she says dismissively. "I take my food seriously. I'm no trend."

One factor that often means the difference between success and failure for a small restaurant is good press. "We didn't get reviewed for three or four months after we started," reports Wishbone's Nickson. "When the notices appeared, let me tell you they helped a lot. More than a lot."

Knowing this, Amy Wasserman persuaded Gilbert to let her send a promotional mailing to the city's newspapers and magazines as soon as the Savoy Truffle was open. On July 11 they sent out a menu and a flowery letter from Gilbert. "I feel strongly that excellent food should be enjoyed in wonderful surroundings with service to match, and I believe I have succeeded in these endeavors," she wrote. "As for food, I have an array of unsurpassed choices."

Chicago magazine's dining editor, Penny Pollack, had already heard of the Savoy Truffle, and at the end of June she and three companions ate there anonymously ("I never make reservations, and I have credit cards in two different names," she says). She found it "a delightful little place." She assigned Jill and Ron Rohde to check out the premises for the *Daily Herald.* They went one night in July, accompanied by two friends. They liked the food, especially the desserts, and they enjoyed Gilbert. "She did lots of schmoozing," says Jill. "While I normally don't like to be fussed over, she was quite engaging."

Gilbert was nervous about the review. "Here's the thing, what if they say something bad?" she said. "I'm afraid. Who wants to be judged? Who wants to stand in the middle of the street on a soapbox and take your clothes off?" Yet she was also excited. "I know people'll be looking at the *Daily Herald* from coast to coast," she joked.

"Could any restaurant be smaller or snazzier?" wrote the Rohdes in the *Herald*'s August 11 edition. "This charming eight-table bandbox . . . is like hanging at the home of your most fun, flamboyant friend." They hailed the menu as "quirky, enticing, and reasonably priced" and called the *pot de crème* "heaven." The notice was accompanied by a photograph of Gilbert dressed in her cooking whites, lying on the tile floor next to a plate of berries. Yet the review caused barely a blip in Gilbert's business. "I can't imagine people from Arlington Heights coming down to Ashland Avenue," Jill Rohde later observed.

Over the summer the Savoy Truffle's business built steadily, if slowly. Gilbert's friends frequently showed up. Kay Kharasch would materialize about once a week, often with a group. Gilbert's sisters appeared often, as did her mother. "Doris loves it," says Gilbert. "She can come in and talk to strangers and hear wonderful things about her daughter." (Doris says, "Who do you think keeps Wendy in business? It's her mother. When this is over I'm going to weigh two thousand pounds.") And a cluster of regulars developed.

One rule of thumb in the business is that one "turn of the tables"—getting the same number of customers in an evening as you have seats—means you're only breaking even. To make money requires two or two and a half turns. "With two times you can draw a salary," says Donna Knezek. "Otherwise you don't." Erwin Drechsler, whose original restaurant, Metropolis Cafe on North Avenue, had thirty-two seats, says you can get by with less than two turns if your overhead is low enough. "But two turns means you're busy, and you do need to get volume in the door to make money."

The Savoy Truffle saw its first full turn of the tables—twenty-four customers—on August 18. On September 10 it had thirty-three diners. That was during the Around the Coyote art festival, although Gilbert says the customers that night weren't festivalgoers. She ran out of food and had to serve soup to the last couple of the evening.

In late September she said she was generally serving between twelve and fourteen meals a night and running somewhere below the break-even point. She said the gap was narrowing but wouldn't say how wide it was.

She didn't like the two-turns-of-the-tables measure. "Who told you that?" she demanded. "It's wrong." She said having fewer customers often functions to her advantage, because then she can take the time to push the average check—twelve dollars to fifteen dollars per person—higher by selling appetizers or dessert. "Often I can do better with eighteen people than with thirty-three people. It all depends."

On October 4 a second review ran, this time by food writer Steven Pratt in the *Tribune* food section. Pratt called the Savoy Truffle "a catchy little tune of a restaurant" and awarded it three forks out of a possible four.

The prize for any local eatery is to win a place among the 125 restaurants listed in the back of *Chicago*. "We are the standard-bearer in terms of ratings," says Penny Pollack. Unfortunately for restaurants like the Savoy Truffle, Pollack is reluctant to include tiny venues. "I worry about giving a hole-in-the-wall place a whole lot of publicity when it has only twenty-four [seats] and a limited menu. The impact would be too great." Yet she didn't rule out blessing the Savoy Truffle with a listing, and in September she plugged it on WGN radio.

The additional reviews have brought in a lot of people, and Gilbert is now limiting the number of customers each night to twenty-four. "I don't want to screw up," she says.

On a recent Sunday morning, when the restaurant is normally closed, a stout woman in a late-model car saw the metal grates in front pushed apart and stopped to look in the window. Seeing the woman's face pressed against the glass, Gilbert beckoned her inside.

"I heard about you on the radio," said the woman. "I used to know this neighborhood. It's all Mexican now, but it's becoming yuppie. I'll be back for dinner."

Gilbert handed the woman a card and encouraged her to return. But after the woman left she said, "That woman, she's a tourist. I'll serve her, but she's not a *real* customer, a customer who would be my friend."

Gilbert is sanguine about her prospects. "So many restaurants fail, but I won't. Why would I? What would be the point? That would be embarrassing. I set myself up to succeed, not to fail. I never fail—at least by my definition of failure. For eighteen years I've wanted to open a restaurant my way and in Chicago. I've done that. We're up and going. I have a three-year lease. Now I'm just coasting."

But in the next breath she says, "I always need to start something new. When something's done it's done. It becomes a rut, and I lose interest and move on." ▫

STAYIN' ALIVE

Running a business is tough in the South Side neighborhood of Roseland, where fear keeps people off the streets. But Eddie Davis and his family would rather fight than quit.

As the owner-operator of Bass Furniture and Rug Company, at 114th and Michigan, Eddie Davis considers it part of his job to check out the merchandise sold by his competition, big chains in other neighborhoods—Wickes, Aronson's, Harlem Furniture, and Value City Furniture. "I'm looking at styles, what's available, what's movin' and shakin'," he says. "You stay informed by doing that."

One evening in August, after he'd pulled the grates on his own store, Davis headed to a Value City outlet in Calumet City to check out the prices on bedroom items. He noticed a woman shopping for a sleep set, and when she told him what she was looking for Davis passed her his card and said he could give her a better price than Value City.

Two days later the woman, looking vaguely skeptical, showed up at Bass Furniture and asked for Davis. "I'm Beverly White, and I met you at Value City," she said when Davis, a short man in a sport jacket and starched shirt, hustled up with a pleasant smile on his face. He showed her several bedroom sets, and she settled on a contemporary one. He then escorted her to the rear of the store, past the glassed-in office occupied by his wife, Yvette, Bass's bookkeeper-receptionist, to his own worn wooden desk. It was piled with invoices and orders, and the shelves behind it were filled with ledgers, tape decks, ceramic fruit baskets, gym bags.

True to his word, Davis, who'd bought the furniture at a closeout market, told White the set would cost her only $970, less than she'd have paid at Value City.

Kathy Richland

Eddie, Eric, and Yvette Davis

White, a hotel waitress, appeared pleased. "How much is that magazine rack?" she asked, pointing to a gold metal stand on a shelf behind Davis's head. "This will cost you $9.95, and I'll have a guy set it up," said Davis, calling out to Gustavo Barrientos, a salesman everyone calls Goose. "Goose, can you bring this rack quicklike from the basement and put it together for this nice lady here?" White also bought a black leather backpack. Davis picked a wicker basket for carrying silverware off his shelf and presented it to her with a flourish: "This is from me to you."

White then wanted to see samples of carpet, which she needed installed within days. When she picked one, Davis said, "This rug comes from a mill in Georgia, but to be honest I can't get it for you next week. But within my power I will get you whatever you want—and at whatever price you want." White nodded approvingly, but she decided to put off choosing.

Bass Furniture has been a fixture in Roseland for three generations—through the good years and through the lean, when the neighborhood flipped from white to black. The Basses started the store in 1941 and kept it in the family until four years ago, when they sold it to Davis, who'd been with the store for fifteen years. "It's the same store it was years ago," says Eric Davis, Eddie's oldest son and the store manager. "Oh, we do a little painting from time to time, but the same wood steps carry you upstairs and the same swinging door is on Mom's office."

Eddie Davis, who's fifty-eight, hangs on by minimizing overhead, stocking off-brands, cutting prices to the bone when he has to, and catering to his clientele as if they were shopping at Nordstrom's. "Eddie has maintained the Bass name," says Ledall Edwards, executive director of the Roseland Business Development Council, the local chamber of commerce, and owner of a men's store, Edward's Fashions. "He has a good attitude, and he's optimistic about things. He sees the potential of Roseland—and I certainly can't say that about everyone around here."

According to the 1990 U.S. Census, Roseland has fifty-five thousand people, but it has no supermarket, no pizza parlor, no bowling alley, no movie theater. The Roseland business strip, which runs along Michigan Avenue from 111th to 121st, has a few national retailers—a Foot Locker, a Hollywood Video—but it's dominated by small sportswear and shoe shops owned by Koreans, Arabs, or Pakistanis. More than two dozen bars and liquor stores are scattered between 101st and 121st streets. Edwards says ruefully, "We're also a dumping ground for social-service agencies—methadone clinics and battered-women's shelters that bring in undesirables."

The best food on the strip is at Old Fashioned Donuts, a guilty pleasure in Roseland for years. A McDonald's came and went, and the only chain fast-food restaurant is a postage-stamp Pepe's on State Street. There are just two sit-down restaurants, the Ranch Steak House and the Coffee Pot, which are in a small strip mall near Bass Furniture. "Business is shit," says Coffee Pot owner Bill Manikas. "We close at four in the afternoon now—when the sun is shining—because people are scared to come out after that."

The fear is understandable. Some of the most notorious crimes in Chicago in recent years have occurred in Roseland. In 1994 Robert "Yummy" Sandifer, an eleven-year-old fledgling gang member who lived a few blocks from Michigan Avenue, shot and killed a fourteen-year-old girl, then was assassinated by older gang members in a nearby viaduct. This past summer Roseland held its breath as the bodies of six women, allegedly drug users and prostitutes, were discovered in vacant buildings. In July a suspect was finally arrested and charged with one murder. Asked about the serial killings, Ledall Edwards shrugs sadly. "There are a small number of people who wreak havoc in the community."

The strip has police who patrol on foot. "The merchants and the citizens cooperate with the police quite a bit," says Fifth District commander Michael Shields, "but crime occurs anyplace in the city." This summer there were at least two armed stickups on Michigan Avenue, the last one a midmorning heist on August 28 only three blocks from Davis's store. The manager and salesman at Fresh Line, a men's store, were bound with tape in a back room by three robbers who threw leather jackets into garbage bags and fled. Store manager Saeed Ahmed says, "Everybody is scared now."

Bass Furniture has fifteen thousand square feet in two adjoining buildings and a warehouse a block away. On the facade "Bass Furniture Co." is printed in large blue letters against gold paint. A terra-cotta eagle spreads its wings at the cornice. In the display windows are white sofas covered in plastic, an armoire, ceramic piggy banks, and curio cabinets filled with teapots and brass candy dishes. For security, Davis has completely closed off the back of one building.

All summer the entry chime needed a battery, and every time someone opened the front door it went off like a firecracker fizzling to the ground. But even when the battery's new the chime doesn't sound good. Davis says, "It beats the alternative—having nothing at all."

On a July morning the chime marks the arrival of Q. Z. Scott, who strides in without pausing. Like most Bass customers, he's checking out the merchandise—a sign says there's a sale, although the sale goes on all year long. The main showroom contains living-room sets, televisions, and stereos. Pictures of lions lolling in the bush and a woman showing cleavage hang from pastel Peg-Board on the walls. Bedroom and dinette sets, mattresses, bunk beds, washers and dryers, rug samples, and recliners fill the adjoining showroom, the upstairs, and the basement.

Scott, a maintenance worker who lives in the neighborhood, has bought plenty from Bass Furniture over the last half century. "Everything in my house," he says, and he seems to remember each item: a washer and dryer, a couch and love seat, a console TV, end and cocktail tables, and two lamps. Scott ambles back to Yvette Davis's office to make a payment on his latest acquisition, an entertainment center.

"How are you, Mr. Scott?" says Eddie Davis as Scott passes his desk. "How's the wife? I took good care of your sister-in-law."

Yvette announces that Eddie has a call. It's from a Florida manufacturer Davis is pressing to replace broken handles on some dresser drawers. "You see that you wrap them up right away so they don't arrive all smashed up," says Davis, his irritation gradually rising. "You know the handles I'm talking about? . . . I'm Eddie from Bass . . . B-A-S-S . . . no, not 312—773 . . . Eddie Davis . . . what's your name?"

No sooner has Davis hung up than a stout woman approaches him. She says she's trying to buy a building, but the credit bureau is mistaking her for another woman with the same name who's behind on her bills at Bass. "I know your difficulty," Davis tells her. "I once had three Johnnys who had accounts here at the same time—an excellent Johnny, a bad Johnny, and a so-so Johnny. We'll straighten this out and give you a letter to vouch for you." As the woman leaves, Yvette Davis tells her, "Have a blessed day."

Davis sits down at his desk, and Barrientos shuffles up, whispering that he wants Davis to serve as an "Otto" on a prospective sale. It's an old sales technique, an Otto being the person who "approves" a salesman's offer, reassuring the customer that it truly is a deal.

In this case, a woman has found a living-room set for $1,250 plus tax at Value City. "That figure stopped her dead in her tracks," Davis says later. Goose has countered with a price of $1,099 for the same set minus a table or two but including tax and delivery. Good, Davis tells Barrientos, and the woman takes the deal.

"Now we may not have made the profit we could have," Davis explains as the woman, clearly happy, goes out the door. "But part of a loaf is better than no bread at all. If you sell something at 15 to 20 percent less you're better off. Besides, if that customer likes the furniture she'll be back."

The furnishings and appliances Bass sells aren't from brand-name manufacturers, except the televisions, many of which are Zeniths. The fabrics are velvet, chenille, or polyester blends, but not the finest quality. The frames on the beds and sofas tend to be pressed wood, particleboard, Masonite, or polyurethane. "Listen, everybody can't afford a two-, three-, or four-thousand-dollar bedroom set," explains Davis. "Someone coming here may be able to afford seven hundred ninety-nine dollars, if that. What we have looks like wood, only it isn't. And it may have been made by some company in China, not by Thomasville. Our price reflects the difference in material and in where it comes from." He tries to sell people on the notion that cheap isn't necessarily bad. "Thomasville is just a name," he insists. "It's not made any better than other stuff."

In the store the gospel music of WGCI-AM radio is almost always playing. Davis and his family are members of Pleasant Grove Missionary Baptist Church in Lawndale, and they take their religion seriously. Eddie is a deacon who sings in the choir, and before church on Sunday he conducts Bible study at a halfway house for state-prison inmates. One hot July morning only one man showed up, but Davis listened to him describe his disappointment at the mother of his children moving with them to Freeport. "We're going to pray about that," Davis said before he embarked on a lesson. Davis also hosts a weekly cable-access program called *Redeemed and Ransomed*. "That's every Thursday at seven," he notes.

On the glass of Yvette's office are various admonitions: "No refunds, changes, exchanges without your receipt" and "Checks require driver's license or state ID." The office has a desk, a safe, an old cash register, file cabinets (with folders for every customer), and two computers. The store's records haven't all been transferred to the computers—Eddie isn't a wholehearted convert. "If a computer crashes," he says, "you need to take a physical look at a page."

Yvette, who's fifty-seven and always wears a hat, has overseen the office for three years. "I was babysitting family members," she says. "But then I had surgery, and Eddie said he needed me at the store. I came in thinking he was going to hire another girl, but he never did." She handles the Bass paperwork, sends out late notices, answers the phone, and takes customer payments.

Davis, who's soft-spoken yet garrulous, is always either on the phone, coordinating deliveries and orders from suppliers, or gabbing with customers. He keeps several chairs by his desk. "When we were first married Eddie would be all over the place talking," says Yvette. "It was aggravating, but I got used to it. Now when I want to I tune Eddie out, and then he fusses at me. Customers don't have the same problem with him. Sometimes they don't have even a bill to pay—they just want to talk to Eddie."

Davis says that what he loves best is to join his brother-in-law James Robinson and Barrientos on the floor selling. "More than anything, I consider myself a professional salesman," he says. "Personality is key. You have to sell yourself. Nobody wants to deal with somebody with an attitude. If you have a bad night at home, you put a smile on your countenance, and you greet the person cheerfully. Every customer is different. One may say, 'I'm just looking,' and another will tell you, 'If I see something I'm interested in I'll call you.' But you have to keep up the interchange with the person. You smile and keep talking, even if it's just about the weather. 'Did you have something particular in mind?' you finally say. They'll own up to wanting a bedroom set, and then you take them over to the bedroom department and question them as to their needs. What style do they want? Queen Anne or French provincial? You show them a range of styles until they come across the one they like, and then you go from there."

Going from there usually involves Davis making lower and lower offers on price, although he doesn't openly encourage haggling. "You can try it," he says. "I'm just not saying it'll happen."

Nevertheless, he is willing to push the ticket price on goods close to the whole-sale cost—as he did for the woman he found at Value City—because the over-head at Bass is low. He carries what he considers manageable debt, and all of his employees, except Goose and two warehousemen, are relatives, including Eric and daughter Erica Davis-Robinson. But he's quick to point out that employing family doesn't boost the bottom line much: "I still have to pay everyone."

The store's advertising consists of a mailer sent four times a year to people in the surrounding zip codes and spots on WBEE radio and television channels 62 and 47. In general, he says, "I watch and budget. I try to buy goods that will sell. We keep an eye on the pennies and don't splurge. We don't have the same markup as the big guys."

Three-quarters of Bass customers pay on time, and Davis is liberal with cred-it. "I understand that people don't always have A1 standing," he says. "Young people, for example, will take out three or four charge cards during college, and they'll run up awesome debt. I believe that God is the God of the second chance. I try to help people as far as giving them credit." If one of the two finance com-panies that clear prospective customers vetoes someone, Davis will go over the application and likely as not cut the person slack. "We don't OK everybody," he says, "but hopefully we make the right decisions."

Joseph Thomas was one of Davis's first customers at Bass. "When I went to him years ago my wife and I were just starting out," recalls Thomas, who was an appraiser with the Cook County assessor before he retired. "I didn't have bad credit, but it was questionable from a car I'd bought and paid off slowly, shall we say. Sears had turned me down. I explained all this to Eddie, and he said, 'Let me see what I can do.' He did magic, and he told me to come back and pick up my furniture. Little by little we bought everything in our first apartment from Eddie, and eventually he asked to come over. I think he was sizing me up—trying to figure out what else we might need—but we became friends." Both families lived in Avalon Park. Thomas coached Davis's son Eric in Little League, and the two men served together on the Hyde Park Academy local school council, where they sometimes had testy disagreements.

Thomas has continued to buy from Bass; he lists dinette and bedroom sets, two gas ranges, tables, lamps, mattresses, and the table his TV sits on. "It's a darn good table, though it may not have the attractiveness you can get somewhere else," he says. "The fact is, Bass stuck with me, and I'm loyal to them. Eddie's easy to talk with. I trust Yvette and the guys on the truck. There's no drinking and no growling. It's a pleasure to do business with them. Eddie's now selling to my daughter, and he stops by to stake out her place, the same way he did with me."

Esther Pierce, a drug counselor, is loyal to Bass too. "My mother started going to Bass in the early eighties, when we were living in Altgeld Gardens. She was on Social Security, and it was hard for her to pay her bills on time. She was open with Eddie, and he worked out a payment plan. When I came to him I didn't have credit either—I was a volunteer in the schools, but I was out of a job. I needed a washer and some bunk beds. I explained to him that I could afford about fifty dollars a month, and he worked out a plan for me too. Sometimes I pay more, or I'll go double up for a month. But if I'm late I'll just explain it to him."

His willingness to extend people credit sometimes lands Davis in trouble. Around 15 percent of his customers stop paying, and Davis has to refer the matter to an attorney. He admits that the percentage of nonpayers has risen in the last couple of years, and he acknowledges that he's too trusting "in some instances."

Some customers shop at Bass simply because they like Davis. "Eddie's a churchgoing man, and I like dealing with the right people," says Q. Z. Scott. Others come to Bass because it's convenient, including Ninth Ward alderman Anthony Beale, who bought both a dining-room and a living-room set at Bass. "You get in your car and you're taking your dollars outside the community," he says. "That's the uniqueness of Bass—it's here."

It doesn't hurt that Davis is one of the few African American store owners on Michigan Avenue, or that he's willing to make house calls. "A granddaughter bought a sleeper for her grandmother," he says. "We had it delivered, and the grandmother had it for four or five months when the granddaughter called to complain that the sleeper wouldn't close. So I went out to the grandmother's apartment in Calumet City only to find that she wasn't pushing this bar down right. I showed the grandmother the way. We're always helping people with their TVs—programming a set the customer had deprogrammed or pointing out how to use the mute button. This one woman said her TV wasn't working, and I went by and looked behind the set to discover she'd unplugged it. She felt real small."

Deborah Jackson, a teacher trainer for the Board of Education who became a friend of the Davises, bought her first piece of furniture from Bass fifteen years ago. "Eddie just tells me what's best," she says. The only item in her North Pullman row house that came without Davis's input is a bar table her son made. "I just got those slipcovers yesterday," she says one afternoon, pointing to some champagne-colored plastic covering a couch. "Eddie picked them out, called me in, and said I had to have them."

Jackson was invited to the wedding of Davis's daughter, and Davis tries to attend events that involve his customers. "When someone dies Dad takes an hour to go to Gatling's [a funeral home on South Halsted]," says Eric Davis. "He shows his face and signs the guest book, and the bereaved know that Bass Furniture was there. They don't do that at Aronson's."

In 1849 a group of Dutch immigrants purchased 160 acres southwest of what's now 103rd and State and established a settlement. Abraham Lincoln called the place Hope, but that name was scuttled in 1875 when Colonel James Bowen, a German-born retailer and banker active in founding the Pullman Company, chose the name Roseland, after the wild roses he found growing there in profusion. Roseland became part of Chicago in 1889. Residents first made a living in cattle and vegetable farming, and later worked at Pullman, Sherwin-Williams, and the steel mills.

The retail strip along Michigan Avenue flourished, and by the time Roseland marked its centenary in 1949, it could call itself the third-best shopping area in the city. It seemed to have it all—grocery stores, camera and jewelry shops, pharmacies, fur salons, and three movie theaters, including the thousand-seat Roseland at 113th and Michigan. Monarch Cleaners, on 111th Street, advertised stainless-steel washers, and Gordons Women's Apparel boasted of summer dresses in "silk, Bemberg sheers, linens, chambrays, pique, shantungs, and more." Roseland natives say you could find almost any household or personal item at department stores such as the Home Store and Gately's, so there was no need to shop downtown. Bass Furniture was only one of several stores that sold strictly furnishings.

Maurice "Morrie" Bass, who'd helped his father in a furniture store on Milwaukee Avenue, struck out on his own in 1941, opening a store at 114th and Michigan in what had once been a five-and-dime. Bass Furniture specialized in "all-wood furniture for working people," in the words of Gilbert Levy, who started working for his father-in-law in 1948. Levy remembers that Michigan Avenue bustled with trade through the next two decades. "The streets were crowded with people—why, you could hardly walk on the sidewalks. People didn't drive the way they do now, and besides Gately's had a big parking structure. You had a Kresge and a JC Penney, and the Roseland Theatre was nothing but first-run. We did well."

Bass did well enough to take over the building next door. A big factor in the store's prosperity was Bass himself. "Morrie Bass could sell any product to anybody at any time," Levy says. "He could have sold houses or airplanes. He could have sold ice to the Eskimos. He just happened to like selling furniture. How do I explain this? I can't. I'm no psychologist. But he was as good a salesman as you can imagine. I backed him up—taking care of the office, doing the buying, keeping the deliveries flowing. I held my own as a salesman, but I was nothing compared to my father-in-law."

Like Eddie Davis, Bass extended credit and encouraged loyalty among his customers. Ruth Liggett began buying furniture at Bass in the 1940s. "My father worked the mills, but he wouldn't bring any money home," says her son Jerome. "Then he got sick and went on Social Security. My mom would scrape up money playing policy. Mr. Bass looked out for her because she was a poor person." Levy recalls, "Mrs. Liggett came in like clockwork to pay. If it was the fifteenth, there she'd be with a smile on her face—you could figure out what day of the month it was by her showing up." Davis says that only recently did she stop appearing to retire her debt; now ninety-six years old, she's confined to a wheelchair at her Altgeld Gardens row house, yet her son says her eyes still brighten at the mention of Bass Furniture.

"We would get people and then their children and grandchildren," says Levy. "With a family business like ours, repeaters are very, very important." He guesses that a quarter of Bass customers had bought from the store before, and Davis says the same is true today.

In the mid-1970s the Pullman Company began laying people off, and the steel mills started closing. The whites who'd dominated Roseland began heading for the suburbs, and blacks, depending on federally insured mortgages because they'd been redlined by conventional lenders, moved in. But hundreds of people defaulted, leaving Roseland strewn with abandoned houses and buildings. Many of the retail businesses along Michigan Avenue chose to leave.

Gately's, headed by John Gately, opened a suburban outlet in Tinley Park, and in 1981 the Roseland store closed. "Mr. Gately had lots of theft," recalls John Edwards, Ledall's father and the founder of Edward's Fashions. "Some snowblowers were stolen off his dock, and that was it. He came to the chamber of commerce and told us he was leaving. He was very distraught. Six months later Gately's was gone." After Gately's went, other stores quickly followed.

But not Bass Furniture. In 1979 Morrie Bass sold the business to his son-in-law. "It was strictly a business deal," says Levy. "He didn't give anything away." Levy was determined to stay. "I have lived and worked with blacks all my life," he says. "I've been in their houses, and I have an idea of what they want. If you know what the income level is, you know what to buy. So Roseland changed. Instead of stocking Thomasville and Drexel, we went to a lower-priced product across the board. Maybe a bedroom set would run several hundred bucks on the low end, although there was a point where we wouldn't go cheaper because we could no longer guarantee the product."

Levy's wife, Roslyn, came in to do the office work, and the next year Levy hired Eddie Davis as a salesman.

In 1950, when Eddie Davis was seven years old, his father moved his family north from the small town of Morton, Mississippi. The son of a farmer, Jacob Davis was seeking the promised land in Chicago, and he found it as a mechanic for a company that assembled truck trailers.

Jacob and his wife, Rhodine, raised Eddie and his three sisters in apartments on the South Side, primarily in Kenwood. They were members of the storefront Friendly Baptist Church at Forty-second and Cottage Grove, which eventually became Pleasant Grove Missionary Baptist. "My father was the Sunday-school superintendent," says Eddie. "Every Sunday when the church door opened, he opened it."

Jacob Davis, now seventy-eight and retired but still as talkative as his son, says he always had a simple personal philosophy: "Whatever you want to be in life, be the very best. This started with my great-grandfather on my mother's side, who was a blacksmith and made molasses. In my work I was always the top. I told my daughters, 'If you want to be a prostitute, well, I may not like it, but be the best at it.'" He was a strict father. "I was firm, very firm—we had rules and regulations to keep them out of trouble. They couldn't be out at certain times. We had meals together. When I got home from work they were home, washed up, and ready to eat." The Blackstone Rangers and Vice Lords were around when Eddie was young, and he credits his father's influence with keeping him out of them. He remembers one of the things his parents taught him was that "to gain respect, you must show respect, and it doesn't matter who the other person is."

Jacob remembers Eddie as "a little puny child and sickly." When he was nine his limbs suddenly weakened, and he ended up in Cook County Hospital. "They examined me so much my body was like a pincushion," Davis says. The doctors thought he might have polio, and his family and their minister prayed for him. Jacob remembers, "One day I went in to see Eddie, and he said, 'Daddy, if they put me on the floor I can get well.' So they laid him out on a blanket, like he was a baby, and two days later he was able to turn over. Then he sat up. Then he walked, and he came home." Eddie had missed a full year of school and was held back a grade, but he says the experience taught him an important lesson: "I learned to be grateful for each day."

When he was fifteen Davis became a member of the Friendly Gospel Singers, a quartet started by his father and the church pastor that would eventually go on tour and cut three records. After graduating from Hyde Park High School in 1961, he attended Wilson Junior College (now Kennedy-King) and Midway Technical Institute, where he trained to be an auto mechanic. He served as a cook with the army in Germany, and after he came home he took business classes at Prairie State College. He also took a test for the New York Life Insurance Company. "That exam was nothing but adding and subtracting," he says. "Now I may not be scholarly, but I know my numbers. When they called and told me I hadn't passed, I knew what it was—they were prejudiced." So Davis got a job as a mechanic with the CTA.

He met Yvette, then a clerk at Standard Oil, in church. "I wasn't interested in her at first," he says. "I sang in the choir—had since I was nine years old—and she joined up. She was a beautiful young woman. I was seeing a couple other young ladies at the time, but God has a way of making adjustments." They were married on June 1, 1968, shortly after they bought the house in Avalon Park where they still live.

They had no dining-room set, so Eddie headed over to Tasemkin Furniture, then at Forty-sixth and South Ashland. "I went through two or three different salesmen in search of that dining-room set, and the last one gave me to the owner's son, Leslie Steinberg," says Davis. "I said I'd give them X dollars down, and I'd pay off the furniture in ninety days." Steinberg asked Davis if he'd ever done any selling, then offered him a part-time job. Davis says, "They needed a black face on the floor because they didn't have one."

At the end of 1968 Davis quit the CTA to go with Tasemkin full-time. "There were five salesmen," he says. "The first salesman would get the first customer, the second salesman would get the second person, and so on. Well, when it came my turn they wouldn't call me, unless some lady was looking for a plant stand. They just didn't want to relinquish me their turn." Often he'd be handed the black customers, whom he says the other salesmen looked down on. "A guy would come in the store, a black, and the others weren't in any hurry to get up. But I didn't let any of that deter me. One day a little lady came in and wanted a dinette chair. 'You should take her,' a salesman told me. I did, and she bought a gas range and a refrigerator too—and paid cash for it all. Another time I sold a bedroom set for three thousand or four thousand dollars. I rubbed the other guys' noses in my success."

But he also learned from them. "I'd stand within earshot of the other salesmen, and I would take bits and pieces from each one," he says. "How to qualify a buyer—are you working, for who, and how long? I picked up a little about decorating. I would incorporate it all into my own style. I would go out on the dock and get my hands on the furniture. I knew who made what and how it was constructed. Leslie Steinberg taught me about paperwork." Davis was promoted and for eight years managed the store's outlet in Chicago Heights. "I treated the place like it was mine," he says. "It took forty-five minutes to get there from my house, but if the alarm went off at three in the morning they called me, not the Steinbergs."

In 1981 Davis was back at the Ashland store as manager. Before Thanksgiving that year, Michael Steinberg, Leslie's brother, asked Davis if he would put off a trip he'd planned so the Steinbergs could go on a trip to Europe. Davis agreed, but noted that the weekend after Thanksgiving he was already committed to go to Mississippi with the Friendly Gospel Singers. "I was gone Saturday and Sunday," he says. "I was back Monday morning at eight thirty—the store opened at nine. I walked into the office, and Michael says, 'You're fired.' I gave him the two or three keys I had to the store, and I went home and fell into bed—I was exhausted from my trip. On Thursday I called Michael and asked him if his decision was final. He started hemming and hawing and said he couldn't stop me from filling out an application for salesperson. In that way he let me know it was over."

Five years earlier, Gil Levy had asked Davis whether he wanted to work at Bass, and now Levy made another offer. Davis liked his new job. The store was closed on Sunday, enabling him to go to church, and Levy gave him plenty of responsibility, including sending him to national furniture shows. "Soon I was managing the store—pricing, doing inventory and buying, and signing the checks," says Davis. "I was here six or eight months tops when Gil and Roz went on the first vacation they'd had since he had bought the store from Morrie. After that they never stopped."

Levy, who's Jewish, says he valued Davis's commitment to his faith and appreciated his live-and-let-live attitude. "That's where you don't try to convert me, and I don't try to convert you," he says. "Everybody was happy." A warm friendship developed between the two men. "Oh, we had arguments and discussions, but we had a good rapport," says Levy. "Eddie's knowledgeable about the business—he's a much better salesman than I ever was. If you want to know, he's as good as Morrie Bass was. And Eddie's as fine a gentleman as I know. After working with the man for fifteen years, give or take, he became part of me, a friend and almost a son—you can leave out the 'almost.'"

Levy and his wife had three sons of their own, yet none of them showed any interest in taking over Bass Furniture. Levy says that when he was in his sixties he thought about going out of business. "Then, I thought—maybe Eddie. I started talking to him."

In the early 1990s Davis, with Levy's encouragement, approached banks for financial backing to buy the store, its inventory and accounts receivable as well as the buildings. Harris Bank offered Davis a seven-year loan, but Davis wanted a fifteen-year one. Pullman and South Shore banks turned him down. He went to Seaway National Bank of Chicago, now the nation's second-largest black-owned bank. "I filled out all the forms, and they kept upping the amount they wanted me to put down," says Davis. "When they got to $125,000, Gil said, 'Screw them—you don't need them.'"

Even South Holland Bank, where Bass Furniture kept its account, turned him down. "I had some type of experience and good credit—excellent credit, really," says Davis. "No one gave me a satisfactory answer about being turned down. I don't think it all had to do with Roseland, but with my being African American."

Levy found the rejection by South Holland Bank "surprising and perplexing." (South Holland Bank president Dan Ward declined to comment.) In the end Levy financed Davis's purchase of the business, and Jacob Davis contributed too. Morrie Bass financed the purchase of the buildings, which he still owned, and Davis paid Bass directly until he died last year. Since then Davis has engineered the acquisition of the buildings through a loan from South Shore Bank. Levy, now seventy-four, often returns to Bass Furniture to visit. "When I walk in the store," he says, "it's like going home again."

The old Gately's sign still hangs over Michigan Avenue like a ghost. In July cement slabs on the building's exterior loosened, and the exterior had to be removed. The grand old Roseland Theatre, sold at a tax sale, is empty and decaying. Rents on Michigan Avenue are low—$6.50 a square foot—but there are plenty of vacancies. "We used to sell to the worker, but there isn't anybody engaged in industrial work now," says Don Cohen, proprietor of Herman's Army Store, which has been on Michigan Avenue for seventy-five years. "Two-thirds of our dollars come during the cold months, but the winters are warm now. I like this business, but you can't go on forever. My knees are wearing out."

Gately's massive parking garage is closed, even though merchants complain about the lack of parking. "That's the number one need—parking, with a security guard around it," says Cohen. Other retailers carp about the Arab and Pakistani stores, whose employees openly hawk their wares on the street. "We are upset about it," says Myung Yang, who owns Chicago Shoe Mart. "It's not right to grab customers on the street."

Bass is the only furniture store left in the area now. Venditti Furniture and the Home Store closed in the late nineties. "Business had fallen off very badly, and we saw our future in Country Club Hills and the south suburbs," says Renee Kaminsky, co-owner of the Home Store. "It was difficult for my husband. He was the third generation, and his father was—and is—still alive. There were mixed emotions."

Since 1992 a Walgreens has dominated the corner of 111th and Michigan, and the Foot Locker is reportedly prosperous. The local chamber of commerce has tried to improve the retail strip's image by putting up decorative street banners, and it has tried to bolster solidarity with merchant meetings and an annual awards banquet. But Ledall Edwards says the chamber's efforts can't have much of an effect because consumers still have to go outside the neighborhood to get good clothes and groceries or to see a movie. The large number of bars and liquor stores doesn't help. "Nobody wants to locate in an area when the number one industry is liquor," says Reverend James Meeks, pastor of the eleven-thousand-member Salem Baptist Church. In November 1998 Meeks led a successful campaign to vote four precincts in the area dry. But the stores banded together and sued, and the case is now before the Illinois Appellate Court. To Meeks's dismay, the liquor retailers are still open for business.

The local merchants are also frequently the object of thieves. "We're broken into twice a year," says Yang. "They get in through the roof, they come through the walls—everywhere. And as soon as you figure out some other way to protect yourself, they come up with something new. We have a problem with stealing too, even by our employees."

Levy says that when he was still at Bass, "We had minor problems. You'd walk around the store and a lamp would be gone. A car came through the front window once, but the insurance company took care of that." Davis says that since he's owned the business, thieves came through the roof once to steal a couple VCRs, and he had to fire someone he suspected of taking an air conditioner and some televisions.

Meeks blames the problems in Roseland on former Ninth Ward alderman Robert Shaw, who was in office from 1979 to 1998. "Shaw was an independent alderman who strived hard not to be connected to the machine," says Meeks. "When that is your posture, your power to get things done will suffer." Shaw, now a commissioner on Cook County's tax-review board and an occasional Bass customer, counters that he tried to stop white flight, which he says doomed Roseland commercially. "The white businesses that left preferred that black dollars come to them," he says. "It's a form of racism in reverse, and you see it in every changing neighborhood. But the new businesses that are there—the Walgreens, for instance—I brought in."

Alderman Beale, who was supported by Meeks, says, "What you have now on Michigan Avenue is a bunch of garbage. We've taken a downslide with nothing there to stabilize things. The only people who shop there now are hip-hop teenagers. Our working-class dollars go outside the community. Roseland has hit rock bottom. There's no place to go but up—and Bass Furniture is going to be one of the key parts in that."

Davis says that when he bought Bass Furniture he never thought about changing its name. "Bass has a good name and reputation in the neighborhood," he says. And he's never considered moving the store or closing it. "I can personally go to any furniture store and get a job, but if I have a choice I want to work and maintain what's already here," he says. "Customers shouldn't have to go to the malls forty-five minutes away. And I believe that if you set your mind to something you can survive in slow times."

The store now grosses roughly one million dollars a year in sales, a little less than what it took in at the end of the period when Levy was there. By comparison, figures from *Furniture/Today* show that in 1999 Wickes Furniture, headquartered in Wheeling, grossed $8.2 million per store and Plunkett Furniture, based in Hoffman Estates, grossed $5.2 million per store. Davis says the unit sales for those chains are higher in part because they sell their products for more money. "I make an honest living," he says, "and when my debts are paid off I'll make a comfortable one."

Jacob Davis says, "The way I see it, you lay down your bucket where you are," a saying of Booker T. Washington, the original apostle of black economic empowerment. "If old Mr. Bass made out all right and Gil did too, why can't Eddie make a living out of the store? It isn't going to happen overnight. You have to be long-suffering sometimes. He may work a lifetime there, and his children will reap the harvest."

Davis is on the floor from 9:30 A.M. until 6 P.M. six days a week, breaking only to eat a brown-bag lunch and, two afternoons a month, to tape *Redeemed and Ransomed*. After closing he and Yvette spend time on administrative matters before heading home. Davis is proud of the jobs he provides. Barrientos was a Guatemalan immigrant with only a slim grasp of English when Levy hired him as a salesman in 1991. "Back then I went by the name of David," says Barrientos, who was in the United States illegally. After almost three years Levy learned the truth. "Get your papers in order, and you can come back," he told Barrientos, who quickly got resident-alien status and returned.

Barrientos, who's now thirty-three, mastered English by studying a language textbook and reading the *Sun-Times*. When he's not selling, he often listens to the problems of other Hispanic immigrants at his desk by the display windows. "A lot of people get letters from the city and the government, and I figure things out for them," he says. Davis doesn't mind. "Even though he's assisting people on my time," he says, "I don't hold that against Goose. We have to help each other when we can."

Davis wants to help turn around Roseland. He attends meetings sponsored by Beale and meetings at schools, and he's treasurer of the Roseland Business Development Council and a member of the Roseland Redevelopment Planning Board, a two-year-old community organization. He recently joined a business advisory panel Beale organized.

Davis is hopeful about the community's prospects, but the neighborhood is still decrepit. Beale says it has three hundred or so abandoned buildings, and a *Sun-Times* study published last year showed that Roseland had 696 bank fore-closures in 1998, more than any other city zip-code area. The 1990 census put the median annual household income at $28,600, more than $2,000 below the city median.

But a recent study by Social Compact, a nonprofit based in Washington, D.C., that studies poor neighborhoods, shows that the median household income in a large section of Roseland is $50,881 and that 73 percent of houses in that section are owner occupied. "There are people in Roseland with purchasing power and a population able to support business," says Issa Lara Combs, Social Compact's managing director.

Two years ago the development arm of Salem Baptist Church turned a building at 115th and Michigan that had been occupied by a drug and liquor store into the House of Peace, an upscale Christian bookstore. "I wanted to take over the largest liquor store, and I wanted to show developers that we are serious about redevelopment," says Meeks, who oversaw the spending of one million dollars on the project and persuaded Mayor Daley to attend the opening in November 1998. Salem Baptist also intends to build forty-five houses at 101st and Michigan, and the nonprofit Neighborhood Housing Services is now finishing forty rental town houses and apartments at 105th and Michigan. And Southside College Prepara-tory Academy—one of six new regional magnet high schools, located in the old Mendel High School—is getting a twenty-five million-dollar-refurbishing.

Beale pushed through an ordinance, approved by the city council in July 1999, that allows the city to condemn 273 parcels of land along Michigan Av-enue, three-quarters of them vacant; the buildings include the Roseland Theatre and the old Gately's building. "When you can assemble a lot of properties into a package," says Pete Scales, spokesman for the planning department, "it's more attractive for developers." Beale says the land or rehabbed buildings might be used for a community center, parking lots, a Dominick's grocery store. "We are actively talking to Dominick's," he says, although Mike Mallon, Dominick's real estate vice president, will say only, "We continue to look at lots of opportunities throughout the area." The Matanky Realty Group wants to build a small mall near 111th Street, and Beale says businesses such as Old Navy, Denny's, and

Applebee's have shown some interest. But one developer says, "It'll be a special type of operator to be the first to come in." Beale is also looking into making the area a tax-increment financing district, which would allow the city to sell bonds to pay for infrastructure improvements and development.

Eddie Davis plans to apply for a city rebate grant that would let him redo the front of his store—put in new windows, decorative brick trim, and security grates on tracks inside the store. He also wants to acquire the overgrown vacant lot across 114th Street for parking. "Eddie has a vision," says Beale.

But upgrading his property isn't the most important thing for Davis. "Whether we look good or bad, we'll still be around selling furniture," he says. "Bass has been here for sixty years, and we want to be here for another sixty—selling good merchandise at affordable prices and being kind to our customers." ■

Crime

GROWING OLD
IN PRISON

A generation apart from their fellow prisoners, four elderly inmates
come to terms with the fear of never getting out.

Before they were sent to prison, they answered to common names: Dick
or Floyd or Jimmy. Inside, they have been labeled with nicknames like "Skinny"
or "Scoots." Over time, however, the nicknames have given way to another sobri-
quet, "Pop."

These are the elderly behind bars.

As with their younger counterparts, the patriarchs of prison hardly love their
lot. At best, they voice resignation, at worst, a deep bitterness. John is a snowy-
haired old man put away in an Illinois penitentiary years ago for taking indecent
liberties with a child. "I have never found one goddamn good thing about prison,
from the day I came in until now," he says. "What kind of person can come in
here and not realize that this is a place intended to destroy people?"

Elderly inmates are, to a considerable degree, a forgotten minority. To start
with, there are so few of them. Of the thirty thousand residents currently in U.S.
prisons, only 320 are over sixty-five: Illinois has thirty-one older prisoners out of
14,400 inmates.

In many ways, prison's senior citizens are like other inmates. They are mostly
male, and they have been convicted of misdeeds ranging from armed robbery to
murder. Some of them resemble benign grandfathers, but their criminal records
catch that impression up short.

Surprisingly, these older prisoners have been locked away for more violent crimes than their younger counterparts. Ann Goetting, a sociologist at Western Kentucky University, analyzed profiles of state and federal inmates taken by the U.S. government in 1979 and found out that 70 percent of those fifty-five and over were incarcerated for violent offenses, compared to only 56 percent of those under fifty-five.

There are theories, of course, to explain the disparity. Goetting figures the higher proportion of elderly violent offenders reflects the fact that judges and juries are more lenient with older people. A senior accused of a lesser crime can usually avoid prison. But because the rate of violent crime among Americans over fifty-five is skyrocketing—it doubled between 1974 and 1981 alone, according to one major study of FBI statistics—it may be that fewer judges are handing down lighter sentences to older offenders.

Notwithstanding the crimes that send them to the pen, elderly inmates are often unaccustomed to the setting. Goetting reports that 40 percent of those she studied were first-time offenders. And there they are, housed with a mass of convicts whose average age hovers in the midtwenties in state prisons. (The average age of federal prison inmates is thirty.)

Like the elderly everywhere, older inmates face the encumbrances of age—failing eyes and fading hearts—only more so. "Prison is a very stressful existence," says Ronald Shansky, medical director of the Illinois Department of Corrections, "and it brings on symptoms." Shansky cites headaches, dizziness, and gastrointestinal ailments as common complaints.

Prisons do make special provisions for the old and infirm. The Illinois system, for instance, authorizes a yearly checkup for everyone over forty and keeps special watch over the sickly. The U.S. Bureau of Prisons runs a federal hospital facility in Springfield, Missouri, and maintains two minimum-security outposts—at Lexington, Kentucky, and Fort Worth, Texas—for those with drug and chronic medical problems; a higher-than-average portion of all three hospital populations is aged. A handful of states have established similar hospital facilities, notably South Carolina, where the Goodman Correctional Institution in Columbia is devoted largely to the ailing.

Occasionally, a prison system assigns separate quarters for inmates strictly on the basis of age rather than a decline in health. For years, the West Virginia Penitentiary in Moundsville has set aside one dormitory—known as "the old man's colony"—for men fifty and up. "They all live in one giant room with a fairly high ceiling, and they serve out their time in a relaxed atmosphere," says Joe Cometti, executive assistant to the state corrections commissioner. "There is low supervision and a garden in summer. Look, some of these old fellas—our oldest is ninety-one—are country boys out of the hollows convicted of one thing or another back into the forties. Most everyone's trustworthy. They look after each other, and a good feeling gets going."

By and large, though, old prisoners in America remain part of the general mix, and there they tend to become isolated. "Generally, the old guys have their heads in different places," says Neal MacDonald, warden of Illinois' Sheridan Correctional Center. "They have lifestyles and habits that separate them from the younger guys, and, besides, the age gap is so great that the younger ones don't pay attention to the old guys anyway. I'll say this: the gangs leave the old guys alone, and as to sexual harassment, that's pretty much for youth—and youth tends to be attracted to youth. But the usual objective of prison, rehabilitation through education and training, is extraneous to people over sixty-five. The only expectation of the older inmate is to do the time."

"Now I'm not a hermit here, not an island," offers John. "But the youngsters, they look at me, and it's impossible for them to envision being so far along in a lifetime. So perhaps in self-defense, I draw away. What kind of friendship can you have in prison, anyway? People are here today, gone tomorrow. Here someone may want to be my friend, but I don't allow it to go beyond a certain point."

Contact with the outside world does little to diminish the loneliness. John, a career criminal who has spent a total of four decades closeted away, once went seventeen and a half years without a single visitor. "I got a cousin in Florida," he says, "and once in a while she writes me."

Gnawing at each senior is the fear of dying before walking on free pavement. Many states and the U.S. Bureau of Prisons often let terminally ill inmates return home for their last days, but the dread of perishing before they are released haunts elderly inmates. "Everybody fears dying," says Judy Anderson, warden of South Carolina's Goodman prison. "In here, people have to come to terms with their own mortality, and that they'll be in jail when the proof [of their mortality] comes."

Perhaps because of this sense of time running out, elderly inmates are amazingly, and often painfully, articulate about their lives. These are the stories of four of them.

Tom Butler: Menard Correctional Center, Chester, Illinois

It would be wrong to say that Tom Butler likes prison. Rather, after a lifetime in jail, the regimen of confinement suits him.

Butler is impounded at Menard Correctional Center, the largest prison in Illinois, a sprawling sandstone complex that perches over the Mississippi River and contains the state's fifty-man death row. He lives alone in a room in a concrete-and-steel dormitory that used to function as the prison's isolation unit.

The child of a miner, Butler was raised in a small town in southern Illinois. At sixteen, he was sent to prison the first time for, he claims, stealing "a few candy bars and cigarettes." Over the years he has become well acquainted with prison, in particular Menard—having served time for three robberies, a burglary, and attendant parole violations. In 1977, however, his future seemed promising. Trained as an ambulance driver at a minimum-security prison in Vienna, Illinois, he was retained as a driver after his release.

"One night it was late," Butler remembers, "and I drove into this gas station. I was drunk—drinking's been my problem since I was a kid—and this guy [the station attendant] kept hollering about his not having change. We got into an argument, we got to scuffling, and I put a pistol on him. Then I took his money, too. Once they arrested me, I knew I couldn't beat it, and so I pled guilty. The judge was an old Christian judge, and he sentenced me to sixty years."

The length of his punishment disappointed Butler's friends, but it didn't surprise them. "Tom's probably the smartest man you or I will ever meet," says Reverend William G. Johnson, who once ran a statewide prison project for the Methodist Church and has known Butler twenty years. "He has special gifts that would make him a viable part of society. But he drank, something that was hidden for years but then became a heavy problem. Really, the system made a con out of Tom. He can get along excellently in jail, but not on the street. He's used to being taken care of, to being without responsibilities."

In fact, Butler agrees with the minister. "In jail, I have escaped boredom and pain through my own efforts," he allows, "but outside I don't know if I can do it."

Skilled in shorthand, he works as a clerk to a prison guard captain, but other than that he stays aloof. "I'm a loner, strictly," explains Butler, a tall man with a mustache and a Roman hairstyle who appears two decades younger than his sixty-seven years. "This place is full of garbage. I have a lot of acquaintances here, but no friends." He seems fondest of his electronic chess game, which is programmed to duplicate a grand-master level of play, and a pair of Nike court shoes, with which he jogs six to seven miles a day.

Though he didn't get through fifth grade, Butler has always read voraciously, from modern novelists like Hemingway to the ancient philosophers. His present interest is science. He subscribes to *Scientific American, Science Digest,* and *Science 84,* and he has come to embrace the theory of evolution wholeheartedly. In a memoir about his boyhood that Butler wrote for the Menard newspaper, he created a fictional sage who forecasted the future. "The older you become," the sage tells the young Tom, "the more you'll come to realize that life isn't such a bargain. The best part of your life will be the latter, when you will become extremely interested in the universe, space, time, and matter, in consequence of which you will become a firm believer in the only thing that makes sense—evolution.

"Although it is very difficult for man to believe that there is 'personal' meaning to life and he thinks he longs for immortality (there's no such thing in nature), you will come to see this is mere egotistical nonsense."

Butler is definitely a man alone. No relatives visit him. The last Butler heard of his mother she resided in a nursing home somewhere. During the thirties, he was married for a few years, but while he was at Menard he advised his wife, "I'll be in these f—ing joints my entire life, so divorce me." She did. Butler is estranged from a middle-aged son, and as to the possibility that he might have grandchildren, he snaps, "Be better off if they never saw this terrible world."

Butler's sole visitor is a teacher of the handicapped, Myra McCabe, who met Butler when he was in prison at Vienna. McCabe, who is fifty-five, comes to Menard several times a year from her home upstate, and she writes to Butler daily. "Tom said, 'Write and tell me what you and yours are up to,' and I do that," says McCabe. Butler enjoys the letters, but he never quite knows what to write Myra in return.

He harbors many conclusions about society's ills: "If children were raised right, we wouldn't have so many illiterates and so much worship of the buck." He is writing a book filled with his ideas and tales of his life, a life that will likely dead-end at Menard, given that his earliest release date arrives past the turn of the century.

"Just say I'm not going to make it to freedom," Butler muses. "Doesn't bother me a bit. I've learned that life is no prize or blessing. It's phenomenal, but we're no better off than tumblebugs. Like the old Greek philosopher said, probably the best thing that could happen to you is to have never been born; the next thing, to die young."

James Phillips: Sheridan Correctional Institution, Sheridan, Illinois

James Phillips's birthday falls on the Fourth of July; he was either seventy-six or eighty on his last one, depending on whether you believe him or prison records. Either way, Phillips ranks as one of the oldest residents in an Illinois prison. Among administrators, guards, and fellow inmates at the Sheridan Correctional Institution, a medium-security facility west of Chicago, he is one of the most beloved.

Last July 4, like seven before it, Phillips celebrated his birthday behind bars. He received a load of gifts: an album of family pictures, a black-and-white TV from Sheridan's assistant warden, and, courtesy of a friendly lieutenant of the guards, a green-and-white billed cap with "Pop Phillips" written up top in block letters.

"Everybody here calls me 'Pop'—women and men, black and white, all of them," Phillips explains. "Fact is, I'm well liked."

Pop, who had his right leg amputated three years ago, lives in a single cell in a small, cross-shaped block. The loss of his leg cost Phillips his job in the Sheridan dining hall. Although he has an artificial leg, his stump is too sensitive and he cannot wear it, so he moves around in a wheelchair.

The son of a farmer, Phillips grew up in Alabama. He was convicted of robbery as a teenager and received a life sentence, but he eventually charmed his way to privileged status as a cafeteria aide in the state capitol and, at last, he received a pardon.

In the 1940s, Phillips moved north to Chicago, where he became a laborer. "My wife, she died, and we never did have kids," says Phillips, who nonetheless has three daughters and two sons by three common-law wives. In 1959, he resettled in East St. Louis, Illinois, to be near relatives. There he worked on a riverboat, but soon was back in prison—this time for four years in Missouri—for armed robbery.

It was another robbery that landed Phillips in Sheridan. Early one morning in 1975, two young men robbed an East St. Louis grocery store at gunpoint. The two owners handed over $8,600 and begged for their lives, but the gunmen shot them to death. Unfortunately for the perpetrators, the whole affair was recorded on the store's security system. The two robbers were soon arrested, along with an accomplice who had allegedly driven the getaway car: Pop Phillips.

"I didn't kill anybody," Phillips swears. "These two boys I barely knew—they were friends of my niece—held up the store and did the killing. I was just the driver." But Clyde Kuehn, then the district attorney, who prosecuted Phillips, characterizes him as the mastermind, staking out the grocery store in advance, noticing its traffic in food stamp dollars, and arranging for the heist. Kuehn scoffs at Phillips's memory of his role in the crime. "That's the image he's relied on his whole life," observes Kuehn. "And it's served him well. At trial, he was this old Uncle Tom type."

Both of Phillips's partners in the grocery robbery and murders were convicted and got sentences of several hundred years each. Phillips got twenty to sixty years.

The major feature of Phillips's stay in prison has been his failing health. He has sustained two heart attacks, the insertion of plastic veins into both legs to restore circulation, and then, when the right leg rapidly became gangrenous, its amputation.

Phillips longs for release, to see a cousin in East St. Louis and to visit his last common-law family, a young son and daughter, and their thirty-three-year-old mother who reside in Michigan. But although his first date with the parole board is approaching ("I'll just tell them I'm ready to go home"), Phillips's discharge this soon is unlikely. A petition for executive clemency filed by some inmate friends has already been rejected.

But Phillips is philosophical about the course of things: "I never wanted to be no criminal. But funny things happen. . . . I don't know."

Kenneth Sanders: Sheridan Correctional Institution, Sheridan, Illinois

A guard refers to Kenneth Sanders as "that small, stubby guy." His fellow prisoners call him "Pops" or "Colonel Sanders."

Sanders, who is four feet eleven and has a sly laugh, lives in a separate wing of the same cell house that James Phillips calls home. But unlike Phillips, the seventy-four-year-old Sanders finds prison an ordeal to be shouldered stoically.

Sanders began a four-year sentence at Sheridan last March. For a while, he was assigned to a ground-maintenance crew. "You know," he says, "going around with a plastic bag picking up paper. I didn't mind the job, except I have two artificial hips, and the bending got my hips to aching." So now Sanders goes to school to learn how to repair the engines of lawn mowers and motorcycles.

Sanders was born in Wisconsin, the son of a farmer, but he trained in electrical maintenance and moved to Rockford, Illinois, in 1937, to do that type of work. He enjoyed a career that took him in and out of several companies until his retirement in 1969. "The president of that last place even asked me to stay on," Sanders recollects, "but I was so crippled with arthritis I wanted to go." And go he did, back to his wife of twenty-five years and the four-unit apartment building he owned in a quiet neighborhood of east Rockford.

His wife died in 1971, but otherwise Sanders's life was placid. It was a jolt, then, when he was arrested for taking indecent liberties with a young girl. Sanders pled guilty and received probation. But in 1982, Sanders was arrested again, this time for molesting the two-year-old daughter of a man renting a house from him. Sanders maintains that the accusation was trumped up by a disgruntled tenant and that the confession he signed was invalid because he had not been read his rights. Still, a judge convicted Sanders last February and consigned him to prison, his first experience there.

"When you come in here, you have nothing," Sanders says of Sheridan, "not even a pair of shoes. You are allowed a few things after a while. I have a hot pot, to heat myself water for coffee, which you can buy in the commissary. Now I also have a hook to hang my coat on."

He keeps to himself. The day room, he says, is usually filled with "yelling and hollering" by younger prisoners, and Sanders prefers to steal back to his cell to listen to the radio: "I like the ball games, the news and, of course, there's music." At night, he gets into a card game.

"I can't say I've made friends here," he says, "although I haven't made any enemies, either. But everybody's so much younger, in their teens and twenties. I just don't fit in with that young bunch."

It is the regimentation of jail that rankles Sanders most. Eating, for instance, has some discomfiting aspects: "When they call chow, I'm almost the last to get over to the dining room, and because I wear dentures I'm usually the last one done. The guards yell at me to finish, but I've learned to just sit there and finish up through the shouting. Sometimes I don't even go to meals; I'd rather just sit in my cell."

Visiting arrangements are cumbersome, and some procedures are humiliating. "I have a friend from Rockford who comes to see me, and I've had to strip down beforehand. The guard looks in your underwear, and asks you to bend over. I can see where that's necessary with some of the young punks, but with me?"

Back in Rockford, a friend is minding Sanders's property. Sanders looks forward to a release date he has set for himself: February 1985 (or half of his full term). "I'm ready to go tomorrow," he reflects. "They need the space without devoting it to people like me. I've never done anything wrong in life; I've led a decent life.

"This has all certainly taken a lot of years off my life—the tension, the sitting in my cell, never getting any exercise.

"In Rockford, so many people are cruel, and they think this [his last crime is all he brings up] was true. I do have friends who really know *me*, but even they feel sorry for me. Now all I want is to lead a nice, quiet, good sort of life."

Charles Williams: Stateville Correctional Institution, Joliet, Illinois

At seventy, Charles Williams is bald, with a thin mustache wrapping around his mouth, wisps of hair underneath his lower lip, and thick-lensed eyeglasses, which aren't that necessary anymore since glaucoma has claimed his left eye and rendered him nearly blind in the right.

The Jamaica native has hopscotched in and out of prison since he spent four years as a lad in a New Jersey reformatory for "atrocious assault and robbery." ("I knocked a woman down running around a corner," is Williams's explanation.) Other prison engagements on his rap sheet include two and a half years in a federal pen in the 1940s for joyriding and a couple years in a state prison a decade later for car theft.

He is currently doing fifty to seventy-five years inside the graystone Stateville Correctional Institution in Joliet, Illinois, for a murder committed in 1967.

Williams has an involved explanation of how the body of a man got inside his burning Plymouth Fury on a Chicago street during that year's historic snowfall, but it is evidently not one a Cook County jury believed.

Williams's sixteen years at Stateville—which houses 2,250 inmates—makes him one of the two or three senior convicts on the premises, a select bunch that also includes mass murderer Richard Speck.

At first, Williams was a bricklayer inside Stateville (that and shoemaking had been his primary occupations on the street), but his failing sight and good conduct has earned him a spot at the prison's adjoining honor farm as a cook for prison officials. "I can cook and that's a proven fact," Williams boasts. "Ravioli and meatballs, fried chicken, peach cobbler, and apple pie—I can make any dish you can name."

Williams concocts his specialties from 4 A.M. until 1 P.M. "Then I catch a nap or two, play a little chess, and listen to recordings for the blind on my cassette tape." He has been given permission to use a parcel of land near the farm clothing room for a garden, and there he grows cabbage, spinach, cucumbers, and tomatoes. Inside, he shares a dormitory with three other seniors, and though he refuses to count his roomies as friends—("It's best not to have friends here, you understand me?")—he does fall into long bull sessions with them.

But unlike many older inmates, Williams has frequent contact with the outside world. About five years ago in a Stateville visiting room, through another prisoner, Williams was introduced to Juanita Baker, a licensed practical nurse from Chicago. The pair was soon wed in a prison ceremony, and now Juanita Williams comes calling once a week.

"Actually, I think sympathy was the main issue in my marrying Charles," allows Juanita, sixty. "I'm not saying I don't love him, but sympathy was primary. He has no one—he never established a family in Chicago, and he told me he once went fourteen years without a visit."

Juanita says her husband is "very affectionate" during their four-hour visits, but there are limits to the ardor either can display. "We can put our arms around each other, and we can kiss," says Charles, "but a man knows how to go here."

On one occasion three years ago, the guards prohibited inmates and their guests from repairing to the visitors' yard, and to his wife's amazement Williams objected strenuously, with no regard for the consequences. "We have a right to relax with our families," he argued, and the yard was opened.

Williams's championing of prison rights has surfaced in court, too. This year, he and two other Illinois inmates became the name plaintiffs in a class-action suit challenging the state's intention to transfer prisoners to other states to relieve overcrowding; in September the litigants won. Williams, through his attorney, has also sued to complain that rehabilitation, not the seriousness of his offense, ought to be the determining factor in his winning or losing release. So far, he has been denied parole.

The prospect of dying in Stateville is repugnant to Williams: "Death always crosses my mind in here, but I want to die on the outside, in peace and harmony. I'm not content here. I'm not like the guy they always joke about who leaves prison after so many years, sees a plane, and goes back inside, saying, 'I can't deal with that.' I could deal with it."

Editor's note: Shortly after this interview, Williams was given parole and since October has been living in Chicago with his wife. "I'm out," says Williams. "I'm not able to do anything because I'm nearly blind. But I'm glad to be out. I don't see how you could have any other opinion."

IT'S
INSANITY!

Landlord shouts, "You're out!" Tenants say, "We won't go!"
Everyone agrees: It's insanity! How a simple rent dispute became
a five-year blood feud.

The yellow brick building at 6128 South Kilpatrick in West Lawn contains two apartments and a basement recreation room. The roof over the entry porch has a slight tilt to it—a Prairie School touch perhaps. With its pine tree in the front yard and garage on the alley, the building resembles thousands of two-flats that dot Chicago's working-class neighborhoods.

In December 1993 Georgia Speredakos, who is now sixty, rented the three-bedroom unit on the first floor to David and Bambi McMillion, a pair of small-time evangelists. By the following spring she'd embarked on a quest to evict them because they'd paid only one month's rent—they wouldn't pay another month's rent for four and a half years.

The McMillions promptly charged Speredakos with being a bad landlord, and they eventually countersued, insisting that she owed them for their pain and suffering. As the case proceeded, they portrayed themselves as advocates for put-upon tenants. "We are standing up for the right of all people to have a legitimate landlord who obeys the law," said David McMillion during the trial that finally began in December 1997.

Speredakos v. McMillion, which would involve five lawyers and three judges and innumerable court appearances before it was over, ranks as the longest-running eviction dispute in memory in Cook County—such disputes normally conclude quickly in the landlord's favor. As the case dragged on, Michael Pensack,

David and Bambi McMillion and Connie Fernandez

executive director of the Illinois Tenants Union, said, "This is a weird, freaky case." Robert Gordon, who was briefly Speredakos's lawyer, said, "It's insanity."

"I came to this country forty years ago with no clothes to wear," said Speredakos this past May. "My husband and I struggled so we could have something for our later years. Now these people owe me $27,825 in back rent, and if I lose, everything I own could be taken away from me. I don't sleep much at night, and all day I'm in court with Bambi and David McMillion."

Georgia Bisbikis immigrated to Chicago from Greece in 1958 to join her family, then living at Fifty-fifth and Halsted. Her first job, as a seamstress for a dress company, paid thirty-seven dollars a week. She met John Speredakos in an evening English-language class, and they married in 1966. At first the couple lived with Speredakos's two bachelor uncles, but they soon wanted a place of their own.

County records show that the two-flat on Kilpatrick, which is only blocks from Midway Airport, was built in 1965 and bought by a man named Eugene Sullivan. "He lived there with his wife and his son and daughter-in-law," says Georgia. "But the mother and the daughter-in-law didn't get along, and they decided to sell." In November 1966 the Speredakoses purchased the two-flat for $47,000 through a land trust that named Georgia's parents, John and Anastasia Bisbikis, as partners.

"It was a quiet neighborhood, except for the noise from the airplanes taking off in the afternoon," says Georgia. She was then pregnant with the first of four children, and she and her husband took the first floor. Her parents lived upstairs, and everyone shared the rec room in the basement. Georgia says the building was always a break-even proposition, yet its value gradually rose as time passed. By 1979 the first-floor apartment was crowded with eight adults and children, including John's sister and her son, so they all bought a house in the southwest suburb of Palos Park. The Speredakoses kept the two-flat; Georgia's parents went on living upstairs, and the first floor was rented out.

At the time Georgia operated a beauty shop, and John was a loader for Nabisco. He eventually also became owner of the Nevada restaurant at Sixty-eighth and South Pulaski. In 1977 the restaurant was grossing $250,000 a month, although it went through leaner periods. In 1990 John suffered a debilitating stroke, and responsibility for managing the restaurant, renamed the New Nevada, fell to Georgia, her children, and some business partners. Late the following year the McMillions started to patronize the place.

You couldn't miss them. David McMillion is a large, bearded man with shaggy brown hair and a southern twang. He has a cross tattooed on his right hand and sometimes walks with a cane. Bambi has lacquered bright blond hair and dresses girlishly in bright dresses, Mary Janes, and false eyelashes. The McMillions went to the New Nevada for lunch and supper. "Those barbecue ribs were just tremendous," remembers David. Often they stayed till closing.

The pair told the short and stout Speredakos, who was often there as hostess, that they were Pentecostal preachers, had set up a tent in a lot on Eighty-seventh Street near the Dan Ryan Expressway, and were attracting a following. Slowly they became not just good customers but friends. When the McMillions told Speredakos that they were unhappy with the apartment they were renting on Archer Avenue, she told them she had a vacancy at 6128 South Kilpatrick. Soon they negotiated a month-to-month lease that stated that the McMillions were to pay $525 a month in rent plus utilities. No security deposit was required. David signed the lease on November 30, 1993, and paid the first month's rent.

The McMillions' tenancy began pleasantly enough. Georgia Speredakos invited them out to her house in Palos Park for pizza, and they appeared to get along with Georgia's elderly parents, who still lived upstairs. Speredakos even talked with Bambi about starting a flea market.

Speredakos says the relationship soured over the winter and spring of 1994, when the McMillions failed to deliver any more rent. We're waiting for money to arrive from the South, she would later say they told her in January. Nothing came, and in March Speredakos asked for the money again. We're waiting for some checks to clear, she says they told her.

The McMillions would later testify that they hadn't paid the rent because the apartment had numerous problems—not enough heat, so much frost around the freezer door that it wouldn't shut, no rubber seal around the oven door, low water pressure in the shower and kitchen sink, no smoke detector, a broken air conditioner, cracked windows, no dead bolt locks on the exterior door, and water bugs, centipedes, and mice.

The McMillions would also state that they were being forced to pay extra for gas and electricity for the building's hallways, the basement rec room, and the utility room—they would later insist that the amount was more than two hundred dollars a month above what they thought they should be paying. And they would contend that Speredakos reneged on a promise to let them park their van in the garage behind the building. All these problems, they said, had exacerbated their medical problems: David had a heart condition, arthritis, and diabetes, and Bambi had Graves' disease. The McMillions say they complained to Speredakos's father, John Bisbikis, and to Speredakos herself. They contend she flat-out refused to repair anything. "Mrs. Speredakos, you will never get rent out of us until you fix what's broken," David McMillion says he told her.

The McMillions say they put down their position in a series of letters, composed in Bambi's bold longhand on ruled paper and mailed to Speredakos. (Bambi would testify that she'd kept copies of the letters.) In a letter dated December 27, 1993, that is part of the court file, the McMillions write that they're withholding rent until repairs are made. A letter dated January 10, 1994, reads, "It has become apparent to us that you are uninterested in doing the fair thing as our landlord. . . . We thought you were our friend. You said we were your best customers at your restaurant. Is this how you repay your friends and best customers?"

Speredakos would testify that she never received the letters (she thought the copies the McMillions produced in court were fakes) and that the McMillions didn't complain verbally to her or her father. She also said nothing was ever put in the lease about the use of the garage (there's no note of it in the lease that's in the court record). "But they were welcome to it. Is it my fault their van didn't fit?"

Whatever their complaints, the McMillions contend that Speredakos never came to look at their apartment. She admits, "I called a couple of times, and they never called back." She says she still has no idea whether the gas and electricity for the common areas of the building are hooked up to the first-floor apartment. And she admits to not knowing what the city code requires apartments to have. "I didn't know an apartment needed dead bolt locks or peepholes," she says. Asked if she's a good landlord, Speredakos answers, "I'm a good person."

In April 1994 Speredakos asked again for the rent, and when it didn't materialize she wrote out a five-day notice—a standard form—demanding payment and threatening eviction, and sent it to the McMillions by registered mail. Speredakos had worked as a real estate agent in the suburbs, so she might have been expected to know what she was doing. But when she and the McMillions met in court at the Daley Center later that month, circuit court judge D. Adolphus Rivers threw out the notice because Speredakos had attached an expiration date and the McMillions had picked it up a week after that date.

By this time the New Nevada restaurant had gone bankrupt because sales taxes hadn't been paid. Speredakos and her partners were feuding, and she hired a downtown lawyer, Barry Barnett, to help her. She told him about the McMillions, but he advised her not to move against the couple because the Cook County Sheriff's Department said they were needed by the FBI as witnesses in another case.

A year later, in May 1995, Barnett filled out another five-day notice on Speredakos's behalf and had it delivered to the McMillions. It too was tossed out on a technicality.

Then Barnett vanished on Speredakos. "He never returned my phone calls, either on the eviction or my restaurant bankruptcy," she says. (Barnett is now facing charges of unprofessional conduct under a five-count complaint filed with the Illinois Attorney Registration and Disciplinary Commission. One count relates to Speredakos, who alleges that he misused money she'd given him to pay creditors in the bankruptcy case. Barnett could not be reached for comment.)

Discouraged by this second failure and her losses, Speredakos let another year pass during which the McMillions paid no rent. In April 1996 she and her daughter Maria, a schoolteacher, filled out yet another five-day notice and posted it, along with a thirty-day notice, on the McMillions' door. This time Speredakos was sure she'd done it right. On June 11 the case came before Judge Rivers, and he instructed Speredakos and the McMillions—none of whom had a lawyer—to go into the jury room to try to work out a settlement. David McMillion recalls telling her, "Georgia, here's my deal—we'll pay you seven thousand dollars, and you give us until August to move out." Speredakos doesn't remember that he made a monetary offer, but she was in no mood to bargain—her sixty-four-year-old husband, who'd already suffered several strokes, was in the hospital. She told the McMillions she wanted all the rent due her. That angered David McMillion, who says, "Here we'd offered money, and we were willing to stay two months and be gone. I told Georgia, 'Now we're going to the ropes. This is going into the "Swiss Book of World Records." It's only going to end when the last witness is heard.'" They went back into the courtroom, and Speredakos asked to be allowed to get a new attorney.

That night John Speredakos, who'd been discharged by the hospital and was waiting in a wheelchair by an elevator to go home, died of a heart attack.

David McMillion's career high came early. He began preaching in earnest when he was seven and for the next few years led crusades across the country under the banner: David McMillion's International Flames of Revival Ministries. "I knew Billy Graham and Oral Roberts," he says. "I was on six hundred radio stations. I traveled to thirty-nine countries."

After serving in Vietnam, David entered the Assemblies of God Theological Seminary in Springfield, Missouri. He didn't last long. Asked why, he says he flunked public speaking because he stood too far behind the podium. He says for a while he worked as a private investigator, then as a country-and-western singer. He claims to have opened for Ronnie Milsap and Eddie Rabbitt under the name Johnny Lee Diamond, but Rabbitt's former manager and Milsap say they don't remember him. Then, he says, he became a magician, Jonathan Champagne. He says, "They put me in a steamer trunk, and an assistant set it on fire. Then a Mack truck came along and smashed the trunk to pieces. When the truck stopped, there I was inside the truck." In 1985 he returned to a traveling ministry, preaching at "little churches to little-size crowds."

Bambi recalls that as a girl she saw David preach in Toledo, Ohio. She never forgot the experience, although she later strayed far from her religion. "By the time I was twenty I was an alcoholic," she says, "and by the next year I was dealing drugs." For a while she was a go-go dancer in California. She remembers herself as a "materialistic hippie" who loved Cadillacs and designer jeans, who abandoned her given name (which she refuses to divulge) for Bambi Cherry, and who associated with "white-collar criminals." Yet she says she had her limits. "I never got involved in sexual things. It wasn't that my morals were so high— I just felt anybody who was going to pay for sex was either too old, too ugly, or too dangerous."

Bambi says that when she was thirty or so she was the owner of the Red Eye Head Shop in South Knoxville and was selling cocaine, heroin, and marijuana to street dealers on the side. Then one day, after attending a rock concert, she got down on her knees in the Red Eye bathroom and asked God to take over her life. "When I came up off my knees my outlook had changed," she says. "I'd found peace. Everything I've done since 1975 has been on the right side of the law."

She converted the head shop to a jewelry store and in 1985 moved to Sevierville, Tennessee, to sell vacation time-shares. While there she traced David to Miami, and in 1987 she called him up. "Hello, this is Bambi," she said. "Am I talking to Walt Disney's deer?" David remembers replying. "She told me her story. We got together, did a couple of crusades together, and then we got married." It was the fourth marriage for each of them.

In the early years of their marriage David and Bambi preached on the road, subsisting on offerings and living in motels. As Pentecostals, they believe that the Holy Ghost takes over worshippers during services and has them speak in tongues decipherable only by God. "We also believe that divine healings and miracles are for today," says David. He claims his ministry has healed AIDS and cancer patients and made the lame rise from their wheelchairs.

In June 1991 the McMillions drove to Chicago and set up their tent on Eighty-seventh Street. "There was a TV report on us, and we kept that tent full every night until October, when it got too cold," says David. The McMillions then rented a storefront on Halsted in Park Manor and opened the Higher Ground Christian Center, which attracted a small, racially mixed congregation. That Christmas David was accused of pulling a gun on a fellow minister, whom he describes as his church organist, and of later assaulting the man outside a courthouse. He and Bambi were arrested. The McMillions denied the charges, and court records show that they were eventually dismissed.

The couple now conducts a Friday-evening Bible reading and a Sunday service at a recreation center in Highland, Indiana. David, who's now fifty-four, leads the modest affairs, and Bambi, who's fifty-three, is his backup. "We are born not to be sick, but the devil convinces us that as humans we will get sick," he intoned on a Friday in June. "But we have dominion over sickness." Speaking in tongues, David will lay his hands on people who are sick. The regulars say it works. Valparaiso insurance agent Marty Glennon has been attending services for a year. He cites someone whose back pain was eased and a ninety-year-old woman with gangrene who was told she was going to die but is still living. "We ourselves were in debt because our eighth child had blood-pressure problems after birth," says Glennon. "David laid his hands over my checkbook, and the next week a man we knew came by and gave us five thousand dollars to fix our septic sewer."

David says that since 1971 he's been affiliated with the United Christian Church Ministerial Association, a seventeen-thousand-member organization based in Cleveland, Tennessee. According to Margie Minton, the association's general secretary, acceptance as a teacher-preacher in the organization requires only that two other ordained ministers vouch for the applicant. Association president H. Richard Hall says he doesn't know the McMillions personally and that the association is reevaluating David's affiliation because he's lived in so many places—Florida, Tennessee, Michigan, and now Illinois—and because his contact with the group has been only intermittent.

The first six months the McMillions were in Chicago they roomed in a motel. Then they moved into a garden apartment on Archer. "The apartment got too small because my son joined us from North Carolina," says David, "and we went looking for a new place." However, court records show that the McMillions' landlord, Maria Zehak, filed an eviction suit because they owed $2,475 in back rent. "Actually," says Bambi, "we paid the rent, but she paid the rent back because we were going to be foster parents to a black child, a cocaine baby." Zehak says she didn't do that; she says the McMillions kept giving excuses for being behind on the rent—David was sick and couldn't preach, money was late coming from an inheritance in Germany. "I just needed the rent, and they were always late." In November 1993 a judge evicted the McMillions, although the judicial order shows that no back rent had to be paid.

In June 1996, two years after she'd tried to deliver the first five-day notice, Speredakos hired Mark Wetterquist as her second lawyer. The McMillions, who'd been representing themselves, signed on with the fiery Connie Fernandez, whom they'd encountered by chance one day in the hallway outside of court. But Fernandez had once confronted Judge Rivers, suggesting that he'd had a conflict of interest when he ruled against her. "Your Honor, is that your judgment as a judge or as a landlord?" she'd asked. The judge had refused to hear any more of her cases, so Speredakos's case was transferred to Judge Sheldon Garber.

When the case came before Garber that July he expressed some sympathy for Speredakos, but he threw out the five-day notice she and her daughter had posted on the McMillions' door. Garber said they should have handed the papers to the McMillions in person, as is required by law.

"Good God—delivering a five-day notice isn't rocket science," says Michael Pensack of the Illinois Tenants Union, an aggressive champion of renters. "People with grade-school educations do this every day. How long does it take to get it right?" Later Fernandez would say, "The reason this kept going was that Georgia kept losing in court. Why should the McMillions do anything when they're winning?"

Speredakos tried again. On the morning of August 10, a Saturday, the McMillions were in bed asleep when they heard someone knocking on their door. Bambi looked out to see Nick Zattair, an off-duty Chicago police officer who worked as a process server for El-Ko Investigations. She refused to open the door, but Speredakos, who was standing behind Zattair, unlocked the door with her key. The safety chain still blocked Zattair's entrance, but according to Speredakos, he handed Bambi a new five-day notice. "She was yelling and screaming at Nick Zattair," says Speredakos. "'I'll call the police,' she said. 'I am the police,' he said."

Bambi would insist in court that she never got served the notice because she slammed the door shut on Zattair before he could hand it to her. She also says he was abusive and never adequately identified himself. (Zattair didn't return calls for this story.) The McMillions would later testify that when they went out they saw a piece of paper lying at the top of the stairs, and David would state that he thought it was a five-day notice. "But we didn't see a name on it, so we let it be," Bambi says. "When we returned, the piece of paper was gone."

Yet within days the McMillions hand-delivered a letter to Speredakos in Palos Park. "This letter is to respond to your request for rent to be paid received by us on or about August 10, 1996," they wrote, but went on to inform Speredakos that even more had gone wrong with their apartment. The refrigerator had broken down, forcing them to buy ice to cool their food, and they were incensed that Speredakos had taken steps to turn off their gas. They stated that they didn't owe her $15,750 in back rent, rather she owed them $5,261.30 in damages and fees. The letter wrapped up: "Please contact our attorney, Connie R. Fernandez, if you have any questions."

Connie Fernandez handles some divorce and criminal cases, but her specialty is helping tenants who have complaints about landlords. "Whoever has a question about landlord-tenant issues, they call me," she says. "My friends and clients think I'm a genius." And indeed, even her detractors admit that she's smart and knows landlord-tenant law.

"I'm one of the few women attorneys who are reputed to have balls," says the forty-year-old Fernandez. "Oh yeah, brass ones. I'm aggressive. I fear God, but no one else." Some judges haven't been impressed. "Every case I've ever been involved in with her runs longer than it should—and it's not due to her thoroughness," says Sheldon Garber. "She's not well organized. She's very argumentative. Every ruling requires a long discussion of the law."

A native of Fort Wayne, Indiana, Fernandez dropped out of high school to get married at age seventeen. She got a correspondence high school degree and later earned a law degree from Oregon's Willamette University. She did worker's comp law in southern California, then five years ago moved to Chicago with her husband and started her own practice. Now twice divorced and a grandmother, she works out of a loft in East Garfield Park that she rents with an option to buy; she renovates on weekends.

Early on Fernandez got referrals through the Illinois Tenants Union, and if she won a case she'd take a contingency fee. "In the beginning I tangled with landlord attorneys, and with that came a level of persecution," she says. "I got attacked all the time, personally and professionally." Indeed, she says, the Chicago Property Owners' Coalition, a now-defunct confederation of two hundred landlords, wrote to the eviction court alleging that she'd misused the city's Residential Landlord and Tenant Ordinance, a law passed in 1986 to protect tenants' rights.

Asked to describe some of her significant ITU cases, Fernandez mentions a building in Rogers Park where she helped eleven tenants who were unhappy with the condition of their building stage a rent strike. The landlord ultimately lost the building to the bank, and all but one of the renters ended up with judgments against them. The case has gone through four judges and is still technically alive.

Fernandez's handling of the case irritated Ken Ditkowsky, the landlord's attorney. "Connie Fernandez doesn't believe in the common courtesies that lawyers normally give each other," he says. "She fights every single motion you make, and she asks for mounds of information. You can't imagine how long it all takes. She attacked every judge we were before and every attorney, including me. It was a nightmare."

"Ken Ditkowsky just doesn't think I have rights as a litigant," Fernandez responds. "I fight his motions because they aren't well grounded in fact. I challenge judges—I don't attack them."

One day Fernandez tried to fax Ditkowsky eighty pages of violations she'd allegedly found in the building. "We're talking two thousand items, mostly little things like the stair railings being too low or the stair treads being a millimeter off," says Ditkowsky. The fax machine in his office broke down after twenty-five pages. In response he wrote Fernandez a letter that became part of the court record: "You are the first attorney that we have ever dealt with who has ever resorted to the tactic of sending page after page of unintelligible gibberish to a brother attorney's office with what appears to be the express purpose of overwhelming the fax machine."

Around the same time Ditkowsky wrote another letter, also in the court records, accusing Fernandez of using "voluminous pleadings and outrageous demands for discovery" to win against "'little people' who have invested their hard-earned money in a building to seek and obtain a small return on their investment. Because of their small capitalization and weak financial condition they are prime targets for the nefarious conduct that is attributed to you."

"I don't target small landlords," replies Fernandez. "Big landlord, small landlord—I treat everybody the same." Fernandez's relationship with the ITU lasted only a year, says Pensack, in part because he believed her behavior had deeply offended a judge handling the Rogers Park case. "You can't win by being confrontational with a judge," Pensack says. "He's got the power." Fernandez also appealed a circuit court judge's ruling that severely limited judgments against landlords who fail to pay interest on security deposits. "We told her not to appeal, that if she lost it would set a precedent," says Pensack. "But she said, 'I'm going to win.'" (Fernandez says Pensack never cautioned her against appealing.) In April 1996 the Illinois Appellate Court ruled for the landlord, saying that as a penalty a wronged tenant can collect only double the security deposit for one year, no matter how long the tenant has been in the apartment (tenants had been able to collect double for every year they were in an apartment). Fernandez's only regret is that her client backed off, preventing her from taking the case to the Illinois Supreme Court.

Then last August the state Attorney Registration and Disciplinary Commission filed a twenty-one-count complaint against Fernandez, charging her with, among other things, failing to follow client instructions and "conduct involving dishonesty, fraud, deceit, or misrepresentation."

One of the cases the ARDC complaint detailed involved roommates Kurt Engleman and Matt Cravets, two pharmaceutical-company statisticians who went to Fernandez to recover their security deposit from the Northbrook landlord in 1995. The following July everyone agreed to a settlement, and nine months later Fernandez received a check for her fee and Engleman's and Cravets's deposits of $650 apiece, all of which she deposited in a client trust account. The complaint alleges that neither man ever received his cut. "She assured us it would be a short turnaround in receiving our share," says Engleman, who now works in Maryland, "but we never heard a word. We called after two and a half months, and she wouldn't take our phone calls."

The ARDC complaint has since been amended and now includes a total of thirty-one counts. ARDC chief counsel James Grogan says that the number of accusations is unusually high. If a three-person panel of hearing officers finds them credible, Fernandez could face a number of penalties, including disbarment. "She gives us other advocates a bad name," says Richard Wheelock, housing supervisory attorney for the Legal Assistance Foundation of Chicago.

Contesting ARDC charges isn't easy, but Fernandez vows to fight. She does say, "I haven't taken care of business properly. A lot of people owed me a lot of money." She adds that she'd also had a couple of miscarriages and had been depressed and had had her laptop computer stolen out of her car. She insists she'll pay her clients once the people who owe her money reimburse her. But then she says, "The whole judicial system is going to be put on trial." She's already filed a list of sixty potential witnesses with the ARDC—attorneys, judges, former clients, opposing parties (including Speredakos), plus "God, Heaven," and "Jesus Christ, c/o God in Heaven."

Fernandez's relationship with God and his son has been strengthened by her association with the McMillions—she functions as both their attorney and their devoted acolyte. "I was raised as an evangelical, a Methodist, and a Mennonite, and then I had a falling out with the church and became an agnostic," she says. "But I got a message that it was time to return." In February 1997 Fernandez started accompanying the McMillions to services. "Now I follow God's direction and that of Jesus Christ," she says. (Last October, she says, God directed her to fast on hot tea and water and lemon juice, and she lost forty pounds in forty days.) Bambi says, "You know, Connie is very smart, and we have sat her down and said, 'You know the law, but we know the Bible.' She respects our knowledge in religion. We have become like spiritual parents to her." The three of them regularly dine out together, and Fernandez says she's given money to the McMillions' ministry.

"A lot of people put Connie down and portray her as a nut," says attorney Dan Starr, who often represents tenants and is a grudging fan of Fernandez. "She pisses off lots of judges and doesn't know when to settle. But she's a zealous attorney who isn't afraid to litigate."

Some forty-three thousand eviction cases, including public-housing cases, were filed in Cook County in 1997. Judging by what happened in previous years, most of them ended very quickly and in the landlord's favor. A 1996 study by the Lawyers' Committee for Better Housing found that landlords are victorious over mostly poor, minority tenants—few of whom have a lawyer—in 95 percent of eviction cases heard at the Daley Center. "Tenants may show up and try to assert their rights—they did pay rent or their apartment was maintained in a substandard fashion—but judges tend to dismiss tenants because by and large they aren't represented by counsel," says Julie Ansell, executive director of LCBH. The five eviction judges who hear matters at the Daley Center take three minutes to dispose of the average case, the LCBH study reports—less time, notes Ansell, than traffic-court cases take.

Occasionally a case will go further, but the dispute is still resolved relatively quickly, with negotiations between the two sides taking place in the jury room or out in the hallway. "You'll take a haircut on the rent, and you'll give the tenant a certain amount of time to vacate," says Ron Roman, Speredakos's current lawyer. "Everybody feels a little shafted, but the numbers work out and it's over."

Speredakos v. McMillion proved far more complicated. When the McMillions didn't pay any rent after the five-day notice was delivered on August 10, 1996, Mark Wetterquist filed an eviction suit against them and on the second try got a court summons delivered. But that December Wetterquist signed off as Speredakos's lawyer. "The judge [Raymond Funderburk, who'd been assigned the case in October] doesn't like me," Wetterquist told her. "With me you're going to lose."

Speredakos then hired another lawyer, Robert Gordon, and in January 1997 everyone from both sides gathered in the conference room off the courtroom to consider a settlement. Fernandez says she made an offer—the McMillions would owe no rent but would vacate the apartment within ninety days, and Speredakos would pay Fernandez's $2,500 fee. Bambi would later testify that Speredakos was so irritated that she told her own father, "Shut up, Pa," slapped him on the arm, and screamed at Fernandez. They never came close to a settlement.

Burdened by debt after the New Nevada folded, Speredakos had recently filed for personal bankruptcy, and the bankruptcy trustee, Andrew Maxwell, now fired Gordon. "I would have settled this thing," says Gordon, "but [Maxwell] wanted his own guy in there." His guy was forty-five-year-old Ron Roman—Speredakos's fourth lawyer. A veteran in tenant-landlord cases, Roman doesn't care to name his clients, although he does say that he once represented two of Chicago's most notorious landlords, Lou Wolf and Ken Goldberg.

The next round of negotiations occurred that May, when Fernandez put a new offer on the table. According to Fernandez, Speredakos would get no rent and would pay the McMillions five thousand dollars for aggravating their medical problems. "Plus Bambi had fallen down the stairs because the building didn't have handrails," Fernandez says. In addition, the McMillions would have at least three months to get out, and Fernandez would be paid $9,500. Roman thought it made sense to accept the offer, if only to get rid of Fernandez. But Maxwell didn't like the agreement. "First of all, Mrs. Speredakos didn't want to accept the deal," he explains. "It was expensive, and it left the McMillions in the property. What if they decided not to move? We'd have been back where we started."

The case went back before Judge Funderburk. Now in his midfifties, Funderburk had driven a CTA bus to get through junior college. He graduated from the University of Illinois at Chicago at thirty, then went on to earn his law degree at the university's law school in Champaign. He was a staff attorney for the Cook County Legal Assistance Foundation, becoming an expert in eviction cases through defending tenants. For a time he managed the Harvey office of the foundation, then sat on its board after leaving to join Earl Neal and Associates. "He was always very professional and conscientious," says Ellen Johnson, executive director of the foundation.

Appointed to the circuit court in 1993, Funderburk was elected to a six-year term the next year with sound ratings from the Chicago Bar Association and the Chicago Council of Lawyers. He served in traffic and domestic violence court before moving to eviction court. He maintains a somber and proper air, refers to himself constantly as "the court," and seldom gets into discussions with lawyers, emerging from his chambers only when a session is about to start. "Funderburk is a straitlaced, even puritanical person with high morals," says Pensack, "though he's not as protenant as we thought he'd be."

At the time of the McMillions' trial Funderburk was presiding in room 1406 of the Daley Center. He referred tenants without lawyers to legal-clinic attorneys, although few took the option. He often framed his decisions in legal language that tenants couldn't comprehend. "Judgment for plaintiff," he would say. "Order for possession. Writ of execution stayed for fourteen days. Do you understand this?" If the tenant said no, the judge tended to repeat what he said in the same words. He often told tenants to take their hands out of their pockets when they approached the bench and shushed them whenever they addressed him directly. Landlords and their lawyers tolerated his cold demeanor, but less-sophisticated tenants often seemed undone by it.

In April a woman, who was six months behind in her rent after being laid off, was summoned before Funderburk. The woman had just been hired by a cable television firm, although she wouldn't start for several weeks. "I was hoping I could come before you and make a payment arrangement," she told Funderburk. He replied sharply, "This court doesn't get involved in settlement arrangements. I have determined that you have not raised a meritorious defense."

The woman had no idea what a "meritorious defense" might be. "I do have a daughter, sir," she said. Funderburk looked down at her from the bench. "I'm certainly happy to hear that you have a daughter, but that is not a meritorious defense." He gave her twenty-one days—longer than usual—to get out. "There's a judgment against you, ma'am. Have a seat, ma'am, and wait for a copy of the order. Good luck to you, ma'am." When she stepped into the hallway she was in tears.

"He's forgotten that all people don't have his verbal and legal skills," said one attorney who frequently appeared before Funderburk. "He's forgotten where he came from." But tenant lawyer Dan Starr said, "He is sensitive to issues from the tenants' side. I tell my clients when they go before Funderburk that it will seem like he doesn't like you. 'Grin and bear it,' I say, 'and treat the judge with respect. Because when the landlord's side gets up, he'll treat them worse.'"

Last July Funderburk ordered the McMillions to place twenty thousand dollars in an escrow account pending disposition of the case. They said they couldn't. "We didn't have twenty thousand dollars, to be honest with you," says David McMillion. In 1996 he and Bambi had filed a pauper's petition so that they could have their court costs waived; it stated that they were unemployed, had a yearly income of $5,650 from SSI, and had personal property valued at less than $1,000. The McMillions then demanded a jury trial, but Funderburk, as one of the sanctions for failing to put the money in escrow, denied the request, saying he would hear the matter himself.

That summer Fernandez was irritated with Funderburk. When he demanded the escrow money, she recalls, "I was so outraged that I could have reached up and hit that judge." According to a court transcript, she told Funderburk on July 22, "I do not trust you." Funderburk replied, "Counsel, I suggest that you be very careful in the selection of your words because you may well be exhibiting conduct which this court finds extremely offensive."

Fernandez then claimed that the judge's clerk—whom she said was friendly to Speredakos—had refused to process some of Fernandez's paperwork and had instead brought the judge some grapes.

They weren't grapes but plums, Funderburk fired back. "As far as this clerk—the clerk of this court providing and giving this court plums—yes, the clerk provided this court with plums. And this court graciously accepted those plums and ate them with all the succulent plums that were given to this court, counsel, and was quite filled after eating same." He advised Fernandez to raise her objections formally if she wanted to.

On October 20 Funderburk held Fernandez in contempt of court when she went down the hall to take care of some business in another courtroom. "He was very mad," says Fernandez, "but when I got back he vacated his order."

The Residential Landlord and Tenant Ordinance is a powerful tool in cases against landlords, because it enables tenants to withhold rent or terminate a lease if the condition of their apartment becomes intolerable. But the ordinance exempts buildings with fewer than six units if the owner lives in the building. Fernandez argued in court that the ordinance applied because Speredakos, the landlord of record, didn't live in the building. Roman insisted that the law didn't apply because the Bisbikises, who were partners in the land trust and therefore part owners—had lived upstairs when the McMillions moved in. Fernandez countered that the Bisbikises had moved out in October 1995, before the off-duty cop delivered the last five-day notice.

But Fernandez also had other arguments, ones commonly heard in eviction court. *Spring v. Little,* decided by the Illinois Supreme Court in 1972, lays out a doctrine called the "implied warranty of habitability"—which means that a lease automatically obliges a landlord to keep up an apartment; if the landlord doesn't, a tenant can claim that the warranty has been broken and there's no return obligation to pay rent. The state Rental Property Utility Service Act also states that it's unlawful for a landlord to pass on utility fees for common areas of a building unless a renter knows about the arrangement in advance. The city building code also bars landlords from operating buildings without adequate heat or hot water, or without smoke detectors, peepholes, or dead bolt locks.

Roman conceded outside the courtroom during the trial that the McMillions could conceivably have justified withholding some rent from Speredakos because of problems in the building, but he quickly added that they hadn't paid a dime since December 1993, and they had never deposited any of the rent in an escrow account. "The law doesn't give you the ability to occupy somebody else's property without limitation of term and without any payment of rent," he said. "Even if a place is bad, that doesn't mean you can stay there forever for free. I suppose a place could be so bad it has no value, but if it has some value—any value—then you owe rent. The law doesn't permit a life estate on 6128 South Kilpatrick. And if the place is so bad, what are they still doing there? They have, with the exception of one month, basically not paid rent for four and one-half years. To me it's a free lunch."

On December 12, 1997, the McMillions' trial before Judge Funderburk began. It had been scheduled to last three days, sandwiched between other cases—all the time Ron Roman figured it would take.

Roman summoned Nick Zattair, the off-duty cop who'd delivered the five-day notice, Speredakos, the McMillions, and the court reporter who'd taken depositions in Roman's office the prior October. That took only a day or two.

But then Fernandez began her cross-examination. She brought Zattair back for a whole day on the stand. "That's something we'd never experienced," says Francis McCarthy, co-owner of El-Ko Investigations, which employs Zattair. Fernandez also questioned the court reporter intensively. Speredakos had to answer questions for twelve and a half days. When Fernandez presented the defendants' case, she kept Speredakos in the witness box for another fifteen days.

It was already April when Speredakos testified that the McMillions had never complained to her or to her father about the condition of the building. The only gripe she knew of was in the letter the couple had hand-delivered to her on August 15, 1996, which she said she'd passed on to her first lawyer, Barry Barnett. "I was never aware of anything," she said. "They never complained to me." But then she admitted that she'd seen two notes left for her father in the basement; one stated that the washing machine was broken, and the second, dated November 16, 1995, scolded him for tampering with the boiler pump. Speredakos testified that she'd given both notes to Barnett.

Fernandez attacked Speredakos for asserting that the McMillions had used a phone jack in the basement to make personal calls on her father's line, including one that lasted more than four hours. "But when you previously testified that there were calls longer than three hours, you were lying, weren't you, Mrs. Speredakos?" Fernandez asked. Speredakos responded that she would need a calculator to figure out the hours.

Most of the questioning concerned minutiae. On the afternoon of May 8, for instance, Fernandez explored the condition of the back door at Kilpatrick, which Speredakos called a screen door.

"There is no screen door on the premises, is there, Mrs. Speredakos?" Fernandez asked.

"It's a screen door, whether it has glass on it or not," replied Speredakos. "It has glass on it."

"Mrs. Speredakos, you have previously testified that the door was fiberglass," said Fernandez. "You consider glass to be fiberglass?"

"It's under the same family."

But there's no screen, Fernandez pointed out.

"I call it a screen door," said Speredakos.

"That's really a storm door, isn't it, Mrs. Speredakos?"

"You can call it a storm door."

Speredakos testified that the lower panel of the door was cracked but that she'd repaired it after a city building inspector told her to. She also said that somehow it had broken again.

"So, now do you consider the exterior door on the building to be in good working condition, Mrs. Speredakos?" Fernandez said.

"Yes."

"Did you take into account the building code, Mrs. Speredakos?"

"Yes."

"What section of the code?"

"If it opens and closes, that's good working condition," replied Speredakos. "If it's missing glass or a nail, it's still in good working condition."

"So, Mrs. Speredakos," said Fernandez, "it's your testimony that the door is in good working condition and complies with the building code?"

"Yes."

"Specifically, Mrs. Speredakos, with respect to the door, isn't there a requirement in the building code that every window has to be free of open cracks and holes?"

"I don't know," said Speredakos. "What I consider good working condition, like I said, is when a door opens and closes. If a crack is there, I don't consider that to be bad working condition. As far as the code you just mentioned, the building inspector was there, and he said to call the police. I have placed a police report, and I'm waiting for the insurance company to come and estimate."

Speredakos's testimony took even longer because she frequently told Fernandez she didn't understand even the simplest question. "Will you rephrase and reask the question?" Funderburk, who took meticulous notes throughout the trial, would say. Fernandez would make another stab, although one morning she got so frustrated that she said, "Mrs. Speredakos, do you need a Greek interpreter?" Speredakos just looked at her coldly.

Relations between Fernandez and Roman also grew strained as the trial progressed. On April 29 she accused him of prompting Speredakos's responses with his body language when he stood up. "She doesn't answer a question unless she looks at her attorney," Fernandez told the judge. "I'm standing next to the witness, and I can see her every movement." Roman then told the judge, "Your Honor, it's easier on my back if I can stand." The judge allowed Roman to stand, but not before Fernandez advised Funderburk to watch him carefully.

Whenever it was Roman's turn to examine a witness, Fernandez would raise innumerable objections. Once, just before the lunch break, Roman attempted to question Speredakos about conversations she'd had with her parents about the McMillions. Fernandez objected fifteen times in fifteen minutes—"That's hearsay, Your Honor," "That calls for speculation." Finally Roman sullenly slumped into his seat, and Funderburk adjourned the session. When Fernandez again had the floor Roman began interrupting her with objections.

In court on May 15 Roman moved to quash a subpoena Fernandez had filed asking Mark Wetterquist, Speredakos's second attorney, to testify, and Fernandez asked the judge to disqualify Roman because he was acting in opposition to his client's interests. "I have to listen to this crap coming out of her mouth," said Roman, springing from his seat. Funderburk said, "Crap? I'm not sure of the definition of the term, but I certainly think it's inappropriate to misuse the term."

Roman is ordinarily carefully spoken, but he said outside court, "I just want to grab Connie by the throat and punch her." Fernandez later countered, "I'm very angry with Ron Roman because he lies." She claimed that Roman had said he hadn't received documents that he had, that he'd prompted Speredakos on the stand then denied it, and that he'd once said he'd arrived at court at ten thirty when he'd shown up at ten forty-five.

All spring the McMillions remained in the Kilpatrick apartment without paying rent. (The electric bill wasn't paid either, and in May Commonwealth Edison would turn off the electricity.) In April the place seemed comfortable enough. The front room contained sofas, a couple of televisions, pictures of cupids and angels. Drapes covered the large picture window overlooking the street, and a frieze of fake pink roses ran across the top. "If she [Speredakos] wasn't such an appalling woman we wouldn't still be here," Bambi insisted. Then she conducted a tour of the apartment, pointing out the peeling paint, the lack of a seal around the oven, the tap that dribbled water, the lights that were out in a hallway.

On court days David tended to stay home—the proceedings got him too angry, he said. Bambi always showed up and took careful notes on a pink legal pad. Speredakos also showed up daily and would knit during every break. The two women rarely spoke. Bambi said, "I feel sorry for her because she's in a lot of trouble with God. When someone goes after somebody else with lies and maliciousness, God takes care of them."

Meanwhile Roman was growing increasingly worried about his wife, who was having a difficult first pregnancy. Bambi had begun praying for the baby at an October deposition session in Roman's office. "Ron said his wife was doing bad that day, and there was a chance the baby might not make it," recalls Bambi. "David and I and Connie all prayed for that baby." In late May the baby was in danger again, and a distraught Roman fled the courtroom one day to be with his wife. Bambi wasn't sure it was proper, but she chased after him, stopped him in the hallway, and offered to pray for the baby. She says he took the offer kindly.

But most of the time ill feeling prevailed. After the session on Good Friday ended, both sides trooped from Funderburk's courtroom to the seventh floor to get copies of an order made. On the way down Bambi tore into Roman: "I hate you for what you are doing, but we're going to win." Speredakos says that Roman didn't respond, but once they arrived at the copy machine she couldn't restrain herself. "Pay me before you make any other documents," she said. Bambi threw a quarter Roman's way. "Well, Miss Christian," said Speredakos. Bambi shot back, "Well, Miss Orthodox."

Speredakos is Greek Orthodox. Bambi remembers that Speredakos then said, "What kind of God do you serve?" Bambi uncorked a lecture about the God of the Old Testament. She says Speredakos said something in Greek that Bambi figured was a curse. "I reverse that curse that you tried to send," she told Speredakos, "and I decree it work one hundred times worse than you decreed on me."

Bambi McMillion sat down to testify on May 11. She said that the Kilpatrick apartment was run-down and that Speredakos had billed her and David for common utility costs, deprived them of the use of the garage and the basement, tried to shut off their electricity and gas, and failed to fix a broken washing machine. She said Speredakos had told her, "This is Chicago. Landlords do it all the time. Nobody is going to believe you. You can go to court and do anything you want, and nothing is going to happen." Bambi also said she'd been horrified that Speredakos had once asked about hiring her as a cashier at the New Nevada and suggested that she not record some sales so the restaurant could avoid paying taxes on them. Speredakos later denied saying anything of the sort.

When Bambi spoke from the stand, her voice slowed to a snail's pace and she included every detail. On May 15, for instance, she described how she'd sent a letter to Speredakos: "I folded the letter in thirds. I placed it in a business envelope. On the business-size envelope I placed Mrs. Speredakos's address . . . and then I moistened the inside flap of the envelope and sealed the envelope. Then I placed one or more stamps on the envelope. Then I placed the envelope in a mailbox, or where they pick up the mail." Days later Fernandez had Bambi drone on for hours describing some of the 127 photographs the lawyer had taken of 6128 South Kilpatrick; the high point was the description of how a string through a wall-mounted toothbrush holder held open the stopper in the McMillions' bathroom sink.

Fernandez seemed to know nearly all of the facts surrounding the case; to fill in lapses she consulted papers stuffed in the worn briefcase she toted to court each day. During questioning she referred to scores of exhibits.

Funderburk's irritation with Fernandez often showed. On May 13, in the middle of questioning Bambi, she accused Roman of ignoring a document she'd left for him in court and asked the judge to rule against him. The judge refused, but Fernandez repeated her demand. "Counsel, if you continue to do that, I'm going to end your direct examination," Funderburk said. Fernandez responded, "Your Honor, I'd like to be heard." Funderburk's voice rose sharply. "We're not going to take any more time with innuendos." But Fernandez pressed on, complaining about "Mr. Roman's false statements." The judge looked toward his bailiff. "Mr. Sheriff, stand by. If I hold counsel in contempt of court, take her into custody." Fernandez eyed the judge and said, "Then maybe I'll be heard." Funderburk said nothing, and Fernandez quickly went back to questioning Bambi.

On May 28 Funderburk happened to call her "Mrs." Fernandez, to which she responded, "Your Honor, it's not Mrs. Fernandez. It's Ms. Fernandez. I'm not married." Funderburk could barely control his disdain. "The court stands corrected. It's Ms. Fernandez."

"I'd like not to scream at him," Fernandez later said, "but he has an obligation to listen to what I have to say. When he's rude to me—as he sometimes is—he gets a response that's equal to the rudeness he's shown me."

"With any other judge, her ass would be in the lockup," Roman later said in his office. "For whatever reason, he lets her get away with it." Michael Pensack thought Funderburk was simply protecting himself. "He's bending over backward to let her present her case because she'll take the case on appeal to a higher court, and he doesn't want to be overturned." But an attorney familiar with the case said, "Funderburk could limit her in terms of scope and time. He could say, 'You have fifteen minutes—wrap it up.' The judge is not malicious—he's trying to be fair. But in the process he's not being realistic. With any other judge, this would have been over in an hour or two. What could this be costing the taxpayers?"

By mid-June Speredakos had been in court long enough to knit five afghans— off and on for forty days, two hundred hours or more. Court staff are expensive. Funderburk's annual salary is $112,491. A court clerk makes up to $34,000 a year, as does a bailiff (or sheriff's deputy, the formal title); a court reporter draws up to $50,000. And then there are the costs of heating and cooling and cleaning and record keeping.

The judge had taken limited steps to curtail the trial. In May he requested and was assigned a spare courtroom so that he could hear the Speredakos case all day long for a week. He also ruled that Fernandez couldn't make the Rental Property Utility Service Act part of her defense.

Funderburk refuses to comment on the Speredakos case or his approach to judging. But on May 5, when Speredakos chided Fernandez for repeatedly asking her the same question, "wasting my time and money and the taxpayers'," he interrupted to say, "As far as safeguarding the taxpayers' interest, the court is charged with that responsibility and will take that seriously."

On April 28 Roman had begged Funderburk to curtail the trial. "It's incumbent on the court to control the cadence to these proceedings," he said. "This is turning into a filibuster." June 3 marked the thirty-ninth day of the trial, and

Roman's baby was due two days later. When Funderburk moved to set aside more days for testimony, Roman said, "I do question the unlimited amount of days. This is set for an open-ended trial. This will continue, continue, continue. I plead with this court to put a time limit on this case. It is done every day, and in cases more complicated than the one involving 6128 South Kilpatrick."

"I'm very reluctant to do that," replied Funderburk, although he did say he would strike testimony on "irrelevant matters" or items that had already been explored. The legislature, he noted, intended Illinois trials to be conducted "expeditiously." But he added, "The defense is entitled to present its case in chief. The matter will not go into the millennium, but I'm not sure when it will end." (Earlier Fernandez had insisted that her clients had the right to have their case presented in full, no matter how long it took.)

A few days later Sheldon Garber, the supervising judge in eviction court, said, "I'm incredulous that this could drag on for as long as it has," adding that Fernandez's tactics were partly to blame. But, he pointed out, he had no right to intervene. "We have the right to get into the administration of court calls, but a judge's own courtroom is his sovereignty." Asked whether Funderburk should move the proceedings along faster, Garber said, "I'd rather not comment. But it's part of the function of a judge to expedite the disposition of cases." Asked if this trial had become terribly wasteful, he replied, "Correct."

On June 16 Funderburk at last put his foot down. Garber had once again arranged to give him an empty courtroom where he could hear the case all day, but that morning Fernandez said that Bambi was sick and couldn't testify. Get me another witness, Funderburk told her, then adjourned the session until 2 P.M.

With no regular witness to put on, Fernandez herself prepared to take the stand to describe the 127 photos she'd taken of 6128 South Kilpatrick. But Funderburk said it would violate professional ethics for her to appear as both a witness and a lawyer in a contested case, and he cautioned her several times that if she proceeded he would toss her out as the McMillions' attorney. She sat down in the witness box, and he abruptly disqualified her. She then started describing the photos from the witness box, and Funderburk told her to step down. "Then the judge gave me some minutes to make some points, and I got loud and nasty," says Fernandez, who did step down.

The judge turned to Roman and asked, any rebuttal? When Roman put Speredakos back on, Fernandez raised objection after objection. Funderburk admonished her to stop, and when she didn't he directed her to leave the courtroom. Fernandez yelled at Funderburk, and the judge instructed the bailiff to escort her out. "Let's go, Connie," said the bailiff. But Fernandez insisted she had a right to be in a public place. Soon a half-dozen bailiffs had handcuffed her and were hauling her kicking and screaming into the hallway. Her muffled cries could be heard as Roman gave a short summation and rested his case.

Fernandez was charged with breaching the peace, a minor city infraction. Booked at police headquarters at Eleventh and State, she was released on her own recognizance. She was back in court, although only as a spectator, on June 23 as Funderburk got set to issue his final ruling. The McMillions were absent—car trouble, they later explained—but Speredakos sat at the plaintiff's table, and Roman stood in front of the bench. Funderburk spoke in measured tones.

He said the last five-day notice had been delivered properly. He summarized the McMillions' litany of complaints, noting that they'd failed to provide evidence for some of them—they hadn't, for example, brought in their utility bills to prove they'd paid for power in the common areas. He said they'd also failed to present outside expert witnesses to bolster their claims, and he threw out the goofy ramblings of a follower of the McMillions who'd testified about the condition of the apartment because he'd discussed his testimony with the McMillions in advance.

Funderburk said the McMillions had to vacate the unit on Kilpatrick, and David, whose name was on the lease, owed the back rent—less 40 percent because of the condition of the apartment. He awarded the McMillions a $20 credit for helping to fix the washing machine in 1995, then slapped them with a $16,990 judgment, plus court costs. "Counsel," he told Roman, "if there's nothing further, prepare the order for possession."

So ended the forty-two-day trial and the four-and-a-half-year standoff.

"I feel real bad," said Speredakos afterward. "What's right is right—I should have gotten full rent. The judge was wrong. It's an injustice what he did." The McMillions still claimed they were destitute, and she doubted she'd see a penny of the settlement (she hasn't yet). Roman could go after the McMillions in court, but, he says, "You can't bleed blood from a turnip. The bottom line for Georgia? No money, honey."

Speredakos also worried about what the trial had cost her. Roman's in-court fee was more than twenty thousand dollars—and she'd already paid five thousand dollars to her prior attorneys. Moreover, she'd lost four and a half years of rent. And she was still facing another court battle—the counterclaim the McMillions had filed in 1996, asserting that Speredakos owed them as much as one hundred thousand dollars in damages, attorney fees, and court costs. "This isn't going to come cheap," Speredakos said.

Andrew Maxwell, the bankruptcy trustee, has sold off a piece of property Speredakos owned in suburban Lemont for two hundred thousand dollars, but given all she already owes, her financial state remains precarious. "With Roman's fees yet to come in, we might have to sell something else," says Maxwell. Dominating Speredakos's current portfolio are her $200,000 house, where she lives with three of her grown children, and the building on Kilpatrick, last assessed at $124,000. Speredakos, who contends the trial prevented her from finding work, could end up broke or nearly broke.

The McMillions showed up after Funderburk had left. Bambi scoffed at his ruling, saying, "It's just a piece of paper." David sounded a little smug. "We got our point across that this town won't put up with dishonest landlords," he said. Both McMillions said they had no idea where they'd go, although they were moving out. They apparently broke a pane of glass in the front door when they carried out a couch, and Bambi apologized to Roman. "Apologize to your client for me," she told him, then congratulated him on the birth of his son. The couple is now living with a friend in Indiana.

Meanwhile the case had become the talk of the courthouse. "Oh, the megatrial," said Dan Starr when asked if he knew about it. Tenants' rights groups worried about its implications. "This could become a poster case for how tenant demands are unrealistic in that they drive good landlords out of business," said Julie Ansell of the Lawyers' Committee for Better Housing.

Roman now says, "The amount that was spent here was astronomical—and for what?"

Fernandez, who will be on trial in October for breaching the peace, still insists the McMillions were justified in their actions. "Georgia Speredakos did things wrong, and rather than own up to them, she says, 'I did nothing wrong.' I'll fight to the death." Fernandez has already appealed the case to the Illinois Appellate Court—she's also appealing Funderburk's move to disqualify her as the McMillions' lawyer. "This whole thing is going to come back for a retrial because the judge made so many errors," she insists. She says she's always figured that her skills and God will ensure that she and the McMillions will ultimately be paid what they're owed. "Judge Funderburk wants to be in control, but God is ultimately in control," she says. "No judge is bigger than God."

STILL
DOING TIME

Busted for abusing a teenage girl, Larry will be considered a sexual predator for life.

Larry was in big trouble, and he knew it. For six months he'd been having sex with Laura, the sixteen-year-old daughter of his fiancée, with whom he was living in a town house in the western suburbs. It was mid-December 2000, twelve days before he and Joan were to be married. Laura was talking to Joan in her bedroom, and as he stood in the upstairs hallway he could hear his name being hurled back and forth. Uh-oh, he thought, and fled to the garage in a haze of fear and self-loathing.

There Larry, a short, compact forty-eight-year-old former army sergeant with a military bearing, smoked a cigarette while a heavy snow fell outside. Should I run out the door and never come back? he wondered. Should I stay in the garage? Should I throw myself on a knife?

Half an hour later Joan walked in, disbelief in her eyes. "Is it true?" she asked.

"Yes," he said.

"How could you?"

"I don't know. It's something I never wanted to happen. I wanted to stop, but I couldn't. I was scared what you'd do if I told you."

He asked if he could spend the night downstairs, pointing out that it was snowing hard, but she ordered him to leave immediately. He threw some belongings in a suitcase and drove to a motel. He says he was contemplating suicide.

Wesley Bedrosian

In the months that followed, Larry (whose name has been changed, along with those of other people identified only by a first name) confessed to his crime, spent five months in jail, then entered a strict probation program that includes counseling. The nature of his crime requires him to register his address with the local authorities for the rest of his life. A current photograph, his address, height, and weight are now posted in the sex-offender section of the state police Web site. They're also hanging on the wall of his local police station.

Larry knows that he's an object of scorn, a modern-day leper. He says he's pretty much resigned to that, and he can see that some positive things have come from his conviction. "This hasn't been easy, but now I'm more able to deal with the bad thoughts that come over me," he says. "And in terms of learning how to live honestly with myself and how to treat other human beings, this has been good for me."

But Larry has also had trouble finding a place to live, and although he had a good job for a while, he's now unemployed and is having a hard time finding work. He's particularly worried about his long-term job prospects. He says he's done everything society has asked him to do and hasn't slipped up since his arrest. He wishes that society would someday let him lose the stigma of his crime.

Now Illinois attorney general Lisa Madigan is pushing a bill that wouldn't affect him but could punish future sex offenders like him even more harshly than current laws do and could allow less flexibility in how the terms of an individual's sentence and supervision after his release are determined. "You should judge people on a case-by-case basis," he says. "At some point you have to talk about rehabilitation and giving us a chance. Is it right that I wear a scarlet letter forever?"

The day after Joan kicked him out Larry went back to the town house to apologize, but she threw him out again. And she reported him to the Department of Children and Family Services, which began an investigation.

For over two years Larry had been doing training and process analysis for a shipping-supply firm, where Joan also worked in a higher-level position. Just before Christmas two of his supervisors called and gave him the option of resigning or being fired. "I asked if I could stay until formal charges were brought," he says. "And they said, 'No, we don't think that's a good idea.'"

Larry told his family. "I was in total shock," says his sister Greta, who's a nurse. "I didn't think Larry had any inclinations this way. Can you imagine? Larry and Joan were supposed to be getting married. Lives were being destroyed here. We tried to support him, but it was depressing. When I first saw his face, it was like the aging you see in those pictures of the president at the beginning of his term and then four years later."

Larry moved in with his father, a retired auto-parts store manager who lived near O'Hare. Joan demanded that he tell his two daughters from a previous marriage what he'd done or she would. "Something happened," he says he mumbled over the phone to his older daughter, then in her early twenties. "I did something wrong." He didn't say much more to his younger daughter, but he says she knows what he did and can't quite forgive him.

On January 31, 2001, Larry was indicted by a DuPage County grand jury on four counts of aggravated criminal sexual abuse. He was arrested—he says it was his first arrest since being taken in for curfew violations as a teen—and his father posted the ten-thousand-dollar bail. The story never made the papers or the TV news, and he managed to get J. Michael Fitzsimmons, a former DuPage County state's attorney, to defend him.

Fitzsimmons told Larry to stay away from Joan, but he talked to her regularly, which is how he learned that Laura was in counseling. On his own, he says, he consulted the yellow pages and called a twelve-step program for people with sex addictions. "At the first meeting I was scared shitless," he says. "I thought, do I really belong here?" But within weeks he was attending regularly and soon had a sponsor to lean on for support.

According to Larry, Fitzsimmons told him he'd made a deal with the prosecutor, Mike Reidy, that would keep him out of jail if he agreed to pay for Laura's treatment and undergo treatment himself. He says Fitzsimmons later told him that Reidy's superior had vetoed the plea bargain. Fitzsimmons has since died, but Reidy says neither he nor anyone else in his office ever considered such a deal.

Larry pleaded guilty. He could have gotten three to seven years in prison under state sentencing guidelines. But he had no other convictions, and in early May the judge gave him four years' probation, which included five months in the DuPage County jail, and ordered him to cover Laura's counseling bills. Because his victim was a minor, he was now labeled a "sexual predator."

A couple of weeks later, on the Saturday before Larry was to go to jail, Greta hosted a family dinner. Even Joan was there. "Everybody was trying to be festive, to boost Larry's spirits before he went off," says Greta. "But it was sad."

Larry worried that once in the jail, which adjoins the county courthouse in Wheaton, he'd be the object of "beatings and gang rapes," but he quickly saw that neither was likely. He was housed in a block of eighteen cells on two levels with guys a generation younger, including a man convicted of a double murder. The only people he told what he was in for were two older men also doing time for sex convictions, one of them a communications executive from suburban Denver. "He and I said that we would be there for each other," says Larry, "to keep each other in check and to move forward."

In jail he read a lot, mostly self-help books and a series of romance novels set in medieval Scotland. He enrolled in classes offered by Justice Understanding Service and Teaching, which provides education and social services to inmates. He took a course on emotional healing and an acting class taught by Richard Oberbruner, who'd studied at The Second City.

Oberbruner remembers thinking, "This is an odd candidate for improv." Larry is extremely talkative, but he's also soft-spoken and converses with care and deliberation. One day the class did a skit in which he played a white rider in the backseat of a cab stuck on a ghetto street. Suddenly two young black men approached. "Larry jumped out the door of the car and yelled at the two black guys, and he just seemed to crawl out of his skin," says Oberbruner. "He lost all his self-consciousness. It was half acting and half 'I'm stuck in jail—get me out of here.' He was brilliant. It was his big moment." Larry says it was also cathartic and helped him cope. Before he left jail he suggested that JUST offer other classes, including a creative writing course.

Larry was released late that October and began being supervised by the county's probation department. Since 1995 it has run a special program for sex offenders modeled on one in Maricopa County, Arizona, which includes Phoenix. Larry is required to check in with a probation officer every two or three weeks and to submit to random home and work visits by the officer as well as random drug and alcohol tests. (So far he's had five home visits and two drug tests.) He isn't allowed to drink or look at sexually stimulating material, including that on the Web, and he has to take a polygraph test at least once a year. He's also required to be in therapy until he gets off probation, in May 2006. (The Maricopa County program has even more requirements, including curfews.) He was handed a list of psychologists who were approved to direct his treatment and chose Michael Davison, who has an office in Arlington Heights near his father's place.

The current favored treatment for sex offenders is a form of group therapy called "relapse prevention." Initially used with alcoholics, the program was adapted for sex offenders in the eighties by Janice Marques, a California psychologist, and popularized by her colleague D. Richard Laws in a 1989 book. Its proponents say it's cheaper than one-on-one therapy, and it makes use of a powerful tool—the offenders themselves, who spot each other's lies and rationalizations but also offer real empathy. "When you're facing a half-dozen other people who've been there, so to speak," says Marques, "that's better than your talking to some therapist who hasn't."

Larry has been in one of Davison's sex-offender groups since December 2001. Most of the eight men in it are in their forties. All pleaded guilty or were convicted at trial. They meet every week for an hour and a half with Davison and a social worker in a nondescript room with a couch and some chairs. The leader among the offenders is George, a University of Chicago graduate who molested his stepdaughter. "George is bright, with a genuine wish to get better," says Davison. "He talks frankly about his stuff and gets on you about your own."

The sessions are marked by emotion, tears, and humor. Larry enjoys Davison's caustic wit, although he says not everyone does: "Mike can piss a person off." According to Davison, a molester in another group once announced that he thought he'd been providing sex education to his daughter. "I think you're on to something," said Davison sarcastically, then role-played a school superintendent urging the father to download pornography, share it with his daughter, then fondle her on her bed.

Most newcomers to sex-offender groups, says Davison, "view themselves as normal guys who screwed up, but there's way more to it than that. There is a pattern of behavior that is best looked at in the context of their entire developmental history."

In relapse-prevention therapy the first thing a new member of the group must do is face his "cognitive distortions," the way his mind has framed sexual crimes so he can see them as acceptable. "You come to realize your thinking has been wrong," says Marques, "that the woman you raped didn't want it, that the teenager you had sex with didn't seduce you."

Larry arrived thinking that his relationship with Laura had been "a sexually mutual one." He'd courted Joan quietly because they thought their relationship might be seen as inappropriate at work. He says that to deepen their bond he told her about his infidelities—the brief dalliances he'd had during his marriage, a longer affair, and the inappropriate advance he'd once made to the teenage daughter of a friend. He says Joan seemed to accept his remorse, and in April 2000 she agreed to marry him. That November he moved into her house.

By then he'd been having sex with Laura for five months. She was a petite girl who looked younger than her age, and he helped her with homework, taught her to drive, and advised her on relationships with boys. He persuaded himself she was flirting with him and started rubbing her back and tucking her in at night. Finally he started having sex with her, either when Joan was away or after she'd gone to sleep. He says the sex consisted of mutual masturbation and him giving her oral sex. He admits they once came close to having intercourse but he lost his erection. "Intercourse was a line I couldn't cross," he theorizes. "I told Laura that if she didn't want me to do anything I wouldn't, and that's how I justified it. Part of my thought process was that she wanted it. I never stopped and thought, what are you doing?"

The sex tapered off as Larry's wedding to Joan drew closer. Laura finally told her mother after a dinner-table conversation about a family friend who'd been accused of having sex with a minor. "We told Laura that if anybody did anything of that sort to her," Larry says, "she should come forward." He says he'd never sworn her not to tell about the two of them, but he was horrified when a few days later she did.

Davison's group—particularly George—quickly set Larry straight about his belief that Laura had sought his affections and that her not ordering him to stop had given him license. "The group would say, 'That's bullshit. Who's the adult here? How old was she again?'" Larry says. They also called him on his idea that not having intercourse with her somehow absolved him. "I came to realize that any act causes victimization," he says.

Larry also came to believe that his pursuit of Laura had been complicated by other motives—anger at Joan for keeping their relationship from coworkers and for failing to invite him to accompany her to a party, his need for power and control, the thrill of flirting with danger, a desire to sabotage his own ambitions. "A lot of people have patterns of self-sabotage—getting to a certain level and screwing up," says Davison. "Here you're talking about someone who chose a sexual vehicle."

Davison and the other offenders helped Larry see how he'd repeatedly indulged in the forbidden, felt ashamed, then packed away the shame as a secret. "Laura became my own little other world," he says. He also acknowledged that he'd been guilty of a "grooming pattern"—enticing the mother into his embrace, then slowly enfolding the daughter too. He says he learned to put himself in Laura's position, turning her into a figure of empathy rather than of sexual craving: "My concern turned to Laura and how I hurt her."

That's what his concern should always have been, says Polly Poskin, executive director of the Illinois Coalition Against Sexual Assault, a statewide association of rape-crisis centers. She says sex crimes can be extremely damaging to the victims: "To be reduced to an object for someone else's pleasure—it leaves you with fear, a sense of betrayal, and a lack of safety. It takes an awful lot of time and energy to recover."

Outside of sessions Larry wrote down his personal and sexual history. His family was Catholic, and he'd grown up with his two older sisters near Addison and Cumberland and later in Wheeling. His mother, a receptionist, was an alcoholic. "There were problems related to that," says Greta. "My dad would be upset with my mom, and there was fighting." Larry says his mother's alcoholism diminished her in his eyes: "I had her on a pedestal. How could she?" His relationship with his father was difficult. "I was never real good at sports or academics, and he pointed out my faults," he says. "I always felt like a failure." Only as an adult did he learn that his father had sexually abused his oldest sister when she was a teenager.

Larry briefly attended Harper College in Palatine, then in 1971, just before he turned nineteen, enlisted in the army. He trained as an artillery specialist and shipped out to Germany. "I found the army was something I enjoyed," he says. "I did well in a structured environment, doing work I felt was important. Also, being single and in Europe, I was living the dream of every twenty-year-old, with all the partying and the girls." At twenty-two he married a young woman he'd known back in the States. They eventually had two daughters, and he rose through the ranks—he would win a Bronze Star as a first sergeant during the Gulf War. But he drank excessively. "I was never an abusive drunk," he says. "Instead I wanted to party—and make passes at other women." He had the affair and several one-night stands. And although he listened to the personal problems of the soldiers under him, he never sought help himself. "I was always concerned that if I went to a counselor," he says, "my cheating would come out and it would dissolve my marriage."

He'd first realized that he was intensely attracted to adolescent girls when he was in his midtwenties. He says he didn't act on the impulse until a dozen years ago, when he was visiting an army friend in Germany who had a fifteen-year-old daughter. "The girl's parents had gone to bed," he wrote in his history. "She was in her underwear, and her breasts were visible through her T-shirt. I rubbed her back and got aroused. I fondled her breasts—and scared the hell out of her. I stayed with my friend that night, but afterward the daughter told her parents and that ended the friendship."

He swears this was his only transgression before Laura, but sex offenders are notorious for undercounting their sins. "When they tell you they've done something a time or two, multiply that by several factors," says Linda Grossman, a psychology professor at the University of Illinois College of Medicine and an authority on treating sex offenders.

Larry was a sergeant major and training adviser for the Utah National Guard when he retired from the services in 1997 and hired on with a defense contractor. That November he asked his wife for a divorce. "There was nothing left in the marriage," he says, "and I wasn't willing to put anything new in." Larry's mother was dying of pulmonary disease, and that fall he moved back to Chicago to be with her.

Soon after he arrived Larry found work as a technical writer and started seeing Kathy. Kathy says she liked his sense of humor and gift of gab, and they moved in together, intending to marry. Two years later Larry admitted he was having an affair with Joan, and Kathy tossed him out.

Over several group sessions in early 2002 Larry read his twenty-one-page history aloud. He says he was embarrassed to share the erotic thoughts he'd had about female family members growing up and about adolescent girls later on, the details of all the womanizing, the abuse of the friend's daughter in Germany and of Laura. During one session he broke down crying. Afterward, he says, "I was absolutely drained and exhausted."

The next step in relapse-prevention therapy involves identifying things that might trigger a slipup and then finding ways to head them off. "People have to learn how not to get into trouble," says Marques. Davison says this step is especially important for sex offenders because they're inordinately susceptible to being swept away by lust. "These are people who just get such a charge and a spark from their feelings," he says. "Their physiology goes haywire—offenders talk about this like a crack addict would talk about getting high. There's such an emotional component here."

With the help of the group, Larry came up with a relapse-prevention plan that he wrote down and carried around in his pocket until he could carry it in his head. Most important, he tries to steer clear of situations where he might encounter adolescent girls. He attends Sunday services that are held in a high school in Naperville but says, "If there were to be a school-spirit event going on I wouldn't go to services that day." And he tries to sit up front to avoid seeing teens who might be there. He no longer drinks; he's not allowed to under the terms of his probation, but it also helps him keep control of himself. On Friday night he regularly goes out to dinner and a movie with his sister, her husband, and Kathy, who's remained a friend. He says he makes sure the film they're seeing doesn't have scenes involving teenage girls and that if there is one he'll walk out of the theater. If he sees a provocative picture of a girl on television he'll change the channel.

Some temptations are unavoidable. "If I do see an attractive girl somewhere, with a nice body, and feel something," he says, "I'll recognize that I'm having that thought. And I stop myself and think, 'Now that's a person, an individual.' I'll stop viewing the girl as a sex object."

Davison says even the best-intentioned sex offenders frequently have mental lapses. "These men will get lost in their thoughts and go home to masturbate to them," he says. "It's a private thing—you can't get arrested for it. But that's considered a lapse." Sharing those lapses is vital to preventing future ones. "Sex offenders like to keep secrets—they eat secrets for breakfast," he says. "But once they talk about what they've done it defuses the situation, and a lapse is less likely to take place down the line. You should rely on people who will ask you, 'How are you? When did you last masturbate? What did you masturbate to?'"

Larry says he's had lapses and has quickly talked about them with his therapy group or with his sponsor at the sex-addiction twelve-step program.

Davison says that some of his patients are more likely than others to relapse. He'll put a patient he believes has a strong propensity for relapsing on an antiandrogen, which reduces testosterone and therefore desire. But antiandrogens have side effects—weight gain, depression, headache—and he prefers to use relapse prevention whenever possible. He says that in a decade of treating offenders, only two of his patients have been arrested for a new sex crime, both for "exhibitionism." Sandra White, supervisor of adult sex offenders on probation in DuPage County, says that only "very rarely" has one of her charges been arrested for a new sex offense. In the thirteen years the Maricopa County program has been keeping records, only 2 percent of probationers have been arrested for a new sex crime.

Other research on relapse-prevention therapy shows higher rates of recidivism. According to a study published last year by Canadian researcher Karl Hanson, 10 percent of sex offenders treated primarily with the therapy are arrested or convicted again within five years, compared to 17 percent of offenders who don't get the therapy. That's a 42 percent drop in recidivism, but an analysis of numerous studies by a Kent State University professor showed only a 30 percent drop, making relapse prevention about as successful as antiandrogens. (Hanson points out that all these numbers represent undercounts, since many people who have relapses aren't caught.)

"The public won't find that persuasive," says D. Richard Laws, who wrote the 1989 book touting the therapy but has since developed doubts. He says that in his experience most offenders are in relapse prevention only because they have to be, that in the Florida program he once directed, "the guys were on probation, and they just didn't want to be there." They would show up one week but not the next; half of them simply stopped coming. He also says it's hard for many participants to change their aberrant behavior: "It's all they've known how to do for years." He now prefers a therapy model from New Zealand that puts offenders into four categories based on how capable they are of change, then provides different programs for each category. Asked if he plans to continue therapy once he's off probation, Larry says, "I probably will, though perhaps not on a full-time basis. But it's a tool I will always use."

The statistics on sex offenders get even muddier when all crime categories are considered. The latest figures from the Illinois Department of Corrections show that 50 percent of convicted sex offenders will be charged with or convicted of some new crime, including a parole violation, within three years of their release (about the same rate as all other released prisoners). Davison says one of his patients was arrested for drinking in violation of his probation and another was arrested for domestic battery. The DOC doesn't keep figures on what crimes the sex offenders commit, but a 2002 U.S. Bureau of Justice Statistics study of recidivism in fifteen states, including Illinois, found that 46 percent of released rapists were arrested within three years for another crime (many involving violence and drugs) but only 2.5 percent for another rape.

DuPage County requires sex offenders who are on probation to take a polygraph test at least once a year, but Davison has his patients take one about every six months. He gives the testing service three questions specific to a patient to see if he's relapsing or otherwise slipping up. Larry, who tends toward compulsiveness, gets nervous before each polygraph appointment; he's failed a couple of questions, but the exam has yet to turn up a relapse. Davison says Larry, like all his patients, will have to be vigilant for the rest of his life. "The moment you feel that you've got your problem beat, that's when you probably haven't got it beat," he says. "You're never out of the woods."

Today the public is much more aware of sex crimes than it was a generation ago, and it's no coincidence that many of the stories we hear involve children: according to the Illinois State Police, 85 percent of convicted sex offenders in the state preyed on individuals who were under eighteen.

In 1996—after the kidnapping, rape, and murder of Megan Kanka of New Jersey—Congress enacted Megan's Law, which directed states to give the public access to sex-offender registration information they were already keeping. Illinois' notice law, enacted later that year, required the state police to maintain and make public a database on sex offenders, which is now available on the Internet. The hope was that if the neighbors knew someone had been convicted of a sex crime they'd be able to keep their kids away from him and he'd be less likely to relapse.

In Illinois many offenders, including those who've raped an adult, must register their whereabouts annually with the local police or sheriff's office for ten years after their conviction if they're put on probation or ten years after their release if they're sent to prison. Those who've been judged sexually dangerous (convicted of repeated crimes) or sexually violent (convicted of brutal crimes), or who've been deemed sexual predators (convicted of possessing child pornography, pimping for a child, or assaulting a child) must register for the rest of their lives. The state police provide quarterly lists of all offenders to schools, child-care facilities, and DCFS. Sex offenders can't live within five hundred feet of a day-care center or school, and they can't loiter within five hundred feet of a playground.

According to a survey by the U.S. Bureau of Justice Statistics, rape and other sexual assault rates in the United States went down 52 percent between 1993 and 2000. Michael Rand, chief of victimization statistics with the bureau, says that criminologists cite different reasons for the decline. Some point to increased levels of incarceration of offenders, some to a better economy, others to changes in the drug culture, and still others to registration and treatment programs. But the trend may be shifting again: the Illinois State Police recently reported a 5.8 percent increase in rapes in 2002.

When Larry was released from jail, now a felon convicted of a loathsome crime, he worried about his job prospects. "I thought I'd never be able to get a job," he says, "except to pump gas." He called a former supervisor at the shipping-supply company who'd become an operations manager for a construction-tool manufacturer. "Larry said he needed a job," says Greg. "He came in, we talked, and I hired him as an independent contractor." When a full-time position as a production manager opened up, Larry took Greg aside and told him about his criminal past. Greg says he told Larry, "I know about that. But I also know what your capabilities are, and it's not for me to judge you." He hired Larry for the position.

Larry rented a town house near the company but didn't check the box on the application stating that he'd been convicted of a felony. Two months later, he says, "I was coming home from a twelve-step meeting, and there was a guy who gave me a notice to vacate." There was no box to check on the next application, but he leveled with the manager anyway. He says the manager told him, "Just because you've been arrested doesn't mean you shouldn't have a place to live."

Larry has lived in that town house since October. The place is fastidiously neat, and he always has four place mats and matching napkins on the dining table, even when he isn't expecting guests.

When he moved into his first town house Larry went to the local police station to register. They took his photograph and fingerprints. The photo, with him looking stunned, and his address promptly went up on the state police Web site. He was now one of thirteen thousand sex offenders on the site; another two thousand offenders have been told to register but haven't. After he moved he registered at the new local police station. "I was signing out when I looked up and saw my picture on the wall," he says. "I thought, 'Oh shit. Anybody from work could see that.' Then I thought, 'There's nothing I can do to change this. If a person sees my picture they will ask me about it or they won't.'"

When he finally told his former girlfriend Kathy he'd gone to jail for a sex crime she said she already knew—a friend had come across the information while at the courthouse. But so far no neighbor or acquaintance has confronted him with information gleaned from public records or the Web site.

"When Megan's Law first went into effect I was quite distressed about the implications," says Davison. "I thought we'd get vigilantes forcing sex offenders from their homes, but I haven't seen that." He says only rarely has one of his patients faced outright hostility. "One guy did keep getting his car vandalized, and he was pretty much convinced it was because of the registry," he says. "He was probably right, but then he had a very active presence in the neighborhood. This was someone who'd fondled a boy, and the neighbors hated him. There he'd be outside washing his car and saying hello to all the kids as they walked by. Most offenders' lives aren't so public."

Nevertheless, Davison says, "for the first six months that I see people they are completely paranoid about the registration and notification. At some point they let it go, and the subject comes up less and less. I encourage them to do that. I tell them to live their lives as if everybody knows, because there's evidence that if lots of people know, the less likely you are to offend again." One patient, a residential developer who'd molested his stepdaughter, lost a sale when the buyer found out. "Now he's learned to lead with the information—he tells customers up front," says Davison. "While he's lost deals because of it, that's better than competitors undercutting him with the truth."

Last June, during her campaign for attorney general, Lisa Madigan called for lifetime supervision of sex offenders. Two weeks earlier fourteen-year-old Elizabeth Smart had disappeared from her Salt Lake City home. A few months before, seven-year-old Danielle van Dam had been snatched from her house in suburban San Diego and was soon found dead in the desert.

"Sexual assault of a child is one of all parents' greatest fears," said Madigan, standing with Orland Park's police chief at a press conference. "Far too many women and children are victimized by sexual predators. The recidivism rate for those convicted of sex crimes is too high to ignore. Serious prison sentences are critical to addressing the problem of sex crimes, but prison alone is not enough. Once released from prison, sexual predators must be monitored closely by law enforcement for the rest of their lives."

It wasn't clear how she defined monitoring, but Larry, who wouldn't be affected by any new legislation, was dismayed. "I thought she was just exciting the emotions of people, depicting offenders as the scum of the earth, who have no chance to turn themselves around," he says. "It was an easy platform for her to drum up support."

His sister Greta remembers hearing the news and feeling "disdain. 'That's just not right,' I said to myself. Maybe if Laura had been twelve, sure, I could see it. But she was just short of seventeen, and girls are very advanced at that age today." UIC psychology professor Linda Grossman scoffs at that logic: "It's normal for men to fantasize about sixteen-year-old girls. It's not normal to have sex with them—it's against the law." True, says Greta, "but I see a distinction here between the child molester who abuses a toddler and Larry and what he did to a person who's almost an adult. I'm not excusing him for his actions—and maybe I'd feel differently if it wasn't for him—but Larry shouldn't be supervised for life."

On March 5, seven days before Elizabeth Smart resurfaced, Madigan got more specific about her plan for lifetime monitoring. Her proposal, she said at another press conference, was about "making sure you have people, not just computer databases, that are responsible for keeping track of sex offenders once they're released and back in communities."

State representatives Mary K. O'Brien, a Democrat from Watseka, and Jay Hoffman, a Democrat from Collinsville, put together a bill based on Madigan's proposal and a 1998 Colorado law and submitted it to the General Assembly. They want to make treatment mandatory from the moment a person pleads guilty or is convicted at trial. They want to lengthen sentences for sex offenders, raising the minimum and making each sentence a range, with life always the maximum. They also want to change the way a prisoner's release date is set. Under the current law an offender knows in advance when he'll get out if he behaves well; under the new legislation, whether he got out after serving the minimum would be determined by the Illinois Prisoner Review Board. Illinois abandoned this kind of "indeterminate" sentencing in 1978, but Doug Simpson, chief of the criminal division of the attorney general's office, says, "The idea is to furnish [a bigger] incentive for treatment, for getting a GED, and for staying out of trouble."

Some people who work with offenders worry that the flexibility the system appears to have could be undermined by so much power being given to the PRB, which has a history of inflexibility. The fifteen-member board, which is loaded with former law enforcement officials, now sets the conditions under which prisoners can be released. It also holds hearings on how much additional time inmates who've screwed up have to serve, and it decides whether prisoners confined under the pre-1978 indeterminate sentences can be paroled. In 2002 the PRB held parole hearings for 332 of these aging prisoners and granted parole to only ten.

The PRB members, says Chip Coldren, president of the John Howard Association, an inmate advocacy group, "have been overly conservative. They don't like to let prisoners out, and I predict they won't be lenient with sex offenders—and judges won't either. So many in the justice community operate from the common belief that sex offenders are the most difficult to treat. Some may be, but to lump them all into the same class is absolutely wrong."

The new legislation would also lengthen parole terms for offenders once they're released from prison and would give the power to determine the period to the PRB. Someone who'd been convicted of a grievous crime such as rape would be placed under state supervision for anywhere from twenty years to life. Someone who'd been incarcerated for a less serious sex felony would be placed under supervision for ten years to life. (Offenders who were given only probation would also face long periods of supervision, but the length would be determined by a judge.) This supervision would be more stringent than the current systems and could include curfews, restitution payments, and daily contact with probation officers.

When the mandated supervision period was up the PRB would hold another hearing to determine whether the offender could be released from supervision. The criteria would be spelled out by the Sex Offender Management Board, a group set up in 1997 to recommend ways to treat offenders that is chaired by Simpson and made up of representatives from the DOC, the state Department of Human Services, DCFS, and law enforcement agencies, as well as judges, victims' rights advocates, attorneys, and psychologists.

O'Brien thinks all the new measures in her bill are justified. "Sex offenders do not rehabilitate easily or well," she says. "These are sexual predators, remember. I don't have a lot of sympathy for them." Nor do victims' rights advocates. "A sex offender who's returned to a free society is given a second chance," says Polly Poskin of the Illinois Coalition Against Sexual Assault, which backs the bill. She adds that part of getting another chance is being supervised. "This is America. We believe in safety and freedom of movement. In those rights the victims of sex offenses should have as much access as the offenders, and that's what we're talking about here."

Not everyone is so sanguine. Barry Leavitt, former president of the Illinois chapter of the Association for the Treatment of Sexual Abusers, generally favors the changes but says, "We need to refine the measures here between those who have a high risk and a low risk of reoffending. One size fits all would be a mistake." Davison agrees. He says lifetime supervision makes sense "for somebody who has multiple victims over the years, but consider the twenty-two-year-old who has sex with a fifteen-year-old and is convicted of statutory rape. Should he face scrutiny for life? When the criminal justice system takes a cookie-cutter approach it's not useful."

"Treatment can be effective for many people," says Linda Grossman. "It can reduce someone's chances of recidivating. We can follow and measure a person and apply an end point. Lifetime supervision, be it in a correctional or treatment sense, doesn't allow for an end point that is practicable."

Madigan hasn't responded to repeated requests for comment, but her press secretary, Melissa Merz, wrote in an e-mail that Madigan made lifetime supervision a campaign issue because the "protection of women and children" is a top priority with her. Merz also said that Madigan's supervision plan drew from "research into creative, innovative ways to address the significant problem of recidivism among sex offenders" and noted that treatment is a key component of supervision because "sex offenders—particularly serial offenders—suffer from mental disorders." She said the O'Brien-Hoffman bill allowed for ending supervision if an offender "has made progress in treatment in conjunction with other safeguards to ensure that any risk from him is reduced."

Simpson says the PRB would be given "additional information on treatment" and would take the recommendations of probation officers and people providing treatment into account. "If Colorado is any indication," he says, "sometimes the parole board there agrees with the recommendation, and sometimes it doesn't. The board's no rubber stamp."

As a tough-on-crime measure, the O'Brien-Hoffman bill would normally encounter little opposition in the General Assembly, but these days cost is an issue. Colorado, one of eleven states that have a lifetime-supervision provision, has spent an estimated $3.2 million a year extra for parole, probation, and treatment expenses, along with $8 million for new prison construction. O'Brien says she was told that Illinois might have to spend double what Colorado has—a troubling prospect, she says, in hard economic times. She plans to hold committee hearings on the bill in August, and she says she welcomes testimony from offenders, "especially those who've really made an effort to turn their lives around." She expects the bill to come up for a vote next spring.

Larry says he can understand why people would support lifetime supervision. "I'm a parent as well as an offender," he says, "and though my daughters are both grown, I understand the concern here from a parent's perspective. There are people out there, like I was, who are waiting to groom their next victim."

Yet he still feels the bill would treat many sex offenders too harshly. "Offenders like me want to recover—we're trying to do so," he says. "The process will always be part of my life. I know that. Drug addicts and alcoholics have the same thing—and you think they don't hurt people? Bullshit. How many people do drunk drivers kill? Lots—and they aren't on lifetime supervision. If you put everybody convicted of a felony on lifetime supervision I'd fear for society. Where would it all end?" He pauses, then says, referring to Madigan, "I hope for crap in your closet, lady."

Last November, Larry was laid off from his construction-tool job when the company downsized. He now spends his days reading up on other firms, looking for a job—he's now hoping to find one with UPS—and networking. He isn't using the Internet; he'd subscribed to a Web service, even though having it violated his probation, but he dropped it after he realized he was too tempted to surf porn sites. He's making do financially; he figures his army pension and savings will last him a year.

He got a second blow in November when his father died. "When Larry left home in the first place he was not even a man yet," says Greta. "After Larry's foul-up he and Dad were closer than they'd ever been. Perhaps it was because of what Dad himself had once done with our sister."

Larry has also grown close to his older daughter, now a single mother living in Utah. As a child, she and her father never talked much. "But now we talk about everything," she says. "If we're mad at each other we put it right on the table." Three years ago she pleaded guilty to possession of a stolen credit card. "Back then my dad was very upset with me," she says. Now they commiserate about how hard it is as felons to find jobs.

For several months Larry has been attending Sunday and weekday services, as well as Bible-study classes, at the evangelical Crossroads Community Church. Some people in the church know his history; most don't. "I feel God has forgiven me," he says. "I'm developing a personal relationship with him, and members of the congregation have accepted me." Recently he began training as a "Stephen minister," a layperson who helps other congregants in crisis as Saint Stephen once helped the needy. At a Sunday service in March the speaker talked of God, family, and love, then the music director led the congregation in the hymn "Trading My Sorrows." The lyrics were projected on a large screen, and Larry sang along quietly. "I'm trading my sorrows. I'm trading my shame. I'm laying them down, for the joy of the Lord."

Larry has decided to pursue a master's in counseling at National-Louis University, where he earned an undergraduate business degree three years ago. He starts classes in July and hopes to become a graduate assistant. "There's a part of me that says that's a good idea," says Davison, "but I've also told Larry, 'I don't know if you'll get licensed.'" The state Department of Professional Regulation doesn't outright forbid licensing a felon, but it could deny an application if that were the recommendation of a board of professionals.

Until last summer Larry still saw and sporadically went out with Joan. "A friend of mine used to say, 'Dating is fuck you and good night,'" he says. "That's where my thinking was too, but there's been a major shift in my perspective. Am I going to hurt a person I love because all I want is an orgasm? With Joan now, we could sit down and talk, and I was able to focus on her completely." But he says she decided she didn't want to see him anymore, explaining that she was worried about what it said to Laura and to her younger daughter, who's now a teenager.

Larry has never contacted Laura—the conditions of his parole prohibit it. But he hopes his judge will one day give him permission to apologize to her, in person, although with a supervisor. "I'd tell her she was not to blame at all for this," he says. "It was because I was immature sexually and not an adult. I would tell her I'm absolutely sorry for what I did to her physically and mentally. What I did was a terrible thing." Tears fill his eyes. "This makes me ashamed. But deep down I feel I'm a good person. I think I don't have to be perfect. All I can hope for is that I don't offend again."

Death

ЯEADER CHICAGO'S FREE WEEKLY

The Queen Is Dead

The fast life and slow death of Richard Farnham, a.k.a. "Mother Carol"

By Grant Pick

THIS ISSUE IN FOUR SECTIONS

NEIGHBORHOOD NEWS: disunity in Pilsen PAGE 8
BOBWATCH: Ed Gold in Greene hell PAGE 10
OUR TOWN: stealing across baseball's color line PAGE 13

ЯEADER · CHICAGO'S FREE WEEKLY

Life after Death

BY GRANT PICK

HOW MIKE HEDGES MADE SENSE OF HIS JOB IN THE AUDY HOME AFTER A CRIMINAL KILLED HIS KID.

Henderson: the real cost of campaign finance reform PAGE 12

Margasak: Jae-Ha Kim loses the beat SECTION THREE

THIS ISSUE IN FOUR SECTIONS

ЯEADER · CHICAGO'S FREE WEEKLY

As I Lay Dying

BY GRANT PICK

After a brilliant career teaching other doctors how to save lives, Dr. Roger Bone showed them how to let life go.

THE QUEEN IS DEAD

The fast life and slow death of Richard Farnham, a.k.a. "Mother Carol."

You gotta ring them bells,
You gotta ring them bells,
You gotta make 'em sing
And really ring them bells.
A song by Liza Minnelli

It is toward midnight on October 18 in a dark corner of Carol's Speakeasy, a gay discotheque in Old Town. A tall man in a wool sweater is necking with a man in a silk shirt slit open to the waist, their tongues embracing across the gap between their open mouths. Now the man in the sweater slides his hand ever so slowly down his lover's well-muscled and matted chest, kneading the skin en route. When the massage ends, the lover slips from his mate's grasp and marches to another acquaintance. He slides his stiff hand underneath the new man's crotch in a razorlike motion, and the new man arches his back in a shiver of pleasure.

In the vicinity, a bare-chested man in a top hat fiddles with the ring jutting from his pierced nipple. He's watching the female impersonators who perform on Carol's raised stage. First there's one wearing a crimson dress and black underwear, then another riding in on a hobby horse. The cowgirl, with frizzy hair and a fringed vest, is rewarded with dollar bills from the audience; she acknowledges this acclaim by unholstering her fake six-shooter and drawing it in and out of her mouth.

One female impersonator follows another, all working feverishly to the incessant disco music. A mirror ball sprays dots of light over the dance floor, then the chaser lights go on, then the spinners, then the strobes. The dancers—many touching, some shirtless—gyrate with abandon, while other intriguing actions

David L. Veltkamp

Richard Farnham a.k.a. "Mother Carol"

transpire quietly in the shadows. Off to one side stands a guy in black satin pants, his pectorals underscored by sequin half moons. Eyeing him is a man nude but for a black leather jockstrap and a ring of paint around each nipple. And ogling *him* is a waiter in a tuxedo.

The waiters at Carol's are wearing tuxedos because this is an invitation-mostly party, being thrown to mark the discotheque's first anniversary in business. Everyone with a hand in making Carol's a success is here to celebrate, to dance and drink from the open bar and carry on. Everyone, that is, except Carol.

For Richard Carroll Farnham, "Mother Carol," is dead. The manager of Carol's Speakeasy died a few days before this raucous event, of alcoholism, of overweight, and—some insist—of a wish to die. He was only thirty-seven, but he said he was older and he looked it. In the decade he lived and worked in Chicago, Farnham had cut a broad swath through the city's gay community. He ran three bars under his own name and became known as an extraordinary host, a maven for hundreds—no, thousands—of homosexuals. His signatures were free-flowing booze, lavish buffets, outlandish drag turns, and an unremitting need to "party-party," to use a popular gay phrase. Yet always he had an ear to lend and a hand to help with that first, tentative step out of the closet. His last establishment, this one, Carol's Speakeasy, had just become a cause célèbre, rallying a massive demonstration for gay rights.

But here also was a fat, clownish man who preached a decadent, party-time gospel that many gays found—and still find—abhorrent. "Carol represented everything our mothers always told us gay people were like," remarks one gay bartender. "He was the stereotype of the fat, drunken drag queen. Unfortunately, there's always a kernel of truth in any stereotype, and Carol was that kernel to many of us. He was an argument for *staying* in the closet. It's no accident that the straight community didn't know about him." Beyond his image, and despite the hoopla that accompanied his almost every move, Carol himself was a lonely man who never knew real intimacy.

To climax a ripsnorting evening such as this one at Carol's Speakeasy, Richard Farnham used to retreat to a dressing room sometime before midnight and reappear in drag. Maybe he'd be Dolly Parton. Maybe Cher. As he hit the stage and the music came up, Mother Carol would lip-sync and dance and vamp it up. His eyes would roll back into his head, and his tongue would lunge out toward the audience. This gigantic tongue became Ma Carol's symbol, which is why here at the Speakeasy, as the first anniversary party reaches a crescendo, the dancers dance and the lovers grope against a rear-wall background of tongues, three painted images of Carol's mouth going about its business. These tongues are Mother Carol's legacy—these and the party reeling on before them.

Richard Farnham was born into a different kind of life from this. He arrived on July 13, 1942, at St. Joseph's Hospital in Aurora, the second child of Lillian Farnham and her husband William, a truck driver. The middle name they gave him, Carroll, had been the maiden name of his paternal grandmother. As he grew up, people called him Rich or Dick.

For most of his youth, Rich Farnham lived in a shingled frame house in poor St. Peter's parish on the west side of Aurora. He was a nice, warm kid, by his family's account, who shrank from athletics and liked to play show tunes on his record player and pantomime along. At the parochial schools he attended, he excelled at helping the nuns clean up after the day was done, and when he graduated from eighth grade, he entered a seminary in Techny, Illinois. He lasted there less than a year. His freshman year ended in Hayward, Wisconsin, where his parents by then were running a resort.

The Farnham family was close, although Mrs. Farnham, who's a nice, sixty-year-old woman with henna in her hair, admits to some distance between Richard and his father. "My husband was always working," she says. "He never had a lot of time with Richard, although they always enjoyed each other and there was never any animosity." Richard's deepest bond seems to have been with Marie Farnham, the grandmother who furnished his middle name. On cool summer evenings in Wisconsin, Marie Farnham and her grandson would go fishing together, or else they'd take supper at a roadhouse; afterwards, they'd dance.

Boarding with an aunt, Richard completed his formal education at Aurora's East High School. He went back up to Hayward for a while, then took a job at a gas station in Aurora, and finally signed on as a supermarket clerk. He became at least a produce manager—one friend says he also managed stores—at National groceries in Aurora and Geneva. He kept an apartment in Aurora, dated occasionally, and lived what seemed the straightest of lives—as the pounds began to pile up under his belt. William Farnham, a factory worker when he died in 1966, perished with hardly a thought that his son was gay.

Perhaps Richard himself didn't know in 1966; perhaps he did. When he died, the tale of his struggle with his gayness had been told neither to family nor to friends. All we know for certain is that ten years ago he began showing up at Ruthie's, a gay bar on Clark Street north of Diversey. "He used to come in wearing a business suit and carrying an attaché case, and we were sure he was a copper," recalls John Nicosia, a friend for many years. But Richard's insistence on being included in bar activities swept those fears away. He was a presence: he spoke in a loud, raspy voice, and he was six feet tall and fat.

Indeed, he was very fat. His weight fluctuated within the stratosphere above 250 pounds, with the largest part of it centered in his belly. He wore his hair short, and he dressed in checked shirts, double-knit slacks, and comfortable black leather shoes—he'd soon abandoned his suits. He had a thin mouth and pasty skin, but his eyes were the most distinctive things on his face. They were doleful, drooping eyes that reminded one friend of a cocker spaniel's. In all, Farnham appeared much older than his age, and, as if to deal with that disparity, he always told people he was several years older than he actually was.

Farnham began dressing in drag. The first time was Halloween, 1970. Ruthie, whose real name is Herman Ruiz and who now lives in Los Angeles, shepherded Richard down to Lane Bryant, which sells clothing for large-sized women. They bought Farnham a brassiere, a girdle, high heels, and a dress, and he debuted as an elephant-sized drag queen. Farnham enjoyed dressing up, Ruiz recalls, although not for the sexual thrills; he was always the clown. When Ruthie closed his New Town bar to move farther north, Richard got all dolled up for the farewell party. He wore balloons for breasts, and through the evening he kept popping his tits and inserting larger and larger ones, fanning himself, as he always did then, with a silk scarf. "He wanted to perform," says Ruthie. "This was his way of entertaining people. Really, he wanted to be a figurehead to the gay community."

Which, back then, he wasn't. He was managing go-go dancers in those early days in Chicago, and then he became partner in a couple of bookstores, one on Irving Park and the other on Lawrence. The bookshops sold dirty heterosexual literature, and twice Farnham beat charges that he was peddling obscenity. The impression got around at the time—it still persists—that Farnham had ties to the mob. However, police intelligence commander Lewis Sabella reports his files show nothing on Farnham, and another officer with some knowledge of Farnham shrugs off the rumors this way: "Between you and me, all these joints Farnham was in, from the bookstores to the bars, have money backing them. Sure, some might not be legitimate. The outfit is washing its money in so many businesses today that they can make it seem money comes from an upright place whereas it really comes from narcotics. Anything could be connected to the mob now—or if it isn't, people say it is."

Farnham's big break came in 1972 when Lee Stanley, an investor in bars, followed the recommendation of someone at Ruthie's and hired Richard to manage the Coming Out Pub on Halsted north of Fullerton. It was a small bar that Stanley says he operated for his sister, the real owner. The pub sported wood paneling, yellow lights, and a jukebox; no one—least of all Stanley and his sister—expected much more than a subsistence profit from the joint.

But it was here that Farnham became Mother Carol, and Carol's Coming Out Pub, as the bar subsequently was renamed, developed into a huge success. Carol was the reason. The young patrons found in Carol a good listener, especially in those slow hours when he was free to lounge at the bar, laugh, and gossip. Conversation with him ran to personalities and the bar business, yet he seldom was bitchy or cutting. He frequently dished out counsel on matters of love. Above all, he was accepting, a significant grace in the days when so many homosexuals were emerging from secret lives. Yet for all the secrets he heard, he never reciprocated; a wall went up when it came time for him to return intimacies. "He kept in his innermost feelings," says Clarence "Corky" Corcoran, a nurse who roomed with him for five years. "None of us really knew him well, I guess."

He perfected his drag acts at Carol's Coming Out. Late at night, or whenever the mood struck him, Farnham would don one of his many hats—a picture-frame chapeau, or one dripping with fruit à la Carmen Miranda—and parade up and down in front of the bar. Later, he added dresses, wigs, and blazing-blue eye shadow to his regalia. Once in action, he'd wag his thick tongue, scream "Up your ass!" at his patrons, and toss around cocktail napkins. People expected him to be a klutz as a dancer; his nifty two-step proved a surprise.

He offered free Sunday night buffets at his bar, serving up beef stroganoff and lasagna, rolls and salad, and he slashed drink prices to the bone on Wednesdays. He hired go-go boys, who kept on their jockey shorts, but just barely. Often, he gave away drinks, and even whole rounds. He was a soft touch for loans. "If he had ten dollars in his pocket, he'd give you fifteen dollars," quips one friend. He fired employees frequently, only to hire them back if they failed to find a job by the next day. All his generosity, which came out of the bar's pockets as well as Farnham's, put him in Dutch with owner Lee Stanley, and they quarreled repeatedly during the four-year life span of the place. But Stanley, who now operates a jazz bar called Redford's, found it difficult to quarrel with success. Carol's Coming Out was often wall-to-wall bodies, the sight of which prompted Stanley to try—but fail—to run a spin-off bar across the street called Carol's Annex.

Carol was more than the manager of a bar that suddenly became all the rage. Part of his importance derived from the loftier role a bar fills in the homosexual community—it's simply more pivotal an institution for gays than it is for straights. "You're dealing with a society of oppressed people that society looks down on," says Michael Kucharski, who runs a bar called K's on Clark. "Gays come to a bar to get a sense of solidarity; if they can relate over a cocktail, then that's OK." Yet Carol rose beyond even the status of gay barkeep to become a mother figure, a revered elder. "He was never a sister to me, but always a mother," says John Nicosia, who now manages a hot dog stand. "Carol was the substitute kind of mother people would have liked to have had, but didn't," thinks Norton Knopf, a psychologist who treats gays and pens a column in *Gay Life*, the more political of the community's two weeklies. Observers, including Knopf, agree that such a matriarch is seldom seen; the only names that recur are of the late Roby Landers, a female impersonator who once ran two clubs here, and of Michael Shimandle, who operates the Bushes on North Halsted.

Mother Carol, unfortunately, found no father. When he did his drag bit, he performed to whatever was on the jukebox, but the song he liked was the one by Liza Minnelli called "Ring Them Bells." He always flubbed the words to the upbeat little number, which tells the tale of a lonely New York girl who travels the world to find a man and ends up with the boy next door. Carol linked up with few, if any, real lovers, certainly none of them long-standing.

"When I first came out, someone introduced him to me," says Chuck Lind, a bartender who was his lover briefly in the midseventies. "I was then this lighting fixture representative, and coming out wasn't easy. You have a lot of fears in yourself. That's where I got my nickname, Bambi. Here I was, just having gotten divorced, and Carol helped me understand gay life. He did this by example, not by anything he said in particular. I quit my job and started tending bar on Halsted. I was living on the Southwest Side, but I'd stay at Carol's five nights a week. He'd cook, we'd have dinner together, and then after we'd close at two o'clock, we'd hit other bars.

"We'd sleep together, but basically it wasn't for sex. We'd cuddle, he wanted to be cuddled, he wanted to know somebody really cared about him. He wanted the assurance that I wasn't just with him—like so many people were with him—just because he was the bar manager."

His weight may have prevented him from cementing relationships. "The whole emphasis among gay men is on the body and the meat," observes Marge Summit, owner of His n' Hers on Addison. "First they look at the face, and then they look at what's between the legs; they're always looking for something pretty. If you're not really a good-looking guy or if you're on the obese side, you haven't got a chance. Carol was the opposite of everybody else. He was loud, he drew attention to himself, but he did it to be popular."

Carol's life revolved around his bar and the regulars there, who took a name, the Family. Farnham lived with a few Family members in a succession of New Town apartments and finally in an Old Town town house, all of which he filled with paintings and ceramics of clowns. His routine became a pretty standard one: he'd rise in late morning and go out for a breakfast of doughnuts and milk, spend the afternoon and evening at his bar, with time-out for dinner, and then cruise other taverns; before bed, in the predawn darkness, Carol usually stopped at an all-night restaurant for another fill-up of doughnuts and milk. To break the monotony, he sometimes organized trips out of town for a dozen or more people, booking excursions through a travel agent who gave him a free ride in exchange for the business. The destinations changed, but each winter invariably brought him to a hotel in Fort Lauderdale, Florida, that caters to gays: the Marlon Beach. There, the partying never stopped. Carol drank and drank, put on his wigs and gowns for fully clothed plunges into the pool, and then drank some more.

Carol's trips out of town were a sore point with Lee Stanley. "He had a habit of going off on vacation, of suddenly leaving," grouses Stanley. "He'd leave the whole joint with debts, and I'd have to step in and solve all the problems." Stanley also soured on Carol's casual and free-spending management techniques. Once, toward the end of their relationship, Carol carted home the weekend receipts, but stopped first at the Baton Lounge, a female-impersonation bar near the Loop; thieves broke into his car and got away with about two thousand dollars, which Carol could only pay back to Stanley by taking out a loan. Farnham's friends now accuse Stanley of grossly underpaying Farnham, forcing him ultimately into personal bankruptcy, but Stanley retorts that the bankruptcy, which was declared after the two had split, was of Carol's own making. Carol's Coming Out had other problems. Neighbors complained about the noise and the open sex that took place in the bar's beer garden—Carol's response would be to bellow into the night, "Mind your own business and pull down your blinds!" The neighbors took their gripes to the Forty-third Ward alderman's office, which finally forced an end to the beer garden, although one feisty old lady refused to wait that long. Patrons at Carol's used the alley beside the bar to piss in, a habit the lady knew well, and several times a customer would step out to relieve himself and get doused with a bucket of Pine Sol and water.

Carol had a lousy reputation among his straight neighbors, and despite his opposite standing with gays, he never wrapped himself in the cloak of gay rights. He seldom touched the issue at all. He almost never appeared at political demonstrations, and he was a confirmed nonvoter. He restricted his outside involvements to those that related to the bar business. He and Eddie Dugan, who owns a swish, off-Loop discotheque called Dugan's Bistro, cosponsored the Mr. Windy City beefcake pageant, and they also teamed up to host wild boat rides into the lake each summer. Three years ago, Frank M. Rodde III, a rotund young bartender who worked for Carol, was brutally stabbed to death after he allegedly accompanied a pickup home one night; the murder remains unsolved. Carol helped set up a memorial fund, under the auspices of the predominantly gay Tavern Guild, to finance a gay community center.

Once Lee Stanley and Carol arrived at a final parting of the ways in 1976, Carol quickly found backing for a new bar. Carol's in Exile, funded by John Nicosia and some straight partners, opened in September 1976 on Broadway north of Cornelia. Exile, which survived for two years, was much tackier than Farnham's previous tavern. Some thought it was symbolic that you had to step below street level to enter the place. Carol held huge card games many afternoons, the pot rising to five hundred dollars and higher. Sex played a bigger role at the Exile; the high jinks spilled out into the alley, forcing Nicosia to plop down garbage cans to crimp the action.

Carol was drinking constantly. He favored vodka with grapefruit juice, but when he was going full tilt, he'd opt for Southern Comfort, and when he was on his version of the wagon, he'd drink Rhine wine and seltzer water. He was drunk quite a bit, yet not so drunk that when a cop entered the bar scouting funny business, he couldn't snap to attention as if *he* had just been showered with Pine Sol and water.

Farnham also seemed to increase his use of poppers, drug stimulants that are popular among gays. Of the two varieties—one of which is legal and passes for a room odorizer—Carol usually chose amyl nitrate; it comes in glass capsules and normally is prescribed to heart patients. By several accounts, Carol often broke open poppers while performing, flaring his nostrils to sniff in the open vials of chemical and then letting the drug do its stuff on his dancing feet and flapping tongue.

The Exile closed in February 1978. "Carol was a party person, and she tended to give cocktails away," says Nicosia by way of explanation. Besides, other establishments nearby, like Crystal's Blinkers south on Broadway, had cut severely into the bar's business. It was just as well, for Carol's sake, because by now he had severe medical problems.

In March 1978, Carol checked into Augustana Hospital for liver ailments stemming from his drinking. Farnham's doctor told it to him straight: if you stop drinking now, you've got seven years left to live; if you don't, you have two years. Carol's answer was to host a booze party in his private room, amid the banks of flowers his friends had sent. Word leaked out on how serious it was. Michael Kucharski, then a respiratory therapist at Augustana, sneaked a peek at Carol's chart. "He's got no liver left," Kucharski informed Nicosia. "None."

Carol emerged from Augustana vowing weakly to dry out, but he quickly returned to the sauce. Summer came, and he and some compatriots went on a binge to celebrate what Carol insisted was his forty-fourth birthday. All day, they drank and caroused on the rocks south of Belmont Harbor, then adjourned to Crystal's Blinkers. Someone lined up forty-four shots of Southern Comfort in front of Carol, and he downed the whole lot in fifteen minutes. He was blitzed; he wound up wallowing in a kid's play pool on the disco's second tier, his friends pouring champagne over his head.

There were barkeeps who refused to serve him. Bobby Lee, a bartender at the Redoubt Lounge who'd known Carol from his days at Ruthie's, was able to keep saying no. "I would not give him a drink," recalls Lee. "Many of his so-called friends just poured drinks down him, which is like giving candy to a diabetic. His friends drove him to his grave, is what I think. They had no concern for him as a person." Carol's friends who are willing to talk about it counter that Carol was a big boy, and liquor was, by this point, intrinsic to his nature. "She [Carol] was your mother, and you ain't going to tell your mother what to do," says Nicosia. "Oh, we'd tell him to slow down, but we came to the conclusion that he was twenty-one years old and if he's not going to worry about himself, we can't be standing over him twenty-four hours a day. It's hard to own a bar and not be a drinker; why, we're all big drinkers."

Carol landed a job at Cheeks, a darkly lit bar on Clark Street south of Diversey. His province was the back bar, and he enjoyed the work, if only because he drew a steady paycheck without management responsibilities. But then he was made an offer that someone who hankered for the biggest gay bar in the city could hardly refuse.

Den One, an Old Town club that catered to gay blacks, was floundering. Owner Fred Kraemer approached Carol to become the man behind a new venture. Carol was written in as a very, very limited partner, but he controlled the more than fifty employees who finally worked at the place. The cavernous discotheque, redubbed Carol's Speakeasy, opened in October 1978 at 1355 North Wells. The new Carol's charged a five-dollar membership fee and soon signed up thousands of card carriers. "The Center Stage [a Lakeview disco] had just closed," speculates Kraemer. "We just came at the right time, I guess; the gay community was ready for a new bar to open."

A disco was hardly Carol's style, but he worked hard at the format. His performances grew more and more extravagant, backed now by an in-the-flesh disc jockey and a bigger staff. On Saint Valentine's Day, he played "Ma Capone" in a plum dress and blond wig, and when the mock-hoodlums finally shot him, he keeled over as fake blood spilled from his guts. A parody of the movie *Grease* found him decked out as a high school principal in a violet dress, a green scarf, and half-glasses draped from his neck. Last March, as Dracula in a promotion for the movie *Love at First Bite*, he was being carted to the stage in a coffin, and when the bottom fell out the bar went up for grabs. He rented a surrey for Easter, dressed up in full spring-drag finery, bonnet included, and rode through New Town and Old Town to the cheers of onlookers, a beefcake beauty king at his side; of course he stopped at the bars along the way. In May, he climaxed a Fiorucci promotion party with a spirited dance behind emerald-green glasses. Yet nothing compared to a July benefit for the Frank Rodde fund; it featured Farnham and the giant Michael Shimandle wrestling in a sea of cake mix. Farnham, who that night tipped the scales at 304 pounds, was a gross, outrageous sight as he thrashed around in his boxer shorts, dripping with thick brown crud.

The crowds jammed into Carol's, and Farnham knew he was presiding over a big success. Mostly, he resisted the temptation to brag about it, yet sometimes he gave in. Surveying the madness on New Year's Eve of 1978, he turned to an intimate and said offhandedly, "I think we're probably number one now." He was far from managing porno bookstores. Last winter, he purchased a cowhide coat and matching hat. "He was all impressed with his new outfit," recalls Chuck Lind. "He thought he was walking around in five thousand dollars in furs." After the Fiorucci and *Love at First Bite* parties, Michael Butler, who once squired the film's costar, Susan St. James, invited Farnham and others out to Oak Brook to watch some polo. A photo from that day survives. It shows Farnham wedged in among this horsey set, and there is only one word for the expression on his face: pleased.

Back in Aurora, Richard's family, whom he loved, knew little of his life in the big city. Farnham returned home on special occasions to visit his mother, Lillian Windisch, who had remarried, and his sister, Pat Barkes. A few times he brought along a friend. At Christmas, he lavished gifts on Pat's three children, particularly her youngest, Nicky, who was Richard's godson. The Farnham clan trekked into Chicago each year for Mother's Day, when Richard would cook up a dinner of, say, spaghetti and sausages and fresh fruit compote. Once Richard took his family over to Carol's Coming Out. It was early Sunday evening and not much of anything was going on; they witnessed no performances.

Lillian Windisch was never sure whether her son was gay. "He used to show us wigs and gowns, for instance, but even as a kid he used to pantomime. And at Halloween time at National Tea [grocery store], he'd dress up in a gal's wig and gown. To me, that didn't emphasize anything about his being gay." Pat Barkes was more suspicious; but she, like her mother, insists that if she'd known for sure Richard was homosexual, she'd have cared for him no less. "He was my brother, and I loved him, and maybe if the shoe had been on the other foot, I would have expected him to understand about *me*. I don't feel that gays are that much different from you and me. They have different sexual desires, sure, but there's lots of straight people in the world that like sex acts that I'd have no more to do with than the man in the moon. Yet they walk down the street like you and me; what they do in their bedrooms—like what gays do in their bedrooms—is none of my business."

Richard also kept from his family the seriousness of his physical condition, which only grew worse as 1979 progressed. "About January or February, I noticed he was getting cramps in his hands," says Ida Guevara, a crony Carol used to call "the only cunt in the Family." Guevara, a very big woman, worked for Carol for years and frequently roomed with him. "Understand that he always had cramps in his legs, but not in his hands. One time we were at dinner, and he couldn't even pick up his fork. But he didn't want me to see—he didn't want me to feel sorry for him." His feet stayed swollen, and his long days exhausted him more and more. One early morning, Carol and Jerry Lopez, a doorman at Carol's Speakeasy, were grabbing a bite to eat at the Medinah restaurant at Fullerton and Clark. "If I ever go away, I don't want you to cry," Farnham told his friend. "Just think of the good times." Lopez looked up from his food: "Oh, I'll go way before you." Carol laughed.

Sick as he was, Carol's greatest notoriety lay just ahead. Neighbors had been complaining to police—one complaint was from Alderman Burton Natarus's office—that Carol's Speakeasy was the site of untoward activities. On May 12, undercover agents entered Carol's and found "open masturbation" in a darkened room in the back. One officer reported he'd had his genitals fondled. The cops charged a fifty-three-year-old maître d' with public indecency, Farnham with keeping a disorderly house, and three other men with disorderly conduct for failing to leave the bar when told to do so.

The cops returned a week later to see if that back room was still open. They entered the bar just before 1:30 A.M., interrupting a party that found everyone dressed up as construction workers. Fortunately for Kraemer, he'd shuttered the back room: unfortunately, police, and the fire officials with them, also intended to check for license and fire-code violations. The police locked the doors and told the patrons to keep still for a head count. Almost seven hundred people were packed into the bar, whose designated maximum occupancy was 399—and that was but one of twenty-six infractions the police tallied. The atmosphere in the bar remained calm as police made their determinations, with Carol helping to quiet emotions, and finally the customers were allowed to leave.

The trouble began as the partygoers spilled out onto Wells Street and mingled with the crowd departing the nearby Glory Hole, another gay bar. Some forty more cops rushed in. Accounts differ as to what happened. "People flooded into the street as we cleared the bar," contends Fred Bosse, who was then head of the Eighteenth District tactical unit. "There are a lot of bars in the area, see, and traffic was snarled. To be frank, there were a lot of freak shows walking down the street, and they did attract attention. Some fights broke out and we tried to break them up." Carol's personnel and patrons responded that it wasn't that way at all. Doorman Jerry Lopez insists the cops swore derisively at those attempting to leave and even pushed some people around. Among them was David Veltkamp, a freelance photographer who was tackled and struck in the stomach with a nightstick while attempting to record the scene. Several people were injured, one seriously, and eleven were charged with disorderly conduct. "All the arrests we made were entirely proper and in order," says Bosse, conceding only that "there may or may not have been officers who said things they shouldn't have—sometimes that happens." Mother Carol? Early on, he'd been secreted out of the discotheque to avoid what his employees felt would be his certain arrest on some trumped-up charge.

Ultimately, all charges stemming from the two raids on Carol's were either dropped or dealt with lightly; Kraemer coughed up less than one hundred dollars in fines. But these raids on Carol's climaxed a series of ten that had been made on North Side gay establishments in May, principally by vice control officers. The police said the raids, which yielded thirty-six arrests on charges that ranged from prostitution to disorderly conduct, were merited, not discriminatory. Gay establishments had been relatively free from such intervention for a decade or more, and tavern owners viewed the raids as pure harassment. "The cops see things going on in straight bars, but the cops never raid them," gripes Baton owner Jim Flint, angry even today. "As long as there are places for our type people to go, who not leave us alone? See, the cops think we're an easy bust. They have to have so many busts in a time period, so they think, 'Why not go after gays?'" Fred Kraemer sees no reason why the police, if they knew of code violations at his bar, couldn't have checked them out at a more reasonable time. The early-morning raids obviously were intended to net sex offenders.

Gays organized to halt what they felt was a campaign against them. On May 21, the Gay and Lesbian Coalition convened a meeting at the Second Unitarian Church on Barry Avenue. Fully five hundred persons showed up, and they formed an ad hoc committee, Gays and Lesbians for Action, to organize a parade and publicize it. The march was scheduled for June 5. On June 1, a delegation from the committee met with Mayor Byrne at City Hall. "The mayor told us she would instruct the police to investigate our complaints and to lay off in the meantime," says Doris Shane, a member of the delegation. Byrne spoke even more firmly at a press conference held soon after: "The city will act if there's a violation in a tavern, and that goes for violations of the building and electrical codes, but the city must treat everybody the same. I told the police, 'Don't go find them in one place and let the place across the street go free because it's not gay.'" The raids stopped, at least for a time. (Gay leaders also huddled during these weeks with top police brass and pressed charges against the individual cops with the department's Office of Professional Standards. To date, that office has made no recommendations to the Police Board. In late December, Byrne restated her opposition to the harassment of gay bars following a raid on the Rialto Tap on West Van Buren.)

The march and rally took place on June 5, as planned, although the parade route was changed, the marchers not being allowed on Michigan Avenue. Some 1,500 people massed in Daley Plaza to hear North Side aldermen Marty Oberman and Bruce Young call for passage of a pending gay rights ordinance (it hasn't been passed). Carol was not there. According to his roommate, Corky Corcoran, Carol had flown to Las Vegas the previous weekend and been kept there settling a traffic accident he'd had in a rented car. Carol's Speakeasy was represented by Woody Lorenz, the disco's publicity manager, as the day's events were planned, but it rankled some people that Farnham himself stayed aloof from the massive protest brought about by the raids on his club. Still . . . other gays were relieved. As Doris Shane explains, "Unfortunately, Richard fit the stereotype of the drag queen to the straight community. When the fanatics who oppose gay rights think of us, they think of somebody having sex in an alley or of a diesel-dyke. *I* certainly didn't go down to the mayor's office displaying the diesel-dyke stereotype."

Supposedly, Carol felt that he couldn't get involved because charges were pending against him; yet it certainly fit his style to remain uncommitted in a political scrap. He returned to Chicago the day after the march. That Wednesday, around midnight, he assumed the stage at the Speakeasy and asked for the music to be lowered. Carol thanked his customers for supporting the march, promised his bar would stay open, and pledged that the tavern would stand behind its patrons in the event of another raid. "And now," he said, signaling for the music, "it's time to have a great party."

After the raids, business slumped a little at Carol's Speakeasy, but it wasn't long before the customers flocked back. Carol's physical condition continued to deteriorate, although he made occasional attempts to help himself. In late July, he was at the Bistro emceeing a contest to pick a delegate to the Mr. Blue Boy pageant in New York, and while he was onstage explaining the contest rules, someone shouted for his drink order. Everyone waited for him to ask for a vodka. "I will have a Perrier, please," Carol mugged, and the audience applauded. Such demonstrations of abstinence were rare, sadly, and applause proved insufficient medicine.

His skin turned yellow with jaundice in early August, and Carol was admitted to Edgewater Hospital. When he checked out two weeks later, he resumed drinking. In late August, he showed up at Chuck Renslow's White Party, thrown each year in the grand style by the proprietor of Man's Country bathhouse and other businesses. He wore a white dress, white hair, and white sunglasses. "Your mother's sick and tired," he complained to Michael Kucharski that night at Navy Pier. "I just need a rest." Several days later, he went back into the hospital.

Richard received as many visitors and flower arrangements as Edgewater would allow—and some it didn't—but they had no power to reverse the medical mess he was in. His liver was gone, his kidneys had shut down, and he suffered from congestive heart failure, swelled lungs, and ulcers. He had trouble breathing, and his blood pressure was terribly weak. He was experiencing a considerable amount of pain, especially from a condition called ascites, in which fluid in the abdomen presses up against the diaphragm. Lying in the intensive care unit, IV tubes plugged into him at various points, Carol tried to maintain his good humor, but his illness was destroying him.

The weekend of September 22, it looked like curtains. A rumor circulated at Dragocious, a benefit held for the Frank Rodde fund at the Baton, that Carol had died. Instead, he rallied. On Sunday, he recognized his mother and sister. By Tuesday, he could eat by himself. On Thursday, he was laughing at TV, so hard that sometimes the nurse on duty had to tell him to cut it out. Pat Barkes, however, knew he was dying—and she knew Richard knew it, although it went unspoken. "I could see it in his eyes," she says.

Sometime during his final days, Richard summoned a priest. The clergyman heard Richard's confession and granted him communion, according to Farnham's mother. Officially, the Catholic Church denies communion to practicing homosexuals, and Carol had never practiced his faith much anyway. The priest, Father Michael Jacobsen, who represents Dignity, Chicago's progressive congregation for gay Catholics, prefers not to say what passed between pastor and penitent. But Farnham's mother was relieved that at least her son had seen a priest: "If he felt like he wanted to confess and the priest forgave him his sins, then as far as I'm concerned, he's absolved. I ain't going to say he isn't going to have to pay for those sins in the afterlife, but we're taught that God forgives, and I think he does."

On Saturday, September 29, Carol slipped into a coma. He died the next day at 9:30 P.M. in the presence of several people, including his sister, his mother, and Woody Lorenz. Doctors listed cirrhosis of the liver as the official cause of death. Carol was waked the next Tuesday at the plush Blake-Lamb funeral home at 1035 North Dearborn. Father Jacobsen officiated at the evening service, which packed the funeral parlor's chapel; there was no special remembrance of Carol in the priest's standard ceremony. Farnham's family returned his body to a funeral home in Aurora, and at 10 A.M. on Thursday, a funeral Mass was held in Aurora's Our Lady of Good Counsel Church. Farnham's funeral drew dozens of his Chicago friends; they filled the right side of the sanctuary while his Aurora family and friends occupied the left. Lillian Windisch remarked to a friend of

Richard's, "My son was fortunate to have had two families." The pallbearers, who were all gay, carried Farnham's casket from the church. He was buried at Mount Olivet Cemetery, laid to rest near the grave of an aunt.

Richard's family had been touched by how loving his friends were as he died, and now the family purchased space in Chicago's gay papers, *Gay Life* and *Gay Chicago*. In *Gay Life* there was a picture of Farnham in a Cheeks T-shirt against a backdrop of rocks; *Gay Chicago* published only the text. It said: "The family of Richard Farnham, known as Mother Carol to his many friends, wishes to thank you for your great concern and prayers during his illness and death. We feel he loved you all very much and would want you to remember him as he was—a thoughtful and loving person."

The formal legacy of Richard Carroll Farnham amounted to a little money, some of it from a life insurance policy, and clothes, furniture, and clown artifacts. The family is divvying up the possessions because Farnham left no will. Carol's Speakeasy continues to do good if not spectacular business, according to proprietor Kraemer; if it faces any harassment today, it is in the form of neighborhood families who have taken their complaints about noise from the bar to the office of the Illinois attorney general. Kraemer fully intends to retain Carol's name on his discotheque, in Farnham's memory.

The meaning of Richard Farnham's life is subject to sharply differing opinions. Michael Kucharski was married and a respiratory therapist when he wandered years ago into Carol's Coming Out, there to be nudged into overt homosexuality. "Carol taught me much about this life that most people don't understand," remarks Michael "K" in the cramped, dark bar he has just opened on Clark Street. "'I'm gay, I'm proud, and I'm going to live life to the fullest'—that was his credo." Robert D'Appley, a psychologist who has treated gay clients for a half dozen years, also endorses Carol's life-of-the-party ways. "Carol was funny and entertaining; he was loose," says D'Appley, who observed Farnham from a distance. "He did things at full blast, and he didn't hide. He was out there—he didn't mask what he was." Ralph Paul Gerhardt, copublisher of *Gay Chicago* and Carol's good friend, eulogized his chum this way in the pages of the newspaper: "He was dedicated to making people happy and achieved his goal through warmth, love, and a touch of tacky zanyness."

But a considerable number of people speak of Carol with derision, feeling his life counted for little in the end. "Frankly, I could never get a sober word out of Carol," says Larry Rolla, the young attorney who represented all but one of those charged in the May 19 altercations outside Carol's Speakeasy. "Carol was the last of the great drag queens, the last one to die. As far as great influence, there wasn't any. It was just personality, that's all." A bartender at one North Side gay establishment thinks Carol symbolized the debilitating frenzy of the party life. "He did like to have a good time," sighs the man, "but that involved sex, drugs, and tearing people's clothes off. He was the center of places where sex, poppers, and disco were points of existence. But it got to the point for him where he'd be drinking vodka and his head would hit a table at ten o'clock, never to rise again in any presentable state. He was perhaps the first mythic person among party people, but not for the rest of us, for the more sober ones." Thinks Grant Ford, "We all have our canonized saints and our canonized sinners—maybe Carol was simply *our* canonized sinner."

Bar owner Marge Summit, lounging in her new Uptown apartment, is familiar with the aspersions that are now cast upon Carol's memory. They disturb her. "Listen," she insists, "what he did for the gay community, as far as giving people a good place to party-party, if it was *so* bad, how come his place was so packed all the time?"

Whatever, the impression of Carol that most tellingly transcends the grave is the inextricable sadness of the man himself. Even his closest associates testify to it. "Sometimes he'd be drinking, sitting at the bar, and you'd see tears coming out of his eyes," recalls Ida Guevara. "You'd ask him what was wrong and he'd just say, 'Nothing, nothing.'" Corky Corcoran recollects similar moments: "There were times when you'd be sitting with him at the bar—there could have been six hundred to seven hundred people in the room—and you had this strange feeling that he was lonely right then. He gave of his personal self very little—he kept everything welled up inside him." To explain Farnham, Guevara introduces the hackneyed image of the clown crying inside; the image, although a cliché, fits Carol.

As you enter Carol's Speakeasy today, above the rack of gay newspapers there hangs a black-and-white photograph of Richard Farnham in drag. He is carrying on in the picture, taken several years ago at a Mr. Windy City contest. His tongue is pressed onto the roof of his wide-open mouth, and his nostrils are flared. The flouncing sleeve of one arm obscures Farnham's left eye, but his right eye appears in the photo. Beneath a pair of fake eyelashes, you can see his eye clearly, a black circle suspended in an oval pool of white. The eyeball is fixed off into space somewhere, yet its expression is clear—it is one of some wisdom and great, great sorrow.

AS I LAY DYING

After a brilliant career teaching other doctors how to save lives,
Dr. Roger Bone showed them how to let life go.

A doctor announces that the cancer has spread or your heart is hopelessly weak. You lose weight and energy, often encounter intense pain. With weeks to go your breath becomes short and you take to your bed, restless, disoriented, your body temperature spiking. Excessive sleep or a coma follows and then you're consigned to history.

We seldom contemplate this trip in advance, preferring to think we'll somehow evade it. Even doctors blind their eyes to this dark territory. Roger Conley Bone, a famed pulmonary physician, recently died of cancer at age fifty-six. He'd studied death at close quarters throughout his medical career, but only as he stood close to his own did he finally fathom it.

"Dying is very hard, the hardest thing in life," said Bone in May, a wasting figure lying on what he anticipated would be his deathbed in a lakefront high-rise. "It's certainly the hardest thing that's ever happened to me. I have pain. I can't do bodily functions. Tumors are all over my body. If I walk, I worry that I might slip my hip out of joint and never be able to walk again." But Bone insisted on making his last days as productive as possible. "I could stay in this bedroom and scream, but that doesn't seem a very constructive way to spend one's final days," he said. "And this can be a tolerable, even a good time."

A generation has passed since the hospice movement surfaced in the United States and Elisabeth Kübler-Ross did her pioneering work on the psychic

237

Roger Bone

process of dying. Perhaps our society is finally coming to terms with death. As the baby boomers age, discussion has increased—about the needless prolonging of life through technology, doctors' improved ability to relieve pain, and the dignified deaths of public figures such as Jacqueline Onassis and Joseph Cardinal Bernardin.

"We can now take dying as the culminating experience of life, rather than the abject, dejected, and solitary farewell that we all fear," says Dr. Linda Emanuel, vice president of ethics standards for the American Medical Association. "If we use technology, we can maximize the quality of the life that people have left, as they accept the inevitability of death. Dying is a very personal matter, but the more we understand how others die the more fulfilling we can make the experience once we get there. And in reaching that understanding someone like Dr. Bone was fabulous."

Roger Bone grew up in Bald Knob, Arkansas, a hamlet set in strawberry and cotton fields sixty miles northeast of Little Rock. His father, Conley, operated one of three grocery stores in town, and his mother ran a beauty shop out of the house. "Dad was very old-fashioned," remembers Roger's younger brother Larry. "He himself had grown up under difficult circumstances, and all he could remember were the hard times. During the summer he worked Roger and me six days at thirty-five cents an hour. By the time we finished scrubbing the floor on Saturday night it would be nine thirty or ten o'clock, and we'd be awfully tired."

The punishing routine fired the ambitions of both boys. "One of my drives was that I didn't want to live my life in Bald Knob," Roger related. "I wanted to be a doctor, though back then Little Rock was as far as I could see." The brothers matriculated at Hendrix College, the state's most prestigious private college, and went on to the University of Arkansas medical school. At Arkansas, recalls Larry, "Roger was always going beyond. I'd be reading a textbook on gross anatomy, and I'd stop to see my brother and he'd be studying three or four textbooks." In 1965, with his sons still in medical school, Conley Bone died of a heart attack at age forty-six. "He worked himself to death," says Roger, "and I inherited the work ethic."

As a decorated army captain and field physician in Vietnam, Bone came up square against the horrors of war. "In Vietnam MASH units there were no clean shots," he said. "You'd always see triple amputees—two legs and one arm gone, or one arm and two legs. It was pure mutilation. I learned that I hated war, but I also learned about medicine." It was in Vietnam that he became fascinated with septic shock, the potentially fatal outgrowth of sepsis, the release of bacteria into the bloodstream.

Back in the United States, Bone took his internship, residency, and a fellowship in pulmonary and critical-care medicine at the University of Texas

Southwestern medical school at Dallas. Beginning in 1972, he taught and practiced at the University of Kansas Medical Center in Kansas City. Then in 1979, not yet forty years old, he was named chief of pulmonary and critical care at the University of Arkansas Medical Center in Little Rock. He directed research into septic shock, a prime cause of death in intensive-care units. He penned a slew of septic-shock articles, although he also wrote pieces on other topics and edited authoritative textbooks, most notably *Pulmonary and Critical Care Medicine,* published in 1993 and updated annually since. "He was a philosopher, a synthesizer," says one longtime colleague. "He didn't do the original research—he wasn't going to be the one to win the Nobel Prize—but he put the hows and whys together." Bone's most significant contribution was probing the pathology and treatment of adult respiratory disease syndrome, a septic-shock-related shutdown of the lungs that had dramatically confronted physicians on the battlefields of Korea and Vietnam.

In 1984 Bone arrived in Chicago as chairman of internal medicine at Rush-Presbyterian-Saint Luke's Medical Center, supervising fifteen specialties. He also served as the pulmonary and critical-care chief, and for a period as the dean of the medical college. At six foot two, Bone was a towering presence, with a pleasant yet formal demeanor and a near photographic memory. He made the most of his opportunities, powered by an almost otherworldly drive that mimicked his father's. "I worked fourteen- to sixteen-hour days because work for me was play," he said, "and I did that more at Rush than anyplace because I had the power base and the resources to develop what I wanted." He oversaw research, lectured widely, directed training, and recruited top doctors.

"Roger's leadership qualities convinced you to share his vision," says Dr. Leo Henikoff, president of Rush. "He was a workaholic, yes. Sometimes that means a person is only into process, but Roger got things done—he was into outcomes. He accomplished more with time than anyone I know." Stuart Levin, an infectious-disease specialist, doubled as Bone's second-in-command of internal medicine. He recalls meetings that one or the other would walk out of on the grounds they both weren't needed there to get the job done; these departures tended to focus the attention of everyone left at the table. "We forced more decisions than you could imagine by walking out to the bathroom to urinate."

Though Bone was often perceived as exceedingly businesslike, he could also be exceedingly encouraging. He was known for the careful way he went over student papers and for the way he dealt with residents. "When Roger talked to you, you felt that here was this person of great accomplishment trying to help you," says Michael Davidson, a former resident who's now president of the Chicago Center for Clinical Research. Says Robert Balk, who trained with Bone in Little

Rock and is now Rush's director of pulmonary medicine, "He invigorated you to reach your potential. He was the epitome of a leader."

"With my patients I was a good, compassionate physician," Bone said of himself. "But to a limit. We would make grand rounds, and there I was, the chief doctor, the leader of the team, like [fabled Texas heart surgeon] Michael DeBakey. DeBakey might know each chest—and the physical problems it posed—but he wouldn't necessarily know each person, and so it was with me. I'd lay out a patient's treatment plan for the day and then leave the particulars to my interns and residents."

Bone insisted on his devotion to his wife (and high school sweetheart), Rosemary, and to their daughters, Mary Katherine and Cynthia. Despite his schedule, he usually managed to return home to Oak Park each night for dinner, and he relished twilight jogs with Mary Katherine. Rumbling along, he exhibited a goofy sense of humor, yelling "hello girls" to preadolescent boys who responded by swearing at him.

But the outside world invariably intruded. When he got on his Exercycle in the basement he tuned in a half-dozen TV sets, muting some while raising the volume on others. "After dinner he would sit down, either in the basement or up in the attic, and out would come a huge stack of paper," remembers Mary Katherine. "He would go through the documents, and if I wanted help with my math homework I had to be firm. 'I need you now,' I'd say, and then he was there for me."

While he relished being out in the backyard in his T-shirt and shorts (an adequate backyard was a necessity of any house the Bones owned), he didn't shoot the breeze much with the neighbors. He wasn't involved in his community, and beyond jogging he didn't have hobbies to speak of, although he listened to self-improvement tapes on art and music. Raised as a Methodist, and once a state officer in a denominational youth organization, Bone let the church go as an adult. "It was predominantly Rosemary and the girls who went to church," he said. Socializing for Roger and Rosemary, a nurse who later became a part-time travel and real estate agent, centered on Rush; at parties he did small talk poorly, preferring to discuss medicine. His friendships tended to involve a few colleagues at Rush, notably Levin and Eubanks, and professionals he bumped into at medical gatherings. "I knew Roger for twenty-five years," recounts Tom Petty, a Denver pulmonary physician who has taught part-time at Rush. "At meetings or conferences he and I would sit down, laugh, and talk. But he was a hard guy to know."

In 1993 Bone, frustrated with cost-cutting at Rush, responded to an offer to become president of Toledo's Medical College of Ohio. "It was a step up, and I was glad for Roger," says Henikoff. Bone and Rosemary settled into a brick

colonial house on a bluff over the Maumee River. At fifty-two, he had a satisfying marriage, two grown, productive daughters, a salary of nearly four hundred
thousand dollars, and a national reputation.

That Christmas Day he fell while unpacking books, and blood turned up in his
urine. Days later, during a long meeting on campus, he experienced riveting back
pain, and when he went to the bathroom his discharge now consisted only of blood
and blood clots. An exam revealed a cancerous tumor the size of an orange in his
right kidney. A surgeon removed the kidney and an adjoining adrenal gland, and
Bone felt the problem had been solved. "I went back to work within a week," he
says. "I thought to myself, I'm cured. I had hoped the tumor had been totally resected. The initial scans were negative. You might as well be an optimist."

But in October 1995 a routine chest X-ray showed that the cancer had metas-
tasized to his lungs, which were now filled with two dozen small tumors. Bone
read the X-ray and realized, at least intellectually, what his prospects were.
"With renal cell cancer the survival rate is only 1 percent."

Bone returned to the house on the bluff. It was 4 P.M. on a warm Friday. He
took off his coat and tie, sat in a lawn chair, and shared the news with Rosemary.
"She was devastated, and she was also in disbelief," he recalled. "I had seen
hundreds of people with my disease and I knew the prognosis, but I wasn't about
to burst her bubble. As for me, I don't recollect denial. I knew it was happening, so why deny it? I'd seen too much sickness in others to pretend it couldn't
happen to me. There wasn't anger, either—I had had fifty-four good years, with
excellent health. But there was sorrow, definitely."

Rosemary handed him a glass of lemonade. "Suddenly the lemonade became
the point," Bone said. "I tasted the sweetness of the drink, and though I felt my
life passing before me I tried to savor the moment."

The emotional process of dying is a pathway charted by Kübler-Ross in the late
1960s. For four years the Swiss-trained Kübler-Ross interviewed terminally
ill patients at the University of Chicago's Billings Hospital. Her *On Death and
Dying*, published in 1969, defined dying's five stages: denial and isolation; rage,
envy, and resentment; bargaining, largely with one's Maker; depression; and finally acceptance, albeit tired and unfeeling. Although Kübler-Ross wrote that
the stages "will last for different periods of time and will replace each other or
exist at times side by side," the general impression remains that the phases are
to be passed through in sequence.

Many of today's experts on dying prefer to think of dying as a period to be
profited from. Charles Corr, a professor of philosophy at Southern Illinois University at Edwardsville and a longtime hospice volunteer, hates the theory of

stages. "They make it sound like you're being pulled along through a car wash, and at the end you'll be clean," he says. Corr says many of the terminally ill take on tasks. "For some it involves dealing with pain and nausea. For others it may mean being with someone they love or restoring an old hurt. This is all about maximizing the quality of life you have left." Corr likes to repeat an end-of-life maxim he attributes to a hospice patient in England: "I only hope to be able to say to the people who are important to me, 'Thank you, I'm sorry, I love you, good-bye.'"

Experts also say that people remain who they were as they die; seldom does a scrooge become a saint. "Basically we die the way we live," says Martha Twaddle, medical director of the Hospice of the North Shore. "You can't, in the good ol' American tradition, pull an all-nighter. The essence of who you are remains and, if anything, becomes more vivid. If you have lived like a son of a bitch you'll die like a son of a bitch."

From the outset Bone confronted his dying as an experience to put to use. He'd already written articles for the *Journal of the American Medical Association* (*JAMA*), where he'd served as a consulting editor. After he was diagnosed with kidney cancer, but before he learned it would kill him, he sent the magazine an article of a different sort.

In it he offered four cautionary observations: "1. Good health is often taken for granted; however, it is the most precious commodity one possesses. 2. One's spouse, children, family, and friends are the essential ingredients that allow one to endure an experience such as a serious and unexpected illness. 3. When faced with death, one recognizes the importance of God and one's relationship to God. 4. The things one does throughout one's life that seem so urgent are, most of the time, not so important." At a convocation at the Medical College of Ohio, Bone had told incoming students to temper their devotion to doctoring. Now, in *JAMA*, he reprised that advice. "I would suggest to the students in my speech that they must find the time to balance the scientific with the humanistic. To find not only the time but also the energy to be with family and friends and to enjoy the arts or a good novel or a fine dinner."

After realizing he was dying, Bone wrote three more essays for *JAMA*. "In my experience it's very unusual for a physician to write eloquently for a public audience about how they feel," says *JAMA* editor George Lundberg. "Roger, you know, has written hundreds of articles of a scientific nature, but here he was poignant, pointed, and in many ways disturbing."

"I saw death more times than I can count," Bone said in his final essay, which appeared last December. "I always thought that death caused a collapse of the dying person inward upon himself. The dying person appeared to be little more than a shrunken shell lying in a hospital bed. Physical collapse meant that there was a collapse of mental and spiritual being as well. I know now I could not have been more wrong.

"Death has opened my eyes to life—literally. Since learning that I have a terminal illness, I believe my mind has expanded and its appetite has become insatiable. I want to know and experience everything. I feel at times what Thomas Wolfe described when he first walked into the New York Public Library: I want to grasp everything, read every book, listen to every piece of music. I believe that I will walk toward death with that same quest to know."

Bone was now reading Thoreau and contemplating the broad Maumee River—"his Walden Pond," says his brother Larry—that flowed below his house outside Toledo. In his last *JAMA* essay he described the view at sunset. "I watched the buzzard hawks and a pair of ducks," he wrote. "A woodpecker hammers away at a tree on the other side of the river, taking advantage of the last light to pick a last juicy grub out of the bark. A fish flops somewhere in the black water—probably one of the large carp that school in the shallows."

He dived into John Updike's Rabbit novels and read *Our Town*, Thornton Wilder's rumination on mortality, enjoying the high school classic anew. The Bone stereo system pumped out Mozart, Beethoven, Vivaldi. "I sat on our patio in Toledo and listened to *The Four Seasons* and read," he said. "Did all this have something to teach me about life or about death and dying?" If he came to no certain answer, "at least I could savor what was beautiful."

Though Bone said his cancer didn't send him down the path of Kübler-Ross, his colleagues say the normal emotions did emerge—he was no superman. When his cancer reappeared "he was disappointed, shocked, and angry," recalls David Eubanks, director of education at the Northbrook-based American College of Chest Physicians. "He was mad that the cancer had gone the way it had, and he wondered about the initial diagnosis." Specifically, he thought that chemotherapy could have been started earlier. When Bone informed his friend Tom Petty about the metastasis, resentment was mixed with trepidation about the forthcoming chemotherapy.

Throughout his ordeal, Bone said frankly, he sorrowed. "I've been sad, yes," he said, "because I'd like more time with my wife and family, because I'm dying in my midfifties. Rosemary and I will cry occasionally, over not being able to spend our lives together, over not continuing on." Gallows humor was beyond him. "I don't find humor in anything that's happened to me," he said.

The Bones moved back to Chicago in April 1996, renting an apartment with sweeping views of the lakefront. Rosemary filled the apartment with traditional furniture, Oriental rugs, crystal, and family photographs; her husband assumed a distinguished professorship at Rush. His office was next to the dean's office, and he had no regular duties. But he sounded off, advocating in *JAMA,* for instance, an FDA-imposed moratorium on a risky critical-care technique of catheterization to monitor vascular pressure within the heart. He continued a course of radiation and advanced chemotherapy—interleukin-2, gamma and alpha interferon, and floxuridine—that caused hair loss, nausea, and the weakening of his bones. Much as he valued the efforts of his oncologist, Dr. Robert Kilbourn ("Bob pulled out all the stops for me"), the cancer remained.

He became even more outspoken in his views. "Maybe through what I say people can come to a greater appreciation of this part of life," he said when I first visited him last April. "Not to be morbid, but there are things to do in advance, things to consider." He was lying under a blanket in a four-poster bed, the curtains drawn against the light. A lamp with a burgundy shade cast an eerie glow. A small fan on the nightstand cooled the doctor; a wheelchair stood in a corner. By now there were tumors in Bone's right hand, in his right shoulder, and in his lungs: fluid on his lungs had to be drained periodically by a nurse.

Over the last decade or so drugs pioneered in hospices have begun to relieve the awful pain that can attend one's last days. A morphine pill lasts from eight to twelve hours; an intravenous pump provides extra bursts of liquid morphine when needed; a fentanyl patch offers a narcotic analgesic. "Now your every waking moment needn't be in constant agony," says Steven Rothschild, a family physician at Illinois Masonic Medical Center. "Eighty to 90 percent of the time we can give people a constant floor of pain relief." Morphine relieved some—certainly not all—of Bone's pain.

Each time I came to see him, he extended his left hand. When asked how he occupied his days, Bone said, "I can sit in the other room. I watch television and talk to my wife. The reading is much less now, since it's hard to concentrate. Sometimes I look out the window and see people jogging, like I used to do. Now that my body is racked with pain I realize that vitality is such a precious gift."

As Bone's physical world narrowed, his love of family deepened. "You ask yourself, 'Who am I going to miss?' It's not the hundreds of people you see occasionally. It's my younger daughter [Cindy] in medical school, and Mary Katherine, my daughter who's now an administrator at Rush. It's Rosemary. My own father wasn't very expressive to me or my brother, never telling us he loved us—and given who he was I don't blame him. But I have made it a point to always let them know that I loved them and was there for them, and that tendency is all the stronger now. I tell my children and my family hundreds of times that I love them. This is the time to make such statements."

Mary Katherine told me afterward, "I don't feel he left anything unsaid."

Bone took care of final matters—nailing down his finances (enough money for Rosemary to survive on and enough for Cynthia to finish medical school), figuring out his burial site (in the family plot outside Little Rock), and insisting that no measures be employed to keep him alive beyond reason. Bone wanted to die in bed near Rosemary in their apartment, if need be assisted by a hospice affiliated with Rush. (Hospices, of which there are 103 in Illinois, marshal social workers, nurses, inhalation therapists, and chaplains to provide the dying with palliative care at home.)

Bone said he was thinking more about God and eternal life. Not everyone is like Cardinal Bernardin, who referred to death as "my friend" and believed he was moving "from one state of existence to another"—in the words of his oncologist, Ellen Gaynor. "Still, for many of us there's a new focus on a belief in something greater out there," says Larry Burton, the head chaplain at Rush-Presbyterian-Saint Luke's. "Sometimes it's mere questioning—why is God doing this to me? And other times there comes a new unity with God. Nonbelievers may embrace Christianity or the Muslim religion."

Bone read the Bible diligently. In April, his eyesight failing, he was watching videotapes of the Holy Land lent from his brother Larry and of a rambling late-night Arkansas preacher he'd recorded off cable television. He also listened to an audiotape Burton had given him of a Franciscan priest and spiritual guide named Richard Rohr. He wanted to discuss what he'd read and heard; one afternoon he talked about how Leviticus anticipates modern-day germ theory. He'd been gripped by a book that dealt with biblical prophesies and Christ's second coming. Burton comforted him with metaphor by inviting him to think of his dying as a Sabbath: after his labors he could rest and reflect on the fruits of his creation. Bone said he'd made peace with himself. "I have my own personal confessions that I have made with my God—and will make. I haven't been perfect, nor has anyone."

Much of the satisfaction in Bone's life had revolved around his career, and to a large extent it still did. As I was leaving after our first conversation he handed me his curriculum vitae, a document running to eighty-three pages that noted the books he'd edited or coedited, some 1,108 articles, and his mentions in *Who's Who in America*, *The Best Doctors in America*, and *Town and Country* magazine. Every outside lecture, prize, and committee chairmanship earned an entry.

When he'd written in *JAMA* that the urgent becomes unimportant in the face of death, was he denigrating the accomplishments so carefully detailed in the résumé? I asked him this the next time we met.

"I spent a lot of time in my career worrying about administrative duties, hiring and firing, fellowships, and research projects," he replied. "All those things were priority items, but I now see that my worrying didn't make success in these ventures any more likely. I should have spent more time with my family and had a closer relationship with my God. I may not have been as successful if I'd written one hundred fewer articles. My pride in all the articles I wrote remains. But when my moment actually comes I won't be thinking about them. I'll be thinking about my family, God, and my place in eternity."

The final journey of Roger Bone came as mainstream medicine was rethinking its approach to the terminally ill. Ten years ago the New Jersey–based Robert Wood Johnson Foundation, whose focus is health and health care, undertook a twenty-eight-million-dollar study of ten thousand critically ill patients at eight U.S. medical centers. Its conclusions, published in *JAMA* in November 1995, found that doctors often ignore the wishes of patients. As a result, half the patients studied spent eight or more days either comatose or being mechanically ventilated in an intensive care unit. Half the patients were in moderate to severe pain the last three days of their lives.

Startled by the findings, the Johnson Foundation has launched the Last Acts Campaign, with task forces at work in such areas as doctor and nurse education and palliative care. The American Medical Association is using a Johnson Foundation grant to make physicians and medical students more aware of palliation and acquaint them—and patients—with living wills or at least with a short form some patients are given to fill out stating how they want doctors to handle resuscitation, major surgery, mechanical breathing, and pain. "Yes, we're slow and we're behind," admits Linda Emanuel, who's directing this AMA initiative, "but a generation is relatively short in the history of medicine to come up with a proper intervention." On June 27 the U.S. Supreme Court rejected the notion of a constitutional right to doctor-assisted suicide; the decision, dashing the hopes of supporters of Michigan physician Jack Kevorkian, heightened attention on palliative care.

A paladin of the machinery-filled intensive care unit, Bone was the kind of doctor the Johnson Foundation labeled as cavalier with patients. "You become shell-shocked to the dying around you," he conceded. "Doctors want to cure, to think that for every diagnosis there is a prescription to make things better. But what do you do when the cure is a failure? You may walk away. Doctors need a way to deal with failure. They need to tell their patients, 'We still love you though we can't cure you, and we are not rejecting you as a patient.'"

Last October Bone was invited to deliver the convocation at the annual meeting at the American College of Chest Physicians in San Francisco. As a past president of the group and one of nine masters among the college's fifteen thousand members—a practitioner judged to be greatly gifted—Bone would have been welcomed in any case. As he was dying he drew an especially big crowd at the Moscone Convention Center. Bone wasn't sure he'd be fit enough to speak, so he had taped his remarks.

Dressed in a red tie, white shirt, and dark suit, the doctor looked gauntly into the camera. "I spent my life thinking about medicine. Medicine was everything to me, as it is everything to you." But he told his fellow doctors this: "Take time to be with family and friends. Take time to reflect on nature. Take time to contemplate the fullness of life and to acknowledge death as a natural consequence."

Bone drew a portrait of Harry "Rabbit" Angstrom, the car salesman protagonist of the Updike novels, perishing in an intensive care unit—white-skinned, downcast, tubes running out of his body. Angstrom's wife, upon seeing him, nearly vomited in "a crushing wave of sorrow," said Bone, and continued, "Harry's life was absorbed with the need for something more. Thus, the greatest tragedy in Harry's death was the missed opportunity for a personally fulfilled life. What I hope is that Harry's life is not typical of most of us. Definitely, I would want Harry's life not to be like your life. . . .

"I cannot sit idly by very long," he said. "We must discuss life and death with our patients more. I have been a medical school dean, the chief of a pulmonary section, and we really don't teach the dying process well at all. We are so involved with the scientific that we unconsciously ignore the dying part of life. My first challenge to you is essentially this—you should try to live as if it is your last day. Now you shouldn't live morbidly, but you should live to appreciate the great things that are out there for us. It took a great event like cancer to make me realize that. My other challenge to you is this—you need to look at your patients who are terminally ill and try to help them find the peace that they may be able to find before they die."

"The speech was a barn burner," says Tom Petty. Bone's peers gave him a standing ovation. Later, at a smaller gathering, he unveiled a new theory on how the immune system may be counterproductive in combating sepsis.

Bone became more attentive to patients, less the superior authority than the equal. When he went to Rush to receive radiation, he would approach others waiting for treatment. "I'm a distinguished professor with terminal cancer," he would say, "and I would be happy to share thoughts with you." He said he had many mutually beneficial conversations.

Bone never abandoned hope. "Early on there was hope that my cancer had been resected successfully," he said. "Then I had hope—slim, yes—that radiation and chemotherapy would take care of it." A year ago, with luck running out, Bone traveled to the University of Arkansas to attempt a new technique in which tiny plastic particles would be injected into the arteries leading to the tumors in his lungs to cut off the blood supply. "If this works, you can write it up," Bone told his doctors in Arkansas. "If it kills me, you'll know you shouldn't do it again." After trying the technique, Bone spent three days in a hotel room in the grip of a high fever; the tumors' growth merely paused. "Now there is hope that there will be some last-minute advance, just like an AIDS patient prays for a breakthrough," he said in May. Rosemary flew to Prague this year for an alternative drug, and although Bone doubted its efficacy he tried it; he also took an experimental drug provided by the National Institutes of Health.

Bone returned to Arkansas to receive awards from the University of Arkansas medical school, from Hendrix College, and from the citizenry of Bald Knob. The town proclaimed March 21 as Roger Bone Day. When Rosemary drove the native son up from Little Rock, he saw his name on a banner hung over the main street and a crowd of youngsters, friends, former teachers, and family waiting for him at the high school, where he'd once been captain of the football team and student council president. As he moved inside the auditorium someone gripped his tumor-stricken right hand too hard, and he switched to shaking hands with his left.

He spoke first to the students, telling them that with effort they too could excel. "I understand that at home he never comes out of the bedroom, and I was surprised at his ability to stand and speak like he did," said Bald Knob mayor Earl Strickland some months later. Afterward, refreshments awaited him in a school lounge. He was so tired by noon that he skipped the luncheon planned in his honor; when Rosemary got him back to Little Rock he went straight to bed. But to Bone March 21 was an elixir. "Probably that was the most meaningful day of my life," he told me.

In April Bone and chaplain Larry Burton joined in a lecture to students, faculty, and residents at Rush on death and dying. Bone appeared on videotape, but he managed to get to a seat in the front row, thanks to a cane and Rosemary's arm. Several donors, led by an unnamed colleague, endowed a $1.5 million chair in Bone's name at Rush, the interest on which will go to establish a center on the dying patient at the medical center. For the second year, in May Rush sponsored a Bone-inspired conference on end-of-life issues, with Mary Katherine as one of the organizers. Those in attendance at the Drake Hotel received a booklet called *Reflections* written by Bone. Published by the Evanston-based National Kidney Cancer Association, the handsomely illustrated booklet is written for dying patients and their families. It deals with nitty-gritty issues such as insurance, memorial contributions, hospices, and doctor-assisted suicide, an option he firmly opposed.

"Before we start I'd like to say a few words about Dr. Roger Bone," said Erich Brueschke, Bone's successor as dean of the Rush medical college, welcoming the conferees at the Drake. "This extraordinary human being and physician is dying in our midst. Because of his deteriorating health, he's unable to be with us today, but I'd like to publicly recognize him with a round of applause."

Back at his apartment, Bone, clad in a yellow T-shirt, was propped on pink and yellow pillows in his bed. The blanket pulled high and tight about him, he looked boyish and innocent, despite a hacking cough he couldn't contain. "I feel sorrow a lot now," he said. "I don't want to leave my family. I'd love to see my grandchildren, and I don't have any. I have some fear. You wonder what eternity is like and that sort of thing. How is the final end going to be? I hope for the sake of me and my family that it comes like it did for Beth in *Little Women*. She had a benign look on her face, and then she just closed her eyes."

I had promised Rosemary I'd be short; Bone needed his strength for the nurse coming to drain fluid from his chest. After fifty minutes I rose to leave. "Good-bye," he said in a firm voice, extending his left hand from underneath the covers. I shook it with gratitude for his courage and honesty.

Bone still talked Rush medical business with Stuart Levin, just like always. He told intimates he was hanging on until Cindy completed the semester at the University of Michigan medical school. "He was afraid his death would mess up her finals," says Larry Bone. Cindy earned high marks. During the Memorial Day weekend the Bone brothers watched the Bulls play on television; Roger had made his way from the bedroom to a recliner in the family room, walking slowing with a cane. "He cheered on Michael Jordan and the rest of 'em as if he was going to be around one hundred years," Larry said later. "Roger's a tough old bird. Nobody thought he'd last this long. He knows death is inevitable, and he has made peace with it. His spirits are very good, probably better than yours or mine would be."

On May 29 Bone developed a fever of 105 degrees. He'd wanted to die at home, but "he'd taken a bad turn, and we couldn't let him melt in the bed," said Mary Katherine. Bone was admitted to Rush and tumbled, ironically, into septic shock. "The chances of his surviving the episode were less than 15 percent, but with antibiotics and other drugs, an old way of treating the condition, he prevailed," says Stuart Levin. "We were all amazed." Rosemary and the girls took turns staying with him as his blood pressure dropped and he drifted into incoherence. His new goal was to be around when the Bulls won the NBA championship; he would watch a quarter of a game, fade into semiconsciousness, and then emerge for the last quarter. By now "he was more a tumor than a person, and so very brave" says Levin. Powerful doses of liquid morphine were applied to lessen his pain, and he continued to crumble. "I'm not salvageable," Bone said at last, fulfilling a promise he had made to Larry Burton to indicate when it was over.

He had a rough night on Sunday, June 11. "Finally he got comfortable early that morning," says Mary Katherine. "My mom was with him. He closed his eyes and went to sleep." He died at 11 A.M.

His funeral took place the following Wednesday at the First Presbyterian Church of River Forest. "His accomplishments read like a who's who in the world of medicine," said the Reverend Richard Latta. Bone himself appeared on videotape on a screen set up at the front of the church—Rosemary's idea. He was sitting on a high-backed blue chair, attired in a suit and tie, and looked so thin and drawn that he shocked associates who hadn't seen him in a while. "I should have depended on God rather than on myself, because depending on myself brought me to a meaningless existence," he said, echoing Ecclesiastes. A doctor friend later joked lovingly, "Of course, Roger would deliver the last lecture."

"Roger stayed alive as long as he did to accomplish something," says Leo Henikoff. "As a patient he realized that medicine in specific—and society in general—tends to turn its head from death. His contribution was to make us look this problem in the eye, to view death not as some kind of option but as a natural end to life." Three weeks before he died, Bone and his older daughter had a heart-to-heart talk in which she told him that she was miserable at Rush. "He gave me the OK to leave," says Mary Katherine, who's just started a new job at the American College of Chest Physicians. "He thought that in life you should be happy and be a good person."

LIFE AFTER DEATH

How Mike Hedges made sense of his job in the Audy Home for
juvenile offenders after a criminal killed his child.

We're going to do self-portraits today," says Mike Hedges, as he passes
out sheets of drawing paper and colored charcoal to twenty teenagers at the Cook
County Juvenile Temporary Detention Center, better known as the Audy Home.
"We don't have a mirror here to copy off of, but you know what you look like. If
you draw anything that resembles a gang sign—even vaguely—let me know. A
gang sign could get you in trouble."

The six-foot-two, muscular Hedges, the after-school art and music teacher,
bounces about the room giving advice. "Very good, Nakesha*," he says to one
taciturn girl, who cracks a grin. Most of the juveniles in Audy, which is at Eleventh and Hamilton, are boys, but there are a few girls. "That's the best damn
picture I've ever seen in my life."

Hedges, who's wearing a blue shirt, red shorts, and sandals, scratches his beard
and moves on to a clump of boys. "José, is that a head you're drawing there? A
mushroom or a head? Billy, now you get going."

Billy tells another girl across the room, "You look like a space monkey."

Hedges redirects Billy's attention to his drawing, explaining that a head should
be shaped like an egg and that the proper place for the nose is halfway down the
face, with the corners of the nostrils matched to the corners of the eyes. "Billy, if
you continue to clown around you won't be back here again."

* The names of the juveniles in Audy have been changed with the exception of Adam Gray.

Mike Hedges

During the day the young detainees, who are being held for everything from violating probation to murder, attend the Nancy B. Jefferson Alternative School, operated by the Board of Education on the second floor. Afterward they can play sports and games in the gyms and third-floor recreational yards, but they can also take classes with staff members such as Hedges or with tutors and volunteers.

Hedges, now forty-six, has served as a recreation worker at Audy for more than twenty years. What's remarkable is that he continues working with these troubled youngsters even though two and a half years ago his eighteen-year-old son was killed by a man whose history mirrored many of theirs.

"I'm amazed Mike has the tolerance and patience to still find good in the Audy Home kids," says Dale Janush, his brother-in-law. "Bless his heart. He's a product of the Woodstock Nation."

Hedges grew up in Buffalo, New York, in a working-class household with ten siblings from his father's two marriages. He attended Canisius High School, a prestigious Jesuit institution. "I never did my homework, and I was always in trouble," he says. But he played three sports and taught himself to play the guitar.

The rest of his class went on to college, but Hedges drifted into drugs and petty crime—"burglaries and whatever little thing came along." He was never caught. He traveled aimlessly and eventually came down with a bad case of hepatitis. In 1972, when he was twenty-one, he moved to Chicago to live with his sister Kate, then started studying education and art at Northeastern Illinois University. While there he got involved with BUILD, a gang-intervention program then based in West Town. "I found I was good at getting things across to the kids," he says. He thought he'd found his calling, and in 1976 he took a job at the Audy Home.

Hedges played dodgeball and basketball with the Audy boys. "They told me I broke the stereotype that white guys can't play basketball," he says, laughing. "After the games I'd head up to the units, where I'd play cards, mellow out, and watch TV with the kids. They needed someone who was approachable—and there I was. There were always conversations going on. I got a chance to emphasize the need to read and to get an education. Problems usually came up—with family, staff, or the school—and I addressed them." But he always preferred not to know the specifics of the crimes the kids had committed, fearing it would blind him to whatever positive was left in them.

He began to do drawings for some of the kids to boost their self-esteem. "I'd pick out a kid who nobody would talk to, and I'd say, 'I need to draw your portrait.' I'd give the kid the portrait afterwards, and he'd be thrilled. At Christmastime I also did drawings for the hustlers and the County boys [teenagers who will be tried as adults and are therefore headed for Cook County Jail] so they would have something to send home to their families." Several years ago he and another artist sketched large portraits of, among others, César Chávez, Albert Einstein, Malcolm X, and Hillary Clinton on the dividers between the third-floor yards and had kids fill them in. They're still there.

For several years Hedges remained assigned to the gym, largely, he says, because he openly criticized the administrators when he thought they made bad decisions. The current superintendent, Jesse W. Doyle, says, "Mike's a rebel and can be difficult to deal with. But he's dedicated to the kids, and they respond to love and caring."

But Hedges liked being a gym teacher. "The job was a dream come true. It was fun and satisfying—better than selling insurance, working in a bank, or doing other meaningless jobs. I was making my little dent in the world."

At least he believed he was, although he's never known for sure what influence he's had on the kids at Audy. When he would meet them on the street or on the El after they'd been released, they were friendly and cordial. Once at an art opening on the West Side the young man handling sound for a video walked up to Hedges and said without elaboration, "You changed my life." But such moments have been rare.

Brendan Hedges was born in October 1976, around the time Hedges was hired at Audy. His mother, Maggie Astacio, is a native of the Dominican Republic. A younger sister, Bianca, was born in 1983. The family moved from Rogers Park to Skokie to Oak Park "chasing good schools," according to Maggie. In 1990 they bought a small house just south of the Eisenhower Expressway in Oak Park.

By then Brendan was in high school, a quiet boy who dressed in preppy garb, steered clear of organized sports, and didn't drink or use foul language. When his parents told him to be home at nine o'clock, he'd show up at eight thirty. He was good-looking and fit, but bashful with girls and so modest he was reluctant to take off his shirt during pickup basketball games.

Brendan was an average student, but his teachers remember that he had a heightened moral sense. Marlene Kolz, his physics teacher at Oak Park and River Forest High School, says that when other students got out of line "you could just see he was offended, that he thought that wasn't the way the world should work." Violence of any sort bothered him—he walked out of *Natural Born Killers*. "This guy literally had a guilt-trip stepping on ants," recalls Moran Beasley, Brendan's best friend. But Beasley says Brendan didn't force his opinions on others. "If he thought a movie was lousy, he would immediately start revising his opinion once we got out the door so he wouldn't appear so negative."

Kathy Richland

It was music that captivated Brendan. He sang in the high school a cappella choir and under his father's tutelage took up acoustic guitar. "He was a talented player—pretty much at the top of the class," says Steve Denny, the music teacher who had Brendan as a guitar student his sophomore year. The next year he was playing Beatles songs in the basement, and with just a few formal lessons and his father to guide him, he moved on to piano, drums, and electric guitar. For his seventeenth birthday his parents bought him an upright piano, which he played morning and night, although his instrument of choice was the electric guitar—a green Fender Telecaster. His favorite songwriters were Billy Joel, Elton John, and the Beatles, and his particular favorite was Paul McCartney.

"When Brendy was a little boy he wouldn't let me out of his sight," says Maggie Hedges. "But after a while he sprang away and he became his dad's kid." Even as an adolescent, Brendan stayed close to his father. "He respected that his dad was making a difference," says Beasley.

Mike Hedges says, "He didn't go through any kind of rebellion, at least with me. We were like buddies." One time Hedges took Brendan to see Veruca Salt. He remembers that during one set Brendan turned around, smiled at him, and gave a thumbs-up. The two of them discussed music and watched *David Letterman* and *The Simpsons* together. When they went swimming they would come at each other feet first and then thrust each other in the opposite direction like human torpedoes.

The bond between them impressed Brendan's friends. Beasley says, "The two of them loved each other, truly loved each other. And how many of us can say that of our dads when we're teenagers? I envied the relationship."

Brendan went on to the University of Illinois at Chicago, where he chose to major in music. "He was a nice young man who was interested in jazz and in New Age things," says William Kaplan, his music-theory professor. "A little spark came through. He was gifted."

The summer before he started at UIC Brendan had met guitarist Carter Lee Scott and drummer George Banks, two seasoned street musicians who were playing in the subway at Washington and Dearborn. They called themselves Carter Lee and the Hired Guns and specialized in the songs of Chuck Berry, U2, and the Beatles. "We were looking for a bass player, and Brendan fit right in," says Scott. "He was calm and cordial in the way he interacted, and you couldn't help but love him. I drew on his inner strength."

Scott helped Brendan learn new chords and improve his singing. A tuxedo store loaned the trio evening wear in exchange for distributing promotional flyers. Over the holidays they donned Santa hats. "It's so dark and dank in the subway, but it was festive down there with the band," says Mike Hedges. "People wouldn't be in such a hurry to get home. Sometimes they would let several trains go by just to listen, and sometimes they danced."

"Some of the musicians who play in the El are obnoxious, and others just stink," says Gary Szparkowski, a tactical sergeant with the police mass-transit unit who occasionally stopped to listen. "But these guys were good with their sixties stuff and rock and roll. It was nothing original, you'd have to say. But it was listenable."

On a good day each band member earned fifty dollars or more for several hours' work. Brendan saved three hundred dollars and bought a used Fender with a soft vinyl case.

The band began to attract attention. They performed on the first Thursday of every month at the Deja Vu in Lincoln Park, and they made two appearances on John Landecker's program on WJMK. Brendan sent a demo tape of his own to Atlanta, and a producer wrote back saying he wanted to hear more.

Hedges noticed a change in his son. "It was amazing how loose he was getting. His shoulders were slack, and he would talk to anyone who came along—boys, girls, blacks, whites, it didn't matter. He was growing up."

Brendan had long been proud of his multicultural heritage. "I am the human race," he would say. But Hedges knew he looked Hispanic and worried that gangbangers would "wonder what flag Brendy was flying" and confront him. On Christmas Eve Brendan was out with his guitar and didn't come home when he was supposed to. Hedges drove around looking for him. "Dad, don't worry," Brendan said when he finally materialized. "I'm a big boy now."

On January 15, 1995, at a family brunch, Brendan brought out his guitar and led everyone in singing. At two thirty he put on a blue parka, and Maggie's sister Sonya gave him a ride to Carter Lee Scott's Uptown apartment. The Hired Guns rehearsed for four hours, then, augmented by a keyboard player, they made a demo tape of rockabilly songs. Scott remembers how confident Brendan seemed. In the early evening Scott took Brendan to the El stop at Lawrence. "Carter, take it easy," Brendan called out as the train pulled up.

At midnight, when Brendan still hadn't shown up, Maggie and Mike were worried, but they didn't want to call people, afraid they'd embarrass him. At 2 A.M. Hedges finally phoned Scott, who said he hadn't seen Brendan since early that evening. They began calling everyone in Brendan's circle, and Mike drove over to the house of a friend who didn't have a phone.

Hedges was convinced something awful had happened. "Somebody's hurt my Brendy," he told Maggie. She was calmer. Perhaps he's with a girlfriend, she suggested. No, said Mike. A girlfriend is out of his realm so far, and besides he would have called.

When daylight broke they filed a missing person's report with the Oak Park police. An officer stopped by and suggested that Brendan might have run away.

Late that morning Scott called to say the television news had reported that an unidentified male had been shot on the El and that he'd had a guitar case. Scott advised them to call Cook County Hospital. They called and were told that an unknown person had in fact been brought in during the night.

At around eight forty-five the night before, Brendan had been traveling west on the Congress El, seated in the back of the car by the window, when thirty-two-year-old Ricky Phillips slipped into the seat next to him. According to court records, witnesses later told authorities that Brendan and Phillips engaged in friendly conversation for a couple minutes, then an angry Phillips rose and grabbed the handle of Brendan's guitar case. When Brendan refused to release his grip, the witnesses said, Phillips pulled out a gun. The story that Brendan wouldn't let go is supported by bruises the medical examiner later found at the base of his fingers.

In a statement he subsequently gave police, Phillips said he pulled out a .32-caliber revolver and demanded money, and Brendan gave him several dollars. Phillips then asked for the guitar, and Brendan said no and "got up and hollered to the other people on the El." Phillips then shot Brendan through the left lens of his glasses.

In his statement Phillips said he shot Brendan because he "was mad that the guy 'fucked with him'" by shouting to the other passengers. Witnesses stated that Phillips said, "Everybody sit down. That's what he gets for fucking with me. He shouldn't have fucked with me."

Brendan stumbled out of his seat and fell into the aisle. The other passengers who jumped up to help him told him to be still. The train almost immediately stopped at Western Avenue, and Phillips fled.

Mike Hedges was just getting off work and recalls that as he passed the Western El stop he saw a man carrying a guitar case. He remembers thinking, you don't see many guys carrying guitars in the ghetto. He also thought the man looked like Brendan.

Paramedics drove Brendan to Cook County Hospital, where he was admitted and treated. But he had no identification on him—he often didn't carry a wallet—and doctors couldn't identify him.

"When we walked in, there was Brendan, so quiet, with a patch over his left eye," recollects Hedges. "He was being kept alive by a half a million tubes. Seeing him, Maggie went into a convulsion, and the nurses and technicians had to restrain her."

When Maggie managed to compose herself sufficiently, a doctor took the couple aside and said, "Has anybody talked to you about the organ-donor program?" Hedges figured, my boy is going to get a new eye, but it quickly dawned on him that the physician was speaking of donating Brendan's organs. The doctor said that their son had no brain waves. "He's brain-dead," Hedges remembers mouthing to the doctor, who nodded.

The distraught Hedgeses went home but returned later that afternoon. When an elevator operator wouldn't let Maggie go up because she didn't have a pass, Mike started yelling. Several security officers shoved him against a wall and put handcuffs on him until he managed to explain why they were there.

"We sat there, looked at Brendy, and tried to absorb the madness," recalls Maggie. "We didn't say anything to each other. We just watched our son. Finally I went over and hugged him, kissing his face and fingers. Mike held my hand and then drew me away."

The next afternoon Brendan's heart, liver, and kidneys were donated through the Regional Organ Bank of Illinois. He was buried in a cemetery in Hillside wearing his tuxedo.

Meanwhile police—including Gary Szparkowski, the mass-transit sergeant who'd liked the Hired Guns—were checking pawnshops for Brendan's guitar. They soon located it in a shop at Madison and Ashland. "I had a sixth sense about that guitar," the pawnbroker said later. "I knew what it was." The police ran down the man who'd signed the pawn ticket, Len Dawkins, who told them that Ricky Phillips, an old friend, had persuaded him to hock the guitar for half the take—fifty dollars.

Dawkins sent police to an apartment building in Lawndale, where they found several people with whom Phillips had been staying. Szparkowski found a green army jacket like the one witnesses said the shooter had been wearing.

Then Phillips walked in. "We grabbed him, and believe it or not, he still had a gun on him, with one spent casing," says William Hougesen, a lead detective on the case.

Back at Area Four headquarters Phillips was advised of his rights. He denied that he'd been involved in Brendan's murder. "He first said he'd been with his mother and his sister," says Hougesen. "But I pointed out that we had tested his gun, and its ballistics would match that of the one that killed Brendan. After that he just gave it up. He gave a full oral statement within a half hour."

The confession notes that Phillips can barely read or write; it also says that an assistant state's attorney read him the confession, Phillips stopping her when he didn't understand a word. "This isn't the smartest guy in the world, but he's far from the dumbest," Hougesen would later say. "On the outside he got by. He wasn't under anyone's care. Just because he's illiterate doesn't mean he's stupid."

Even without a confession the police had ample evidence implicating Phillips: the gun and the spent shell casing, a CTA transfer pulled from Phillips's jacket that placed him on the El at the time of the slaying, his fingerprint on the guitar case found at the pawnshop. The pawnbroker had identified Phillips as having accompanied Dawkins into the store, and two witnesses, including a department-store security guard, had identified Phillips in a lineup. "Some cases are from hell, but this one was from heaven," says Hougesen. "Everything worked out. There were no loose ends. The only thing we were missing was a video."

Hougesen called the Hedgeses to say that Phillips had been arrested and would be charged. Hougesen told Mike, "This Phillips is a real bad guy."

As a child Ricky Phillips lived with his mother, brother, and two sisters in a rented brick bungalow on South Oakley, just blocks from the Audy Home. He never knew his father, although for many years his mother, Azzlee Phillips, had lived with another man who gave him some affection.

"Ricky was just one of the kids on the block," says blues guitarist Jimmy Dawkins, Len's father. "He wasn't very bright, and he was a little off in the head anyway. He was always grinning goofylike. He'd lope on down the street, and the cops were usually after him."

Ricky attended Medill Primary School. His kindergarten teacher wrote in a report compiled by the school psychologist, later part of the court record, "He is very immature and fights the children. He has no friends. He is hostile towards all the other children. He keeps his two fingers in his mouth at all times, sucking and slobbering. He cannot do any readiness work, does not show any interest. He can respond to direct questioning about himself but doesn't respond otherwise. Cries very easily." The report also notes that his IQ was 76.

"There has been something wrong with Ricky since kindergarten," says Azzlee Phillips, who worked in factories and as a teacher's aide during this period, "but wherever I went everybody said there was no help for him unless he got in jail." When Ricky was around twelve and had started being stopped by the police, Azzlee tried to persuade a youth counselor to admit her son to the Audy Home. At fifteen, she says, Ricky spent a brief time in the psychiatric ward at Mount Sinai Hospital.

By the time he was seventeen Ricky had been arrested several times—for stealing a car, for falsely reporting a shooting, and for stealing a smoker's kit and toy pistol from a Jewel [grocery store]. Each offense drew probation from a juvenile court judge. Azzlee says Ricky warmed to one female probation officer, but she was soon taken off his case, and he didn't like her replacement. Around this time Ricky's older sister died, at age twenty-two, of what Azzlee describes as poisoning.

In 1979 Ricky, his IQ now measured at 69, was a freshman at Manley High School. His skills hadn't progressed much beyond the kindergarten level; Azzlee says he hadn't learned to read or write beyond the most rudimentary level in his special-education classes. "By the time Ricky was in high school they were always calling me because Ricky had cut class and was walking the hallways. They told me, 'Mrs. Phillips, you might as well be going to school here yourself, you're here so much.'" It would be Ricky's last year in school.

Outside school Ricky was now robbing people at gunpoint on public transportation. Armed robbery on a crowded train is easier to get away with than you might think. "People who have witnessed an armed robbery on the El don't want to be bothered afterwards, or else they're scared out of their minds," says Gary Szparkowski, the mass-transit sergeant. "Anyway, when the doors open, they often walk away." According to police, armed robbery on CTA trains resulted in twenty-seven arrests in 1995, the year Brendan Hedges was killed, and forty-two the next year. But the real numbers may be much higher.

When Ricky Phillips got caught it was because of mistakes he made after his robberies. On February 12, 1981, Nathan Gardner was traveling east on the Roosevelt Road bus when Phillips sat down next to him and struck up a conversation. When Gardner refused to hand over a foreign coin he was carrying, Phillips drew a handgun and demanded his money—all of twenty-one dollars—and his CTA pass. That night Phillips was arrested at a roller rink, carrying a gun and Gardner's pass. Found guilty in a bench trial that December, Phillips received a four-year prison sentence.

Within two years he was out of prison. On July 29, 1983, he robbed a man of $360 on the Lake Street El. Two weeks later the victim saw Phillips on the El and informed police. When Phillips was arrested he was carrying the snub-nosed starter pistol he'd used in the robbery. That November he pleaded guilty and was handed a twelve-year sentence.

Phillips was sent to Menard Correctional Center in downstate Chester, where he was into trouble from the outset. He became affiliated with the Conservative Vice Lords, and in October 1984 he was cited for starting a paper fire and for hiding a shank, or homemade knife, in his shoe. According to Department of Corrections spokesman Nic Howell, the next day he was placed in disciplinary segregation—confined to his cell twenty-three hours a day. A month later Phillips threw hot tea in a corrections officer's face, saying he was going to "kick his motherfucking ass." A few days later he was cited for fighting in the yard. Court records show that he ultimately racked up more than fifty infractions, including theft, forgery, arson, and weapons possession. On March 10, 1987, he lured officer N. W. Bradley into his cell, supposedly to examine some papers, then stabbed Bradley in the top of the head and the wrist. "I am going to fuck you up," Phillips told him. "I will fuck all you mothers up. I'm tired of being fucked with."

"When he was at Menard they kept Ricky in solitary a lot," says Azzlee Phillips. "That's enough to drive you crazy right there." She visited him only once in nine years.

When he was released from Menard in October 1993 Phillips returned to Chicago and moved in with his mother, now on disability with high blood pressure and "seizures," and his niece Tabitha. He found work at Acme Barrel, which made fifty-five-gallon industrial drums, but was eventually fired. He later told a court investigator it was "because someone told the manager I tried to break into their car." He also worked day-labor jobs.

A bond formed between Phillips and Tabitha, then a student at Orr High School. The two of them would go bowling and to the movies, or they'd sit outside on the stoop listening to the radio. "We had fun together," says Tabitha. "We talked about everything, and we got along."

Azzlee, however, found her son had changed. "He would talk back to me. He was meaner." According to court records, he turned violent when he drank, and occasionally he used marijuana and crack cocaine. Sometime before Christmas 1994 Azzlee kicked her son out for having wild parties and for bringing women into the apartment against her wishes.

In February 1995, a couple of weeks after Brendan died, a numb Mike Hedges returned to Audy for a day, then took two more weeks off. He started putting on weight and took to sleeping in twelve- to fourteen-hour stretches. Maggie says he talked about "doing his time and then dying." He couldn't watch Pete Sampras, who resembles Brendan physically, and later he couldn't watch Tiger Woods, whose pride in his multicultural heritage reminded Hedges of his son. Both he and Maggie sought help from a therapist.

"For a long time I was angry at almost everybody—at people at the Audy Home, at people on the street," says Hedges. He'd always been an easy mark for panhandlers knocking on his car window, but now they pissed him off. One afternoon a year after Brendan died Hedges was taking the El home when a CTA teller asked for exact change, then laughed at him when he fumbled for it. Angry, he jumped the turnstile trying to catch the train. He missed it and kicked at the car. Two CTA workers who'd chased him demanded that he give them the $1.50 fare. Instead he jumped on top of the turnstile and yelled his lungs out.

The police arrived and handcuffed him, pushing him up against a wall until he managed to explain what had happened to his son.

In March 1996, after Hedges had returned to Audy full-time, the assistant superintendent asked him to write and lay out Audy's annual report, an opportunity he welcomed. "It was something new," he says. He also began producing the facility's newsletter, the *Perspective*.

He went back to teaching gym, but when he tried to organize a basketball game a kid confronted him, saying, "This isn't your gym anymore." Hedges decided he needed a change. "Gym was losing its allure," he says. "With my age I had lost a step or two, and the kids couldn't help but notice. How humiliating is that? Plus music had been Brendan's life. Jesus, here there had been an intelligent, talented kid with drive and a moral sense, where lots of musicians are limited and dumb as dirt. In my mind I got to thinking that if I could show kids about music or encourage their creativity, that would be in Brendy's memory."

Hedges asked to be assigned to teach art, music, and performance to the kids. Most of the teenagers who came to learn about music just played around with an electronic beat machine, although occasionally someone wanted real lessons. Some kids also took drawing seriously. Once a week on Sunday they would put on a talent show, performing skits, poems, and rap songs they'd written for an audience of other Audy residents.

"Mr. Hedges doesn't swear and cuss at us," Sue, a sixteen-year-old facing murder charges and the possibility of forty-five years in prison, said last summer. "Mr. Hedges doesn't let the audience goof off at the talent show. He gives out information that makes you feel better about yourself. When I have crap with my family I talk to him, and he says to have faith in God and that one day I'll get out. Be good, he tells us, and don't get into no more trouble."

"I'm disappointed when Hedges doesn't come to get me off the unit, because I look forward to drawing and to the talent shows," said Benny, a sixteen-year-old who'd been at Audy for over two years on murder charges that were then dismissed, although he was still being held on drug charges. His delivery of a Luther Vandross song had stolen the previous talent show. "When I first came to the Audy Home I was a bad little shorty, but I'm calm now and can deal with other people better. Hedges has helped me, been like a role model to me, taught me a lot about myself. I can talk to him about what's on my mind."

Amid the clutter of the art and music room—among masks, old drawings, books, a snare drum, a public-address system—was a microphone stand that once belonged to Brendan. Among the tapes the kids played on the boom box were songs Brendan once played. And in one corner of the room, "my inspiration corner," Hedges had hung a photo of Brendan.

"I know about his son, that Brendan was Hedges's idol and his best friend," said Benny. "In his eyes you can see how much he misses him."

One of the most understanding kids was Adam Gray, who at fourteen had been accused of torching the building where his ex-girlfriend lived, killing two of the tenants. He'd had trouble adjusting to Audy and had tried to kill himself by cutting his wrists.

During the summer of 1994 Hedges had been assigned to help Adam, who was often in solitary confinement. They would walk around, talk, and wrestle. Hedges would push Adam around on a cart and crash him into walls. "He was just a young kid really, and he loved to play. We would discuss philosophy, religion, and the meaning of life." Hedges gave the boy books by Sigmund Freud, Konrad Lorenz, and existentialist philosophers. Adam's favorite book was William Goldman's *The Princess Bride*, the moral of which is that life isn't fair.

"We clicked from the very start," Adam wrote me in a letter describing their relationship. "Being around him is a respite from everything that troubles you. He makes you laugh—laugh to tears. My father was incarcerated [for murder] three weeks before I was born. I never knew what it [having a father] was like until I met Mike. He was like a father, and he was my best friend." Adam's mother believes it was Hedges who kept her son from killing himself.

"The night following Brendan's murder Mike came to the Audy Home to let me know what happened," wrote Adam. "I saw it in his eyes. He was gone. Seeing him in pain broke me down. All the dignity, pride, libido for life that he instilled in me—bam! Man, it was gone. I saw life with a new perspective—no matter what's done, no matter what's accomplished, there will always be a fall. So I stopped trying. I became suicidal again."

But slowly the two helped each other. "I did what little I could to get his mind off his sorrow," said Adam. "I would pester him until he would throw something at me. Tell him he was old, make him chase me around the gym. He resumed teaching me things. He attained a state of—I guess you could call it a peaceful or content existentialism."

In February 1995 a grand jury indicted Ricky Phillips for armed robbery, armed violence, and murder, and the case was assigned to criminal court judge James Flannery Jr. Hedges and Maggie hadn't gone to the early hearings, although Hedges's brother-in-law, Dale Janush, had.

Assistant state's attorney Mary Kay Moore, Phillips's prosecutor, decided to ask for the death penalty. Before Brendan's murder Hedges and Maggie had both steadfastly opposed the death penalty, but now Maggie agreed with Moore. Hedges listened to her arguments but couldn't agree. "Mike was way too liberal on this," says Moore. "He was always trying to intellectualize it, to try to understand this situation from a social perspective, to come to terms with the individual who did this."

Because there was so much evidence against Phillips, Jack Carey, the assistant public defender assigned to represent him, says he knew the only options were getting his client ruled unfit for trial, having his confession tossed out, or having him plead guilty in exchange for a lighter sentence. Moore refused to consider a plea bargain.

Meanwhile Phillips waited in Cook County Jail. He was placed on the residential treatment unit there for a year and prescribed an antipsychotic and an antidepressant. In January 1996 he was admitted to Cermak Hospital, claiming he was having hallucinations and feeling paranoid, but after six days the doctors returned him to jail, saying he was faking his symptoms. Carey says Phillips tried to hang himself while in jail and once ended up in restraints for twenty-four hours.

Tabitha Phillips remembers that when she visited her uncle in jail he was sad, but they never talked about anything substantial. "I would just play around with him," she says. Bill Ryan, a vice president of the Hull House Association who's a volunteer counselor for capital-offense defendants at the jail, spent a lot of time with Phillips. "From a young age Ricky had what we would now call attention-deficit disorder," he says. "He was a loner who wound up in Menard, where he had a very difficult time. 'Whenever a guard called "nigger," I would attack him,' he told me. Then he was locked up in isolation. That was the final embitterment of Ricky."

A hearing on whether Phillips was fit for trial was finally held in January 1997. Stafford Henry, a psychiatrist with the Department of Forensic Clinical Services, the psychological-assessment arm of the county courts, testified that he'd examined Phillips four times. "I believe that Mr. Phillips's behavior is very suggestive of antisocial personality disorder, which is essentially characterized by a failure to adhere to social norms of behavior, a florid and flagrant disregard of the rights and responsibilities of others, deceitfulness, impulsivity, aggressiveness, reckless disregard of others, and a lack of remorse for often heinous activities." Paul Fautek, another DFCS psychologist, concurred. But psychiatrist Jeffrey Teich, an Evanston private practitioner frequently summoned as an expert defense witness, testified that Phillips was a paranoid schizophrenic who had mild mental retardation and an antisocial personality disorder. On January 6 Judge Flannery declared that Phillips was fit for trial.

In another hearing, on March 25, Carey argued that Phillips's confession should be thrown out because his mental retardation and psychological impairment had compromised his understanding of his constitutional right to remain silent. Flannery ruled against him.

Around this time, Adam Gray, the boy at Audy who'd been suicidal, was transferred to county jail to await trial. He was to be tried as an adult and his case was to be heard by the same Judge Flannery. Hedges wrote a letter to Flannery:

> *As a 20-year employee of the Audy Home I have been part of the Justice system throughout my adult life. I say adult life because in 1976 I had a son born, and it was his presence, his promise and potential that made me an adult. Despite my two decades of service in the system it is a pair of tragedies that brings me to your courtroom on a regular basis and prompts me to write this letter. . . . My son, a musical genius with a saintly disposition, is gone. Nothing can change that. So I'll spare you the details of his beautiful and promising life. Suffice it to say that his death was a loss for all humanity. Adam is also a genius. A boy-genius who, despite being deprived of schooling and kept in the most solitary of conditions, has continued to grow intellectually, emotionally and spiritually. . . . Please do not infer that, in my grief, I have made some sort of substitution. For it is only in their great potential that Adam and Brendan are similar. Adam truly is a "hard egg to crack." I urge you, though, the keeper of Adam's fate, to take time to crack the egg. With the proper help Adam will achieve greatness. Future generations may thank you for saving him.*

The letter made no difference. A jury found Adam guilty of arson and murder, and Flannery sentenced him to natural life in prison without possibility of parole. Flannery doesn't remember Hedges's letter but says, "Nothing anybody said could have affected the sentence." He says he might have considered a finite prison term for Adam, but mandatory sentencing dictated the punishment. "You have this kid who did something so stupid at fourteen sent away for the rest of his days," says Flannery. "It's so sad." Hedges later visited Adam in prison and noticed that his attitude seemed to be hardening. Adam insisted he was innocent and said his confession was coerced, and Hedges believes a judge or the governor will eventually be persuaded to set him free.

As Ricky Phillips's day in court approached, Jack Carey and Bill Ryan, the volunteer counselor, pressured him to plead guilty, to throw himself on the court's mercy and avoid the death penalty, which was possible for a murder committed in the course of another felony and more likely because of his previous record. But Phillips knew that technically, even if found guilty, he could receive a term of less than natural life, perhaps as few as twenty years. "I want a trial," he told Carey.

On May 12, 1997, the day the trial was to begin, assistant state's attorney Mary Kay Moore had her witnesses assembled and set to testify. Carey was prepared to lay out an insanity defense. A jury stood ready. Finally Phillips began to waver.

For an hour Carey, Azzlee Phillips, and Tabitha Phillips sat in a conference room off Flannery's courtroom, trying to persuade Phillips to plead guilty. Carey yelled, and Azzlee insisted. But Carey says it was Tabitha's words that finally swayed Phillips. She told him, "Ricky, one of these days I'm going to have a baby, and I want to bring that child to see you. I don't want to point to a patch of ground, your grave, and say, 'That is your uncle.'" Back in court Phillips entered a guilty plea.

Afterward Azzlee walked across the room and approached Maggie Hedges. She extended a hand and said, "I'm so sorry what my boy did to your boy." Maggie was shocked, but she shook Azzlee's hand.

Out in the hallway Mike Hedges told Azzlee, "I didn't want your son to be put to death. I'm sorry about Ricky." He went to embrace Azzlee, but she grabbed at her heart and crumpled to the floor. She spent the night at Mount Sinai Hospital, doctors monitoring her to see if she'd had a heart attack; it turned out that she hadn't.

When Hedges went back to work someone who'd heard that he'd wanted to hug Azzlee called him a "chump."

On the afternoon of June 12, both families reassembled in Flannery's courtroom for Phillips's sentencing. Mike Hedges, Maggie, and a few friends and relatives huddled together. Azzlee and her daughter Beverly, but not Tabitha, sat across the way. Bill Ryan sat with them. Phillips and Jack Carey occupied the defense table.

That morning Phillips had been searched on the way to the courthouse; he had a seven-inch shank—a screwdriver with a sharpened point—sticking out of his rectum. "Ricky thought some guy was going to stab him," says Carey. "He's an institutionalized guy—he thought he had to protect himself." So a couple of hulking sheriff's deputies now stood behind Phillips in the courtroom.

Mike Hedges walked up and sat in the witness stand to deliver a brief victim-impact statement. He quoted Earl Woods, Tiger's father, as saying he'd been "personally selected by God himself to nurture this young man and bring him to the point where he can make his contribution to humanity. This is my treasure." In a steady voice he then spoke directly about Brendan. "In my line of work I have met literally thousands and thousands of young men and women, and none even comes close to Brendan Miguel Hedges in talent, drive, and pureness of life. And I don't see anyone to take his place." But he concluded without asking for the death penalty.

Maggie, who'd dictated what she wanted to say to her therapist, had practiced reading her statement until 4 A.M. that morning. Her two sisters accompanied her to the witness box to ensure that she read every line of the statement; if she faltered they were to touch her shoulder. "For the rest of my life and that of my family we will forever try to understand why Brendan would be the target of a messy execution on the day we honor Martin Luther King," she stated, her voice even. "Our Brendan, who had just turned eighteen, was the gentlest soul I have ever known. Brendan never in his life raised a hand to anyone. He was the butt of jokes and teased as a kid at school, and he never raised a hand. The first time Brendan decides to stand up to protect something that was important to him, he ends up dead at the hands of a criminal. How dare this man put a gun in my Brendan's face? How dare he?"

Maggie painted a picture of Brendan as a pianist, band member, UIC student, and son. "Brendan started to play in clubs in Chicago together with Carter Lee and George. Mike would always be with him. Keeping an eye on him. Using our station wagon as a transport, as an excuse to be with him. Brendan was Mike's dream. He lived through Brendy." Her voice rose. "Since my Brendy has vanished, the sun doesn't shine the same. Spring isn't the same. Christmas—nothing's the same, or will it ever be. The fabric that kept our family whole has weakened. What's become of my boy? A plot in the cemetery with his name on it.

"There is nothing, nothing you can possibly do to this man to justify what he has stolen from us. State of Illinois, show me your outrage. Judge Flannery, show me your outrage. And to you, my precious son Brendan, I miss your jokes, I miss your constant laughter and music. We will never grow old together, because you have ceased being in our lives. If I had you for just one more second, I would tell you just how proud I am of you. What I would give to hear you play your guitar and sing your last song."

The courtroom was silent. Later Carey would say that even Ricky Phillips was on the verge of tears.

Assistant state's attorney Moore then detailed all the infractions Phillips had been responsible for at Menard, and as she did, Mike Hedges recoiled. My God, he thought, he did all those horrible things too. He says his shoulders slumped, and for a moment he felt himself flip in favor of the death penalty.

Then Beverly Phillips recounted the fun her brother had shared with Tabitha. And Bill Ryan read a statement in which he said, "I've seen a change in Ricky. He's learned a bit more about reading and writing. He's talked about his behavior, and how it's hurt people. He's expressed remorse and sorrow. He feels for Brendan and his family, but I'm not sure he understands the enormity of this. I'm not sure anybody could."

In her closing argument Moore stated, "I can't describe how brutal and cold his murder was, of such an innocent young man. . . . Ricky hasn't contributed a thing to society except pain and heartache. He's a danger outside the penitentiary and inside the penitentiary. It's my true conviction that no other penalty fits this crime and this defendant than death."

Carey then stood and said, "There's nobody with a drop of humanity who couldn't have been moved by what's happened in this courtroom." But, he went on, Phillips was mentally retarded, unemployed, and homeless, "suffering from emotional distress at the time of the crime." Carey asked that Phillips be given natural life in prison.

Finally it was Phillips's turn. From the witness stand he said, "I'm sorry for what I did. I made a mistake. Words cannot describe how sorry I am for his family. I pray for his family and also for my mother and the pain I have caused her." Then he went back to the defense table.

Flannery called for a recess, and when he returned he delivered his judgment. He said that Phillips had "absolutely no chance of rehabilitation. The defendant is a coward and a bully, an uncivilized person who cannot live in a civilized society. Mr. Phillips must be warehoused. He cannot ever be let out of the Department of Corrections." Later Flannery, who in four years on the criminal bench had never handed out a death sentence, explained why he again hesitated. He said he remembered a 1979 case where a murderer had been given the death sentence, which was later reversed three times, turning the defendant into a capital-offense martyr. If he gave Phillips death, Flannery told the courtroom, "ten or fifteen years from now people will make Mr. Phillips a cause. But Brendan's family doesn't deserve to have to listen about him ever again." Flannery said he was giving Phillips natural life in prison.

Phillips appeared impassive. Hedges, his arms around Maggie, looking relieved, thrust his fist toward Dale Janush, who was sitting in front of him. Bill Ryan approached from the Phillips's side of the courtroom and embraced Maggie.

Carey says that Phillips later asked if he would ever be released from prison. "No Ricky, you got what you got," Carey told him. "Don't push it." He says Phillips looked resigned and asked to see his mother and sister.

Phillips was sent to Menard again on June 26. "There aren't too many people who'd trade places with Ricky now," says Carey. "He's locked up with father killers and mother rapists, and to protect himself he'll be walking around with a shank up his ass. You could say this is a cursed existence—a life worse than death."

Two months later Phillips told Bill Ryan over the phone that he was proud he hadn't been put in segregation. And he said he was trying to read—he rattled off the alphabet as proof. Ryan promised to send him some easy books.

Maggie Hedges says she still can't make simple decisions, even about such things as whether to take a trip or buy a new phone. In some ways Mike isn't doing much better. "He sees a guitar, he sees his kid, and he loses it," says Dale Janush.

But Maggie sets hair for the owners of Hecky's Barbecue, a carryout restaurant in Evanston, and they've set up a thousand-dollar annual music scholarship in Brendan's name that has already helped send two students to college. And Bianca, who plays flute, has just started high school. Mike, who adores his daughter, hopes she'll turn out to be as dedicated a musician as Brendan was.

Asked how she sees Ricky Phillips now, Maggie says, "He's just a disease to me, like polio or HIV. He's not a person at all, so I have no feelings for him at all." Mike says, "This wasn't a young kid who killed my son, but this son of a bitch, this Ricky Phillips. If somebody had gotten to him when he was sixteen and had shown some interest in him he might not have become the person he was."

"Mike has a big, forgiving heart—too forgiving, if you ask me," says Maggie. "He gives people too many chances."

This past July Mike took a supervisor's job at Audy, although he made sure that he could still stage the talent shows and teach art classes once a week. He gave up teaching music.

"Jeez, some of his Audy Home kids are already murderers," says William Hougesen, the police detective who helped solve Brendan's murder. "How can he still do this work knowing that among these kids are potential Ricky Phillipses? It's hard to figure."

"They're a nice bunch of kids," Mike says. "They work well with me. They aren't as smart or creative as I'd like them to be, but they've been dealt a bad deck of cards. They grew up in poverty, and now they have track marks on their arms. In the hallway one time Jack Carey referred to Ricky as a lost soul, and he is, in every sense of that word. Many of the kids I work with are lost souls too, and I know that. My hope has been to engage at least some of them so they don't stay lost souls."

DEATH OF A NEWSMAN

Phil Walters brought a storyteller's voice to whatever subject he took on.

A Channel 2 videotape from the early eighties shows Polish immigrants arriving in Chicago, including, says reporter Phil Walters, "a locksmith from Warsaw, an electrician from Gniezno, a chauffeur from the Krakow area. In Polish they try to explain why they are here."

The camera focuses on one forlorn-looking man. "His name is Ted, and his wife and two children are still in Poland, so he is afraid to give his last name," says Walters. "This may be the age-old American dream, but these refugees will not look so jubilant in the days ahead."

The tape cuts to a shelter on Ashland where the men will stay, and then we see them singing in Polish. "It is difficult to do this story without sounding corny or maudlin, but this, after all, is the American experience," says Walters. The final shot is of him seated on a mattress, saying, "These few simple, barren rooms are a beginning for them but a continuation for the rest of us."

It's not a big story, but it demonstrates Walters's skill at storytelling.

"Phil could take a simple notion and peel it down like an onion so you'd see its facets, its dimensions," says Channel 2's Carol Marin, who worked with Walters for years. "And I don't care if you're talking about a 7-Eleven robbery or the irony in how you market Father's Day. On TV you can't fake it. It's much more revealing than people think—television strips away whether you are the real thing or a fraud. People get that, especially in Chicago. Phil was an authentic voice and gifted writer. He was one of the best working reporters in this city."

Walters, who'd fought the tabloidization of local television news for thirty years, died of lung cancer in September.

He'd grown up in Washington, D.C., the only child of a supervisor at the Federal Home Loan Bank Board and a real estate agent. Walters found his father's bank profession boring. "It seemed a lot to do with numbers—clerical and dry," he once said. "My mother's work was more a part of our life, because there were no absolute hours and things had to be scheduled around her time. Plus she would talk more at home about her tactics. Many a Saturday and Sunday I spent sitting with my mother in some empty house she was showing."

Walters attended Sidwell Friends, a private academy for the children of Washington's elite (Tricia Nixon allegedly had a crush on him). "To me, the two neat things to be were a politician and a newsperson," he said in a 1989 interview. "And the newsmen got the better end of it, because they watched over the politicians." At Williams College he majored in English literature and covered football games with Dave Marash, the future *Nightline* correspondent, for the college radio station. After graduating in 1964, he wrote for the *Providence Journal*, then turned to newswriting at WHDH-TV in Boston.

He came to Channel 5 as a newswriter in 1967 and was soon producing the noon news with host Jorie Lueloff. He was a zealous booker. The day after Black Panthers Fred Hampton and Mark Clark were killed in a December 1969 police raid, Walters got an explosive Bobby Rush to appear live with Lueloff. Yet Walters was disorganized and always running late. His colleagues dubbed him "Captain Chaos," and the nickname stuck.

Walters first got on the air by freelancing movie reviews. In 1976 he was hired to deliver Washington news for Channel 2 and other CBS stations, and three years later he returned to Chicago as a general-assignment reporter, covering crime, politics, and sports and doing features. Bill Kurtis and Walter Jacobson were then anchoring the nightly broadcasts, and reporters had more freedom to choose their pieces than they do today and more time to deliver them, sometimes as much as three minutes.

Walters was no pretty boy. He had a bald spot that grew with the years, a crooked mouth, and a bemused smirk that the camera caught all too often. He dressed in worn tweed, khakis, and ratty shoes, and his colors clashed. "Phil would match up paisley with plaid," says Marash. "He looked like a cloth traffic accident." His appearance improved when Paula Weiss, who became his second wife in 1978, started buying his clothes and laying them out on the bed in the morning.

The TV scripts Walters wrote matched evocative pictures with simple, often ironic words. After Nelson Algren died in 1981, Walters replayed an interview he'd done six years earlier, when Algren left Chicago. Algren described the city he was leaving: "It's like being married to a woman for keeps, and twenty-five years later she's a mess." In a voice-over Walters said, "Never mind that he too looked like a mess, that his times were used up, that his good work was all typed out. We are left with his words and his voice." In other memorable segments Walters rode the Goodyear blimp, probed unemployment in Plano, and memorialized Don Jordan's newsstand in City Hall: "Don reloads his newsstand for the next edition. It's like he's reloading a squirrel feeder."

Eventually the station gave Walters his own platform, *In Other Words*, for which he wrote quirky weekly essays on such things as trees being cut down next to the station, Jesse Jackson's chameleonic tendencies ("Jesse in a Box"), and the meaning of "quintessential." Walters jumped back to Channel 5 in 1986 after a dispute over money. At the time Channel 2's ratings were slipping, "and they were counting their dollars," says Todd Musburger, then Walters's agent.

At Channel 5, Walters continued to insist that his cameramen catch the small as well as the large signs of emotion—the sighs as well as the tears. He carefully wrote his scripts on a yellow legal pad and then, if possible, sat through the editing process, demanding that the piece have the nuances he wanted. "No, I don't like that," he'd tell a video editor. "Back it up three frames." Hal Bernstein, a cameraman who frequently worked with Walters, says, "More often than not they'd finish the piece thirty seconds before it went on the air."

Walters was perfectly capable of doing dumb pieces. One Thanksgiving evening he was dispatched to do a take on last-minute preparations. "The sun is setting and store shoppers are hefting glaciated birds that still must somehow get thawed and roasted in a matter of hours," he said, standing in a grocery aisle. "If misery loves company, this should make you feel better."

He delighted in covering the Chicago cardinals' trips to Rome, the 1996 Democratic National Convention, and the Bulls playoffs, but he also grew frustrated as the emphasis on crime-oriented news increased and time slots shrank. He seldom got along with management. He was direct and was quick to tell his bosses when he was angry.

Though he would win many awards, including eight local Emmys, he was chronically insecure. He worried about being fired, worried about his status. "Do you think they [his bosses] are going to say anything to me?" he'd ask colleagues after a piece he was proud of had aired. Channel 5 political reporter Dick Kay says, "He was like a kid, seeking that approval—in a business where you're only as good as your last story."

In 1998 the Chicago-Midwest chapter of the National Academy of Television Arts and Sciences honored people who'd been in the business for twenty-five years, among them the long-retired Walter Jacobson and Jorie Lueloff. Walters noticed that he wasn't among them. "He read about it in the paper, and he was hurt," says Paula Weiss, a publicist turned realtor. "Somehow he felt overlooked. He wanted to know that his work was valued, but after all, he was a street reporter in a day when anchors drive the business."

The year before, Walters had been appalled when shock-show host Jerry Springer was brought in to do commentaries on the evening broadcast. When an outraged Marin and then coanchor Ron Magers left the station, Walters joined other staff in signing a letter of protest to NBC president Robert Wright. General manager Lyle Banks called him into his office. Dick Kay says Walters told Banks, "I think you're wrong, and I'd sign the letter again." On Marin's final newscast a sullen Walters stood right behind her, but he never really considered leaving. "He had a family to feed," says Marash, adding that Walters took pleasure in the fact that after Marin and Magers left, Channel 5's ratings dropped dramatically.

Walters and Weiss had had a son, Tyce, in 1986, when Walters was forty-four. He taught his son to fish and play chess, and he began going to the theater after Tyce developed an interest in plays. "We were friends and father and son," says Tyce. "I don't know if it can be described, we were so close."

Walters talked incessantly about Tyce, to the point that he became overbearing. "That kid was the sun, the moon, and the stars to Phil," says Marin. "I remember the last night of the Democratic convention. All this glitter was flying from the ceiling. Phil brought Tyce down because he wanted him to experience this amazing night. I remember the look in Phil's eye—he was showing his son one of the rewards of being a reporter."

Gardening was also a passion. Walters began with plots on the farm he and Weiss owned in Janesville, Wisconsin, and at their house in Lincoln Park. After they sold the farm and moved to Northfield, he put in new beds. "The gardening totally relaxed him," says Weiss. "He would come home and go out to his land." In summer and fall he would deposit loads of cucumbers and tomatoes on the desks at Channel 5.

The public seemed to see him as one of them. "You go out with some guys, and they aren't recognizable to people," says Hal Bernstein. "But people always recognized Phil. You'd walk into a coffee shop, and they say, 'Oh, it's Phil.' And he loved being recognized."

Edward R. Murrow had been Walters's childhood idol, and many people thought it odd that he never moved to a network job. "The network had been what Phil aspired to—going to war zones," says Weiss. "But it just never happened for him.

Then Tyce was born, and he was glad he hadn't gone. Most of his friends who were network correspondents had divorced at least once." Stan Bernard, a longtime NBC network reporter, says, "Being a network correspondent is nice, but that wasn't Phil's lot. The industry is expecting more and more of reporters and giving them less time. Phil had Paula and Tyce. He was happy with his life."

Walters had smoked for years. It was an issue for Weiss, and he hid it from Tyce. His son only learned of his father's habit when he was ten and a friend told him he'd seen Walters smoking. Of course everyone at work knew. He smoked in the office at the Merchandise Mart, then in the smoking room near the cafeteria at the NBC Tower. When the smoking room vanished he went outside by the loading dock. Company policy outlawed smoking in the TV trucks, so Walters puffed outdoors. Once he made the mistake of lighting up in a van, and a cameraman kicked him out.

He tried to quit, and in 1998 he finally succeeded. Then last March when his father, who'd come to live with him, was dying of lymphoma, Walters came down with the flu. He had a cough that lingered, and in April he got an X-ray. It showed a tumor in his right lung.

On May 4 Walters posted a memo on the bulletin board in the newsroom and sent copies to everyone by e-mail. He apologized for not sharing his news in person. "But I fear that, at the moment, I seem to possess neither the courage nor the grace of Joseph Cardinal Bernardin or Attorney General Jim Ryan. And so, please understand if I resort to a writer's chief instrument of defense, the typewriter. . . . I am beginning treatment for lung cancer discovered a few weeks ago."

He ended, "While I have your attention, I would like to add two things. To my fellow alumni of the smoking lounge, no one knows better than I how insidious tobacco addiction is, how it can cause otherwise intelligent and rational people to deny and delay. Having finally triumphed but too late, I would be the last to scold or judge. But I would like each of you to give quitting one more try. Neither you nor, more importantly perhaps, those who love you, should have to face a fight like this. It turns out that quitting is not nearly as tough as not quitting. . . .

"And to everyone: I would like to ask that when I return later this week that you treat this as matter-of-factly as possible. Think of it as a cat with a difficult fur ball, if that will help. And we'll talk. In person. It'll be OK. Honest."

Walters embarked on what he called "Phil's excellent adventure." He said he was sure he'd conquer his cancer, and for a time that attitude seemed justified. He took off Tuesdays so he could be treated. He didn't lose any hair, and aggressive chemotherapy and radiation shrank the tumor by 70 percent. In June he threw himself a fifty-seventh birthday party for fifty friends, including a snow-plow driver he'd met while reporting the January blizzard.

And he kept working. In July he did a memorable story about the delivery of the skull of The Second City's Del Close to the Goodman Theatre, where it would be used in *Hamlet*. "Actor-director Del Close is making his first public appearance since dying last March," said Walters. "Talk about a comeback."

In August he took a medical leave of absence and spent time at his family's cabin in Massachusetts, first alone and then with Tyce. His doctors at Evanston Hospital had thought his tumor was inoperable, but then they decided to try surgery. A date was scheduled in early September so that Walters could recover in time for Tyce's bar mitzvah in October.

The first procedure removed part of his right lung. "I talked to him five hours after the surgery," recalls Marash. "He bragged about how he was the hero of the hospital. He had just walked up the hall, and the nurses were standing there with their jaws dropping." But there were complications. A second operation removed the whole lung, and then he got pneumonia. He died September 13.

It was a Sunday, and channels 5 and 2 gave his death prominent play on the nightly news. Kay came in to do an obituary. Marin returned to Channel 5 for the first time since her departure to pay him tribute.

"Phil could construct a piece of art out of a piece of news," says Marin. "What Phil did isn't done by a lot of us today. It's a rare thing." Musburger says, "Many people hired today have gone to video school, have a nice smile, and jump in front of a camera. But they don't know who's in charge or how to tell a story. Where are we going to replace Paul Hogan [a dogged Channel 5 reporter who died in 1993] or Phil?"

Seven hundred mourners attended the memorial service for Walters at Temple Jeremiah in Northfield on September 16. A blown-up publicity photo of him dominated the sanctuary. Marin and Stan Bernard were among those who gave eulogies. A friend read a letter from Marash, who was in the Balkans.

Twelve-year-old Tyce was the last person to speak. He read "Nothing Gold Can Stay" by Robert Frost, his father's favorite poet. And he said, "Dad always said there were too many newscasters in the world, but not enough journalists." ▢

Kathy Richland

John and Grant Pick

Grant Pick (1947–2005) was a freelance writer whose work appeared most frequently in the *Chicago Reader.* He also wrote for the *Chicago Tribune Magazine*, the *Chicago Sun-Times*, *Crain's Chicago Business*, and *Catalyst* until his sudden death.

John Pick is Grant Pick's son and an actor and teacher living in Los Angeles. He graduated from Kenyon College and trained at the Steppenwolf Theatre. He currently teaches acting in the Los Angeles Unified School District and is a member of the Actors' Gang.

Kathy Richland is an acclaimed portrait and editorial photographer and the wife of the late Grant Pick. Most of the photographs in this collection are hers.

Alex Kotlowitz is the author of *Never a City So Real: A Walk in Chicago* and *There Are No Children Here: The Story of Two Boys Growing Up in the Other America*, which was selected as one of the 150 most important books of the century by the New York Public Library.